THE TWO-WHEELED
WORLD OF
GEORGE B. THAYER

The
Two-Wheeled
WORLD
—••• of •••—
GEORGE B.
THAYER

KEVIN J. HAYES

University of Nebraska Press
Lincoln & London

Library of Congress Cataloging-in-Publication Data
Hayes, Kevin J.
The two-wheeled world of
George B. Thayer / Kevin J. Hayes.
pages   cm
Includes bibliographical references and index.
ISBN 978-0-8032-5525-8 (cloth: alk. paper)
ISBN 978-0-8032-8521-7 (epub)
ISBN 978-0-8032-8522-4 (mobi)
ISBN 978-0-8032-8523-1 (pdf)
1. Thayer, George B. (George Burton), 1853–1928. 2. Cyclists—
United States—Biography. 3. Bicycle touring—Anecdotes.
4. Cycling—History. I. Title.
GV1051.T46H39 2015
796.6'2092—dc23
[B]
2015024773

Set in Minion Pro by L. Auten.

For Myung-Sook

CONTENTS

ILLUSTRATIONS

PREFACE

Cycling south through Florida many years ago, I entered the Everglades the week before Christmas with my friends Andy, Gary, and Kyle. Near sunset we reached Long Pine Key Campground in Everglades National Park. As soon as we dismounted, hordes of mean-spirited mosquitoes attacked our bare limbs. We erected our tents, jumped inside, zipped the flaps shut, and then smashed all the mosquitoes trapped with us. Once the last tent-bound bug had met its maker, we grew bored. Unwilling to spend hours within our tents awaiting sleep, we braved the mosquitoes again to pedal to the bar we had passed a few miles back. Returning to the campground after last call, we rode through dense clouds of mosquitoes that stretched across the road. Those menacing little monsters bounced off our arms and legs and hands and faces. As we approached Long Pine Key, Kyle risked a mouthful of mosquitoes to yell: "I feel like Ian Hibell in the Darien Gap!"

We instantly knew what Kyle meant. Ian Hibell, the greatest cyclotourist of his generation, was one of our heroes. He had made a name for himself cycling through the Darien Gap, across the Sahara, and into many other remote places.

Around the time we visited Florida, Hibell was publishing tales of his two-wheeled adventures in the cycling press. It may have been presumptuous for us to compare our modest three-week tour of Florida with Hibell's adventures, which often lasted for months, but our encounters with mosquitoes, alligators, and varmints of the red-necked variety gave us a kinship with him. Whenever we experienced difficulties during the remainder of our Florida tour, we would ask ourselves, "What would Ian Hibell do?"

Since that Christmas vacation tour, I have continued to enjoy bicycle touring, as both a participant and a reader. Lately, many younger cyclotourists have published books about their adventures in far-flung parts of the globe, which have occasionally taken them years to complete (the adventures, not the books). Something bothers me—I had almost said bugs me—about this new generation of bicycle tourists: they seem unaware of their heritage. Most display little knowledge of the adventuresome cyclists who preceded them.

In *The Hungry Cyclist*, for example, Tom Kevill-Davies tells the story of what must be one of the greatest concept tours of all time. Starting from New York, he rode across the northern United States and southwestern Canada to the Pacific coast, which he traced to Panama, where he caught a boat to Colombia and then rode the length of South America, sampling the local cuisine everywhere he went. Sailing from Panama to Colombia aboard a dangerously leaky vessel, Kevill-Davies wondered whether he should have attempted an overland route through the Darien Gap instead. "Is he crazy?" I thought. "Has he never read Hibell's story of his arduous experience in the Darien Gap?" Apparently not. Nowhere in his narrative does the Hungry Cyclist mention Ian Hibell.

Other cyclists of the same generation as Kevill-Davies also seem oblivious of their cycling forbears. Rob Lilwall cycled from Siberia to London via Southeast Asia, Papua New Guinea,

Australia, the Himalayas, and, of all places, Afghanistan. Boasting about his ride through Afghanistan in *Cycling Home from Siberia*, Lilwall appears unaware that Dervla Murphy, a gutsy Irishwoman who cycled from Europe to India, had pedaled through Afghanistan decades before him, an experience she chronicled in *Full Tilt*, the book that launched her career as a travel writer.

The Two-Wheeled World of George B. Thayer is based on the premise that bicycle-touring stories of the past deserve to be remembered and retold. After Thomas Stevens cycled across the United States on the first leg of his round-the-world tour, he inspired several others to cycle across North America. The width of the continent became a way for cyclists to measure their mettle. A dozen years ago I told the story of one of these cyclotourists, George W. Nellis, in *An American Cycling Odyssey, 1887*. Stevens was not the only cyclist to inspire Nellis. The year before he crossed the continent, a Connecticut rider by the name of George B. Thayer pedaled across North America. I first learned about him while researching Nellis's story. Thayer fascinated me, and I grew anxious to learn more.

Though both George Thayer and George Nellis rode the same model bicycle—a high-wheeled Columbia Expert—their stories are otherwise quite different. From the very start, Nellis made up his mind to cross the continent as quickly as possible and, ideally, break the transcontinental record set by Thomas Stevens. Nellis took the train once, but only as a side trip. He made all his forward progress either riding or pushing his bicycle. He grew angry with himself whenever he spent less than ten hours a day in the saddle. His determination and athleticism did indeed take him across the continent in record time, seventy-two days, beating Stevens's record by thirty-three days.

George Thayer was more laid-back. He rode when he wished and took the train when he didn't. Instead of crossing the continent in as straight a line as possible, he took a more circuitous route, seeing sights that sometimes required significant detours. Nellis returned to New York via steamship. Thayer enjoyed his leisurely east-west journey across the continent so much he decided to return home overland, using a combination of cycling and railway travel on his way back to Connecticut.

Whereas Nellis's cycling adventures ended with his transcontinental tour, Thayer continued to enjoy bicycle touring for years to come. He traveled through many other regions by bicycle: New England, Great Britain, Europe, and Canada. In addition to his long-distance cycling adventures, Thayer experienced other aspects of the early history of cycling. Before acquiring his high wheeler, he rode an even earlier kind of bicycle, the aptly named boneshaker. He also witnessed the emergence of the chain-driven safety bicycle, first with hard rubber tires and later with pneumatic tires. Pneumatic tires revolutionized the bicycle and initiated the bicycle boom of the 1890s. As a member of the Connecticut National Guard, Thayer bore witness to early experiments adapting the bicycle for use in combat.

George Thayer related his cycling experience in many different ways. He told the story of his transcontinental tour in *Pedal and Path: Across the Continent Awheel and Afoot.* He wrote several other books, as well. Though none are devoted solely to bicycle touring, they do contain additional cycling anecdotes. Furthermore, Thayer contributed numerous articles to local newspapers and national magazines. He was not a great writer, but he did have a good eye for detail and a good ear for conversation. I have not invented any dialogue for this book. Conversations reported here come from Thayer's writing or, occasionally, from others who encountered him during his travels and recorded their impressions.

Though told as Thayer's personal story, the present work reconstructs the culture of cycling as it existed in the United

States during the last third of the nineteenth century, incorporating the experiences of many other cyclists. After George Thayer, his sister, Florine Thayer McCray, receives the greatest attention. A writer in her own right, McCray wrote two novels but is best known for her controversial biography of Harriet Beecher Stowe. She was an avid cyclist herself. Her first novel, *Wheels and Whims*, is the first cycling novel in American literature. McCray was uniquely poised to tell the story of early women's cycling. Both Florine and her brother George deserve to be better known. My goal in writing this book is to bring alive the nineteenth-century cycling scene by telling the heartfelt story of a major figure from the early days of cycling, a figure who has been neglected for too long.

ACKNOWLEDGMENTS

First published in paperback in 1887, George Thayer's *Pedal and Path* is an extremely rare volume. I had difficulty locating a copy but finally found one in the L. Tom Perry Special Collections, Harold B. Lee Library, Brigham Young University. The book is there for a reason. Thayer's impressions of Salt Lake City form an important record of the city and its Mormon citizenry. I would like to thank the special collections librarians at Brigham Young for making the work available to me. I later located another copy of *Pedal and Path* at the Lilly Library, Indiana University, where the book forms part of the library's excellent collection of materials pertaining to the early history of cycling. I am grateful to the Lilly Library for awarding me an Everett Helm Visiting Fellowship, which let me take advantage of this fine collection of cycling books, manuscripts, and ephemera. In addition, I thank the Lilly Library for their permission to reproduce illustrations from several items in the collection. While researching other projects, I came across additional material useful for telling Thayer's story at several different institutions: Ilion Public Library, Ilion, New York; Library Company of Philadelphia;

Pennsylvania Historical Society, Philadelphia; and Smithsonian Institution, Washington DC. I also thank Gary Sanderson for bringing to my attention Thayer's contributions to the boy's magazine *Youth's Companion*, which I have not seen cited anywhere else. Gary also invited me to present a talk about Thayer at the annual meet of The Wheelmen held at Monmouth University, West Long Branch, New Jersey. Members of The Wheelmen, a group of cyclists devoted to preserving and perpetuating the early history of cycling, provided much feedback, which helped crystallize my thoughts about George Thayer. I also thank Charles Melson of the Interlibrary Loan Department, Max Chambers Library, University of Central Oklahoma, who expeditiously filled my numerous requests. Finally, I thank my wife, Myung-Sook, who never gets tired of hearing me tell bicycle-touring stories, or, if she does, she has the grace and tact not to admit it.

THE TWO-WHEELED
WORLD OF
GEORGE B. THAYER

1

The Century

Perched atop his high-wheeled, nickel-plated Columbia Expert, George B. Thayer pedaled into New Haven late one Sunday morning in August 1884. He found the place a welcome sight. Known as the City of Elms, New Haven presented a handsome appearance to nineteenth-century visitors. A contemporary observer called it "unquestionably one of the most beautiful cities in the world, and one which the stranger always remembers with pleasure."[1] Thayer's experience bears out this observation. Having left his home in Vernon Depot, Connecticut—nearly fifty miles away—at five o'clock that morning, he found himself sorely in need of food and rest. What he really wanted was to treat himself to a fine meal.

Thayer did not want to be too extravagant: he never did. Consequently, he bypassed the New Haven House, the city's finest hotel, choosing instead the Tremont House. Located at the corner of Orange and Court Streets, the Tremont House was neither the second- nor the third- but the fourth-best hotel in New Haven.[2] Seated in its dining room, Thayer had time to consider how far he had come that day. Few physical activities stimulate the appetite or provoke personal reflection more than bicycling. As he sat in this hotel dining room and indulged an appetite whetted by hours of hard cycling, Thayer may have also contemplated the distance he had traveled since his birth thirty-one years earlier.

George B. Thayer—the *B* stood for Burton, after his mother's maiden name—came from old Puritan stock, really old. He was a direct descendant of John Alden and Priscilla Mullins. George's father, John W. Thayer, who had been born in Sterling, Connecticut, on Christmas Day 1819, grew up with the century. After a common school education, he entered the textile trade as a wool sorter. The work was hard: he used to tell George that when he first entered the business, he would work sixteen hours a day sorting wool.[3]

John Thayer's occupation brought him to Waterford, Massachusetts, where he and Adaline Burton met. She had been born at Chepachet, Rhode Island, January 29, 1823. In her childhood, her family had moved to Waterford, where she attended the Bank Village Academy, later continuing her education at the Smithville Seminary, North Scituate, in 1841. On Sunday, April 2, 1843, the Reverend Maxy W. Burlingame married John and Adaline at the Free Will Baptist Church in Waterford, Massachusetts. The following day the newlyweds moved to Rockville, Connecticut.[4]

Rockville suited the young couple. Nelson Sizer—Edgar Allan Poe's phrenologist—visited Rockville in the early 1840s. As a phrenologist, Sizer prided himself on his ability to size up a person's character. His ability to recognize the character of a town was not dissimilar. He called Rockville "a new manufacturing place on the Hockanum river," with "a great fall of water and a number of woolen mills and other works. The people here are young and enterprising, few of them having reached the meridian of life, and most of them range in age from eighteen to thirty years."[5] In other words, the Thayers fit right in. They chose Rockville because John had accepted a position with one of the town's woolen mills—namely, the New England Company. John Thayer rose quickly from wool sorter to superintendent of the plant. Their family grew apace. Adaline gave birth to two sons and a daughter. Adelbert was the oldest, followed by Florine. Two years after Florine's birth, George, their youngest child, was born on Friday, May 13, 1853.

One of George Thayer's earliest memories seems weirdly appropriate for a boy born on Friday the thirteenth, especially one who would earn a reputation as a world traveler. It concerns the first road trip he ever took. When he was four years old, George took the stage coach from Rockville to East Hartford accompanied by a woman whom he described as "an estimable old maid noted for her truthfulness."[6] Thrilled with the passing scenery, young George kept sticking his head out the window. Just before they entered the covered bridge on the road to East Hartford, the old woman warned him to keep his head inside the coach.

"Now, Georgie," she cautioned, "you must keep your head in, for along the inside of this bridge have been placed a lot of hooks to hook off the heads of bad boys who don't mind. The last time I came to Hartford I saw lots of bad boys' heads hanging on these hooks, both sides of the bridge."

Georgie remembered this old woman's gruesome tall tale all his life and retold it several times.[7] Since this experience occurred as part of the earliest travel experience he could remember, it is tempting to consider how the woman's words conditioned the boy's attitude. Travel involves risk. By venturing from the safety of home into the larger world, travelers consciously put themselves in danger. Rigorous, faraway travel becomes a way for them to prove their bravery to themselves and others. George Thayer's attitude cannot be attributed solely to what this old woman said, of course, but he did come to see travel as a way of risking danger to prove himself.

As his family grew, John Thayer became active in politics.

A Republican from the very start of the Republican Party, he was elected to the Connecticut House of Representatives in 1855. His newfound political activism scarcely dulled his business acumen. In 1860 he purchased Ellington Mills, a manufacturing plant located on the Hockanum River about two miles west of Rockville. He also purchased fifty acres of adjoining land onto which he built a number of cottages for his employees and a big yellow-brick home for his family. He named both the company and the village Windermere, after the largest lake in England. Like its namesake, Thayer's Windermere was situated in a scenic area filled with streams and trees, fish and wildlife: a perfect setting for an adolescent boy.

George spent much of his boyhood outdoors, but his parents encouraged him to develop an intellectual life as well. His father's literary tastes were conservative when they came to poetry, progressive when they came to scientific literature. John's favorite poet was Alexander Pope, but he also read *The Origin of Species* after the first American edition came out. John Thayer found Charles Darwin's conclusions absolutely convincing. George remembered his father discussing Darwin's ideas with others. These discussions deeply impressed young George. To him Darwin's thought became closely associated with the place of Darwin's birth. On a British bicycle tour in 1888, he called England "the birthplace of Darwinian theory."[8]

Mrs. Thayer, better educated than her husband, exerted a greater influence on their children when it came to literature. After George's sister, Florine, embarked on a successful literary career, she made sure to thank their "well-read mother" in an interview with the *Ladies' Home Journal.*[9] George called their mother "a woman of rare integrity of character, systematic methods, and of intellectual tastes. Her love of reading was her greatest pleasure through life."[10] Mrs. Thayer obviously made an impact on her children, all of whom became involved in the world of literature in one way or another. Adelbert, the most shadowy member of the family, left home at eighteen to become a newspaperman out West. George himself would write several books, and Florine's foray into literature progressed from newspaper contributions to novels and biography.

Adaline Thayer took her children's education seriously. She could be really tough on them when they neglected their studies. One day she caught George skipping school. With switch in hand, she whipped him all the way to the schoolhouse. He remembered: "Blow upon blow rained down upon my back, arms and legs, and the shower did not blow over till I finally entered the school-room door, half a mile distant." Back home that evening, he bared his back to show the red welts in an effort to evoke some sympathy from her. Florine cried out at the sight of her little brother's injuries, but their mother expressed no regret for what she had done. George said, "Her apparent indifference afterwards hurt worse than the original whipping."[11]

Abraham Lincoln was elected president the year George turned seven. News of Lincoln's victory reached Windermere on Wednesday, November 7, the day after the election. Despite his youth, George remembered precisely how his mother reacted.

"Now there will be a war," Mrs. Thayer starkly predicted when she heard the news.[12] Sure enough, war soon broke out. Mr. Thayer kept the Windermere Woolen Company running day and night during the war to produce blankets for Union soldiers, disaster notwithstanding. When fire destroyed the two upper stories of his five-story mill, he quickly rebuilt the factory and kept it going throughout the conflict.[13]

George was fascinated with the reports of war in the newspapers and magazines. He also enjoyed hearing stories about friends, neighbors, and family members who went to war. His father subscribed to the *Hartford Courant* and *Harper's Weekly*. George vividly remembered the articles he read in the *Courant* and the pictures he saw in *Harper's Weekly*. He used to pore over those pictures, branding its images of war into his brain.[14]

As a boy, he recreated many battles in their home at Windermere, using pennies to stand for soldiers. No doubt his behavior resembled that of many other adolescent boys throughout the war-torn nation. As George later said about himself during the Civil War, "I was full of the military spirit that boys of my age usually are."[15] Remembering the war games he played at their Windermere home, he recalled:

> How many times, for hours and hours, have I gone around those rooms on my hands and knees, building forts out of dominoes, and gunboats and rebel rams out of clothes pins, and manning them with small copper pennies, the red ones for rebels and the light-colored ones representing the Union army. Every penny was a thousand men, and during some naval battle, such as the capture of Fort Jackson and Fort Phillip, below New Orleans, which I fought out over and over again, it was no uncommon thing to lose 1,000 men overboard at a clip. Then, during the Wilderness campaign, with one hand I often turned Lee's flank, and with two hands easily put 10,000 men to flight. Occasionally hostilities would be suspended for a time, owing to the fact that some member of the family who wore long dresses had just passed hurriedly through the room. The strongest fortress would then be laid low and the warships dismasted by the hurricane, and with great loss of life swept out to sea. I never could successfully explode the mine at Petersburg, but all the rest of that struggle, around to Five Forks and Appomattox, was fought out to perfection, time and again.[16]

Some of the stories George heard were quite gruesome. His cousin John W. January, who fought at the First Battle of Bull Run, was one of many Union soldiers who afterward ran toward Washington DC for safety. Only five years older than George, January had enlisted in the Fourteenth Illinois Cavalry when he was sixteen. He was captured in Stoneman's Raid in July 1864 and sent to Andersonville, the notorious Confederate prison camp in Georgia, where he suffered malnutrition, scurvy, and gangrene. As a prisoner, January went from his original weight of 165 down to an amazing 45 pounds. He was ultimately sent to the gangrene hospital in Charleston, South Carolina.

January became convinced that the only way to save his life would be to amputate his black, putrid, gangrenous, maggot-infested feet, but the Confederate surgeon refused to treat him. January obtained a sharp pocket knife and, with the help of a friend, severed his feet himself. After the war, another friend called January "one of the most notable human monuments now surviving of the horrors of our civil war." Not even this gruesome story dissuaded his cousin George Thayer from wanting to become a soldier and go to war. Though he dreamt of doing battle with the enemy in close combat, the biggest enemy George Thayer faced during the war years was the measles, which he caught when he was ten.[17]

He did a lot of growing up between Fort Sumter and Appomattox. What had started as play became serious business. Civic-minded leaders stressed the importance of economy and conservation, and George took their advice to heart. He began searching the heaps of ashes beneath the boilers at Windermere Woolen Mills for usable chunks of coal. He regularly collected considerable amounts, which he sold to his mother at what he called "a fair profit." Of course, the coal he sold to his mother belonged to his father, but at least he kept the profit-and-loss account all in the family.[18] The economic lessons he learned served him all his life: George Thayer economized wherever and whenever he could. His capacity for saving money would later help facilitate his long-distance bicycle touring.

George also began keeping a diary during the Civil War. Some entries derive from his personal experience, others from details culled from the *Courant*. The result is a strange mix, as several entries from 1865 indicate. On Friday, January 27, for example, he recorded that gold was selling for $2.07 a pound. The next day he wrote, "I got three muskrat skins today. They are worth 50 cents apiece." One entry reflects the national economy; the other reflects the private, personal economy of rural boys.[19]

On Monday, February 13, he wrote, "I did not go to school because it was so cold. I went skating and had a fire on the ice."[20] If George, just three months shy of his twelfth birthday, saw any irony in the idea of the weather being too cold to attend school but not too cold to spend the day playing on the ice, he did not admit it to his diary. On Sunday, March 19, he noted that his pet duck laid its first eggs. And on Monday, March 27, he wrote, "I got this pencil over to the store and had it charged to me."[21] Anticipating his life as a writer, he obviously took pride in the tools of the trade.

The next month national news and rumors dominated the pages of his diary:

April 3—Capture of Richmond by our forces.

April 9—Glorious news; surrender of General Lee and his whole army.

April 10—I rung the bell this forenoon because of the surrender of General Lee.

April 11—Father came home from Boston and brought me five oranges.

April 14—Awful calamity. President Lincoln was shot by an assassin tonight. Secretary Seward was also stabbed.

April 15—President Lincoln died this morning at 7:22 o'clock.[22]

Though disturbing, the daily stories of violence in the newspapers did not prevent George from enjoying the pleasures of a rural New England childhood, which he remembered with great fondness and considerable detail. So did his sister, Florine. She retained delightful girlhood memories of walking in the woods and playing in the barnyard. As a child she had several pets, including a turkey, which would "sit on her lap as she read her story book day after day."[23] George remembered two pet pigs—Patrick and Bridget Murphy—which he and Florine used to hold in their laps until they grew too heavy to lift. George also had a horse named Sleepy David, which he sometimes rode to school. Bruiser, a big, scruffy mutt, part Newfoundland and part St. Bernard, was George's favorite pet. In the wintertime, when the ice on the pond out back was thick enough, George used to grab hold of Bruiser's tail and let that gentle beast pull him across the lake on the seat of his pants.[24]

Winter evenings at Windermere offered pleasures of a different sort. Most nights John Thayer would read to his family. Sometimes he read Shakespeare.[25] Charles Dickens was another favorite. John Thayer read all or nearly all of Dickens to his family, often more than once. George later remembered episodes from several novels: *Bleak House, David Copperfield, Nicholas Nickleby, Oliver Twist, Our Mutual Friend, The Pickwick Papers*, and *A Tale of Two Cities*.[26] Though sometimes George would fall asleep as his father read, the promise of snacks usually woke him. He recalled:

> Like the close of a sermon, the sudden stillness that came over the room as father ceased reading, followed soon after by the thin, small voice of the cider down in the cellar directly underneath, a voice that grew in tone deeper and deeper as the pitcher gradually filled up, this, without further warning,

always served to arouse me to the occasion and to the pop-corn and cider. Along towards spring, when the cider had grown hard, a barrel of ale usually found its way into the cel-lar, and those evenings with Dickens, followed by pop-corn, walnuts or apples and the whole topped off with a glass of nose tingling cider or foaming ale, came to be a part of our very life at Windermere.[27]

George enjoyed hard cider and home-brewed ale very much—so much it scared him. Talking about the beer he drank in his youth, he admitted, "From a boy I had always liked the stuff as I did milk."[28] Understanding how easily alco-hol could control people's behavior and dominate their lives, he fought the urge to drink the rest of his life. By and large his fight proved successful. In his professional life as county prosecutor, Thayer would have the responsibility of making sure the laws regulating the sale of liquor were observed and to prosecute any licensed or unlicensed dealers who broke the law. He took his job seriously and went after those who vio-lated Hartford's stringent liquor laws. His dedication would earn him the nickname "Ginger-Ale George."[29]

Mr. and Mrs. Thayer strongly supported their children's interests and enthusiasms. When Florine was selected to play the part of the Goddess of Liberty in a Republican parade, John Thayer supplied the horses to pull her float. Adorned with a long, flowing, white robe, liberty cap, and swept-back wings, Florine as Liberty was the highlight of the whole parade.[30] The Thayers also made sure Florine got a good education. They first sent her to boarding school in Hartford. Later she attended Dr. Dio Lewis's innovative school in Lexington, Massachusetts, where she had as classmates Nathaniel Hawthorne's daughters Rose and Una. Florine Thayer and Rose Hawthorne became close friends at Lexington.[31]

Their teacher, Dr. Lewis, is best known as a pioneer of physical education. At his school he developed a new system of gymnastics especially for women, which used light apparatus such as wooden dumbbells, rings, small clubs, and bean bags. Lewis's system developed both muscle strength and agility. Understanding that physical fitness and intellectual development go hand in hand, Dr. Lewis integrated gymnastics into his daily curriculum, and on Saturdays the girls took long tramps into the countryside, sometimes hiking twelve or sixteen miles.[32] What Florine learned about exercise and physical fitness at school reinforced something she had already learned from her father: exercise is essential for good mental health.

George and Florine were close. They looked like twins. Both were small of stature with blond hair, fair complexions, and bright, pale blue eyes. George missed Florine once she went away to school. He stayed at Windermere for his education, attending the Hall Preparatory School in nearby Ellington. George's reminiscences say little about the curriculum, but he vividly remembered how transgressions were punished. He and his school chum A. W. "Bubby" Sumner got together many years later to reminisce about old times: "We talked over and looked back to the time we spent in Ellington with very much the same feelings, I think, that Nicholas Nickleby had when he recalled his experiences under Squeers at Dotheboys Hall. Still we bear no ill will against the apple-trees in the rear of the school-house, but think it doubtful if those trees themselves have borne anything since, after furnishing so many switches to be used for our moral welfare and physical uplifting."[33] The comparison with Dotheboys Hall, the boarding school operated by the sinister Wackford Squeers in *Nicholas Nickleby*, does not speak well for the Hall Preparatory School, but George Thayer's portrayal of his younger self as a stereotypical bad boy seems like a deliberate exaggeration.

Though his reminiscences indicate a fun-filled boyhood, Thayer had a restless streak in him that no amount of down-home pleasure could satisfy. What prompted him to do so remains a mystery, but he soon ran away to the West. John January may have been an inspiration. Thayer took this, his longest journey so far, when he was around the same age his cousin was when he left home. He could not run off to war as his cousin had, but he could still travel. In early 1869, months before he turned sixteen, George Thayer hopped a train to Omaha. The railroad had always fascinated him; years later he vividly recalled the temporary railway bridge that had been laid across the Missouri River on the ice that winter. Pilings had been driven down through the thick ice and track laid atop the ice to allow passenger trains and even freight trains to cross.[34]

Thayer was still in Omaha when the transcontinental railroad was completed in Utah later that year. The completion of the cross-country railway line meant great economic opportunities for Omaha, whose festive citizens cheered the news in grand style. "A big celebration in Omaha dented my boyish brain," Thayer recalled.[35] His recollection does not explain precisely what he meant by this curious phrase, but apparently the possibility of crossing the continent by rail filled him and thrilled him with thoughts of what the nation could achieve, what technology could achieve, and what the individual could achieve, how far he could go given such extraordinary technology.

Otherwise Thayer's reminiscences say little about his early days in Omaha. He found work in a grocery store and often had to deliver groceries "in the face of the blizzards and sudden changes of Nebraska winters."[36] When he was not delivering groceries, he stayed in the store, devoting his spare moments to reading the local papers, including the *Daily Herald*, *Daily Republican*, and *Evening Times*.[37]

Upon his return to Connecticut the following year, Thayer continued the trade he had learned in Omaha, finding employment as a grocery clerk. This fact is known mainly because Karl Kron—that eccentric, yet indefatigable chronicler of cycling in the nineteenth century——saw fit to ask George Thayer about his early life and recognized that its details were important enough to include in his magnum opus, *Ten Thousand Miles on a Bicycle*.[38] No doubt John Thayer hoped his son would do better than grocery clerk. "There's plenty of room at the top," he used to tell George.[39] But John Thayer's business setbacks were partly responsible for his son going to work instead of going to college. John Thayer did not necessarily see the lack of a college education as a setback: George could get a practical business education by working in business.[40]

During the late 1860s, Windermere Woolen Mills fell on hard times, the victim of fierce competition and unscrupulous business practices on the part of its competitors. John Thayer fought as long and as hard as he could, but the strain proved too much. He sold the business in 1872. Afterward, he checked himself into the Connecticut Hospital for the Insane. Relieved of the strain of business, John Thayer quickly recovered his mental faculties. In a matter of months he went from hospital patient to administrator. He ultimately became supervisor of the institution.[41]

In her first novel, Florine Thayer described the Connecticut Hospital for the Insane in detail. It was beautifully situated a mile or so out of Middletown "upon an eminence which commands an enchanting view of city and river." The character of the Major in the novel is an idealized portrait of John Thayer: "a remarkably fine-looking gentleman of sixty or thereabouts, with a well-filled figure, which was clothed in garments of fashionable style and finest quality. His gray hair, which was receding from his already high forehead, grew thickly upon his temples, and was continued in a full mustache and side-whiskers, which he was prone to clasp and pull to their extreme points when discussing or considering a question. His manners were graceful, and held a flattering deference to all ladies."[42]

Like his sister, George appreciated their father's role of supervisor, but George's tribute is briefer and more specific. He was pleased that John Thayer "instituted a system of outdoor exercise for the patients, which resulted in much good to them."[43]

Outdoor exercise would become the defining feature of George Thayer's life. He told Karl Kron that he rode his first boneshaker in 1870. Invented in France, the boneshaker—or, as it was called at that time, the velocipede—entered the American market in 1868, when traveling performers gave riding exhibitions to demonstrate this pedal-powered machine. The "velocipede mania," as the phenomenon became known, spread quickly. Riding schools were established in major cities across the nation, and the riding rink became a favorite destination for the "fashionables."

The first week of December 1868 one observer described the patrons of a riding academy in New York: "Among the school boys in this new institution are several of those old buffers who are always on the lookout for the fresh things of the world, not a few Wall Street brokers, and down-town merchants, and many young bucks."[44] The description affirms that the young and the athletic were not the only ones riding velocipedes. People of all ages started riding. The fact that several newspaper editors took to cycling fueled the fad. In New York another observer regularly saw a familiar face at one riding school, Charles A. Dana, editor of the New York Sun: "He has velocipedes on the brain, and may almost nightly be seen testing his equestrian powers upon the inanimate steed."[45]

As the contemporary descriptions suggest, those who patronized the riding schools were fairly affluent. They had to be. The machines themselves were quite expensive. According to a Boston journalist, the cost of a velocipede ranged from

$70 to $125, but most of the machines sold were of the $125 variety "as everybody ordering wants the best."[46]

The numerous crashes and spills that took place inside these riding rinks did not discourage people, at least not at first. To characterize the accidents that occurred within the rink, humorist Everett Chamberlain found appropriate some lines Pyramus speaks in *A Midsummer Night's Dream*:

O, wicked wall,
Cursed be thy bricks for thus receiving me![47]

Some of the riders who mastered the velocipede left the confines of the indoor rinks and took to the outdoors. No longer walled in, they could enjoy the freedom of the open road. Flat tires were not a worry in the velocipede days, but saddle sores were: the tires were made from iron bands nailed to wooden wheels. It was not for nothing that velocipedes were called boneshakers.

The velocipede mania died as quickly as it came to life. By the end of 1869, the velocipede was dead, a victim of too much hype. Thayer himself later referred to the phenomenon as "the total failure of the velocipede craze."[48] The mania ended so quickly that retailers were stuck with many unsold velocipedes, which they found almost impossible to unload.[49] Machines that had sold for $125 could be purchased for a tenth the price after the mania ended. Never one to follow fashion, make decisions hastily, or spend money recklessly, Thayer waited until the craze had passed and obtained a discount machine, which he enjoyed very much.

The biggest disadvantage of the velocipede was its slow speed. Like the later high-wheeled bicycles, the crank arms of a velocipede were attached directly to the axle of the front wheel, so the gear was fixed by the wheel's diameter. The velocipede's front wheel was seldom greater than thirty-six inches, roughly equivalent to the lowest gear of a modern multispeed bicycle. Thayer, who was just a smidgen over five feet tall, was more suited to the velocipede than taller riders. He used his boneshaker to deliver groceries but also rode it for pleasure. He kept riding into 1873, when the machine apparently suffered irreparable damage.

During his boneshaker years, Thayer became his own boss. A grocery clerk at fifteen, he rose to grocer at eighteen when he became the proprietor of his own store in Vernon, Connecticut. Given his keen intellect, perhaps Thayer could have set his sights a little higher than small-town grocer, but for the time being the situation suited him. Good natured, happy-go-lucky, never one to rush into anything, Thayer had another personal characteristic that ideally suited his chosen occupation: he loved to talk. Few places are better suited for sitting around and shooting the breeze than the front porch of a rural grocery store.

Ten years passed from the time George Thayer quit his boneshaker to the time he first mounted a high wheeler. At thirty he was older than many others who rode high wheelers, but his behavior reflects his personal belief that it was never too late to start something new. Never did he see age as an obstacle. This impulse he may have received from his mother. The same year her son started riding a high-wheeled bicycle, Mrs. Thayer, now sixty, began taking a Chautauqua course, a correspondence course that represents one of the earliest attempts at distance learning in the United States. She stuck with it and, four years later, earned the equivalent of a college degree.[50]

George Thayer loved riding his high wheeler. Since these bicycles were sized by the diameter of the front wheel, and thus depended on the rider's inseam, taller cyclists had a distinct advantage over shorter ones because they could pedal a bigger gear. Just as Thayer never let his age hinder him, he never let his size hinder him. He rode a forty-six-inch Columbia

Expert—the smallest high wheeler Columbia made. In contrast, George W. Nellis, who was much taller, rode a fifty-two-inch Columbia Expert.[51] To keep up with taller riders, Thayer simply had to pedal faster. By all accounts he did just that.

Besides providing exercise, Thayer realized, bicycles could also speed the exchange of information. As he said a few years later, the bicycle "is, like the telephone, a new means of quick communication."[52] As a cyclist, he did not need to wait for news to come to him—he could go out and get it. Eager to learn whom the Republicans had nominated for president at their national convention in Chicago the first week of June 1884, Thayer mounted his wheel and started off toward Hartford, about twelve miles away by the shortest route. This route was more dangerous than the longer way: it required him to coast down a steep hill, which took a sharp turn at the bottom over the flume of the old red mill.

Thayer normally loved to coast, which, during the high-wheeled era, involved lifting his feet from the ever-turning pedals and throwing his legs over the handlebars. When it came to coasting, Thayer was quite a daredevil. On this ride, he coasted down the hill safely, but once he reached the turn at the bottom, he realized his bicycle frame had gotten bent somehow, making it impossible to steer. With his legs on the handlebars and his feet in front of him, he lost his balance, careening off the road and into the mill flume.

He sank rapidly, coming to a stop as his butt hit bottom. His bicycle followed him into the water, conking him on the head as it descended. He floated to the surface, safe and sound, but now he had a problem to solve: how could he rescue his bike? A beam that crossed over the flume gave him an idea, which his athleticism let him accomplish. Grabbing hold of the beam, he dangled his body into the water, grasped the bike with his feet, and pulled it up with his legs. He walked his broken bike back home, where he had to wait with everyone else to learn that the Republicans had nominated James G. Blaine as their presidential candidate over the incumbent Chester A. Arthur. Later that year Blaine would lose the election to Democratic presidential nominee Grover Cleveland.

The accident at the old red mill did not faze Thayer in the least. Two months later, he began his ride to New Haven, his most ambitious ride yet. Newspaper reporters often haunted hotel lobbies searching for interesting guests to interview. After lunch and a brief rest at the Tremont House, Thayer took time to speak with a representative of the *New Haven Evening Register*, who reported Thayer's impressive ride in an article titled, "Big Bicycle Riding."

"He did not appear to be suffering in the least from fatigue," the New Haven reporter observed. The hardest part of his journey "was over the sandy roads which he struck above North Haven."[53] Recognizing that Thayer's ride was only halfway through, the reporter concluded with understatement: "The feat of riding nearly a hundred miles over country roads in a day is not a job which every bicyclist would care to undertake."[54]

The roundtrip distance from Vernon Depot to New Haven was so close to a hundred miles that Thayer could not resist tacking on an extra loop as he neared home to make the day's ride an even century, which he completed in thirteen hours: not too shabby for someone riding a forty-six-inch gear over dirt roads. In 1884 a century ride remained a newsworthy event. The *Hartford Courant* reported Thayer's ride. The Buffalo papers reported it, too, and, amazingly, so did the *San Francisco Bulletin*.[55]

This, his first century, prompted Thayer to ride even more. Before 1884 ended, as he told Karl Kron, he would ride a total of 1,047 miles for the year.[56] The triumphant completion of his first century helped Thayer foresee other opportunities, off the bicycle as well as on. He began imagining bicycle tours to faraway destinations, but he also started to see that perhaps life held more for him than what a small-town grocery store could offer. He began to dream of bigger things. After completing his first century, George B. Thayer recognized that the world was filled with possibility.

2

The White Mountains

George was not the only member of the Thayer family to catch the cycling bug. His sister, Florine, was "an ardent and graceful tricycle rider." Florine and George often went riding together.[1] She also wrote about cycling. "Love on Wheels," as she titled one of her short stories, tells the tale of a young woman named Belle Morton who takes to cycling, which develops her muscle tone and gives her an apple-cheeked complexion, allowing her to attract the man of her dreams.[2] And in 1884, the year George completed his first century, Florine wrote her first novel, *Wheels and Whims*, which she structured as a cycling tour. Both riding and writing gave Florine a sense of independence she otherwise had difficulty achieving. After all, she first became a writer after her father, John Thayer, quashed her plans to become a schoolteacher.

Once she completed her education at Dio Lewis's Lexington school, a hiring committee from a distant school offered her a teaching position. That was the good news. The bad news was that this position would compel her to live on her own. She was eager to accept the offer, but her father put his foot down. Though normally supportive, John Thayer refused to let his daughter pursue a career as a schoolteacher, at least not one that would take her away from home. There was a term then for single women who lived on their own: women adrift. No way would John Thayer have his unmarried daughter living as a woman adrift. This former Goddess of Liberty now had her wings clipped. To avoid any other tempting offers for employment, he took Florine on an extended tour of California and the Pacific coast.[3]

Upon their return, she began contributing to the newspapers. After submitting a few items to the local paper in Rockville, she contributed a series of letters to the *Hartford Globe* under the pen name "The Bohemiene." Identifying with other Bohemians, Florine chose a pseudonym reflecting the freedom her father denied her. She subsequently wrote for the *Boston Saturday Evening Gazette*, *Brooklyn Times*, and the *New York World*.

Though Florine established a modest reputation with these newspaper contributions, all of her writing to this point remained in the form of fugitive pieces, that is, scattered, largely unrelated items published in the newspapers and magazines. Cycling changed the course of her career. As it did with her brother George, cycling inspired Florine to something greater, and she began work on the novel.

Florine married William B. McCray in 1874. McCray was an insurance executive by profession, but a playful spirit was his defining personal characteristic. George Thayer recorded his brother-in-law's fondness for storytelling and his tremendous ability to make people laugh. The account of a journalist who visited the McCray home to interview Florine confirms George's characterization of William McCray. The interview was frequently interrupted by the "persistent raillery from her fun-loving young husband."[4]

In Hartford, where they settled, Florine Thayer McCray— she kept her maiden name as her middle name after marriage—

settled into a busy life, both social and literary. A society columnist described her as "young, pretty and stylish, a decided blonde, very petite"—a physical appearance the columnist found difficult to reconcile with "the deep thought and often metaphysical analysis seen in her writings."[5] Florine and her husband lived in a graceful house with a vast porch in Asylum Hill, the most desirable neighborhood in the city, a stone's throw from Mark Twain's house and a minute's walk from Harriet Beecher Stowe's.[6]

Wheels and Whims was supposedly cowritten by Florine Thayer McCray and Esther Louise Smith, but McCray did nearly all the writing. Smith drew the illustrations. They dedicated the book to "American Girls," hoping it would inspire them to take up cycling as a means of adding "perfect health" to their other characteristic attributes: beauty, intelligence, and veracity. A prefatory note to the novel reinforces their hope that it would encourage female readers to enjoy vigorous exercise in the open air. Smith's amateurish but not unattractive illustrations further enhanced the appeal of cycle touring. The advertising copy characterizes the book as follows: "The narrative is light and chatty, with a peculiar out-of-door flavor and freshness, teeming with girlish ideas and caprices, which invest it with a delicate humor that cannot fail to entertain the reader."[7]

The novel tells the story of four women who take a cycling tour across Connecticut or, to be precise, a tricycling tour. Few women rode bicycles in the 1880s. No proper woman would dare be seen straddling a bicycle. When some young Hartford women got together to race their trikes in 1885, the *Hartford Courant* reported the event but accidentally printed "bicycle" for "tricycle." The paper subsequently published a retraction: "*The Courant* apologizes. It unfortunately did print bicycle for tricycle, but it protests against the assumption that it would accuse a lady, however young, of straddling."[8]

The social stigma that prevented them from riding high-wheeled bicycles irked some women, perhaps none more than the pioneering photojournalist Frances Benjamin Johnston, who started her journalistic career in the 1880s by drawing illustrations for magazines. She quickly realized that photography would revolutionize magazines and trained herself as a photographer. In an early self-portrait, she dressed in a man's cycling suit and cap, penciled a moustache above her lip, and posed with a high-wheeled bicycle. Her self-portrait offers a wry comment on the social inequality of the times, which prevented women from seeing the world from atop a wheel.

Few women of the time were as daring as Fanny Johnston, but many well-to-do women took to the tricycle, which let them cycle in a decorous manner. The tricyclist sat in the center of her machine, with a small wheel in front and two large wheels on either side of the rider. Keeping her arms at her sides, she would control the mechanisms for steering and braking with her hands as her feet operated treadles, which drove the two large wheels. Madame Morelli, the woman who introduces Belle Morton to the tricycle in "Love on Wheels," calls it "the gr-r-reatest convenience and health-giving mode of locomotion ever vouchsafed to women."[9]

As the title of her novel infers, *Wheels and Whims* tells a whimsical story, but the narrative does possess some documentary value. For one thing, it offers a vivid description of the proper female attire for tricycle touring. To understand Florine's description requires a fair knowledge of fashion vocabulary, including such terms as "postilion basque" (a continuation of a jacket below the waist in the form of short coattails resembling those of a postilion's coat), "frog" (an ornamental, spindle-shaped fastener), and "poke" (a wide hat brim that shades the face).

Beginning their tour, the four women in the novel wear matching gray wool suits trimmed with black braid. The braid

Fig. 1. In this self-portrait (ca. 1887), Frances Benjamin Johnston dresses in men's cycling wear to offer an arch comment on sexual inequality when it came to bike riding. Library of Congress, Prints and Photographs Division, reproduction number LC-DIG-ppmsc-04884.

adorns the edges of their skirts as well as their collars and cuffs and the flaps of their postilion basques. In the front, their jackets are fastened with frogs, which lend their outfits a slightly military air. They all wear black kid gloves that extend well up their wrists. Black poke hats decorated with feathers shade their faces. Their riding outfits cover the women almost completely: "Only the tips of their toes were seen beneath the heavy folds of their skirts as the treadles rose and fell."[10]

Though decorously attired, these four lady cyclists nonetheless provoke comments from those they encounter. Soon after they hit the road, some mischievous boys tease them. "Oh, fellers," cries one boy to his friends, "see the women's righters!" Another boy greets one of the women by saying, "Hullo, Susan Anthony!" A third asks, "When are you going to vote?"[11] This humorous episode obviously has a serious purpose. Cycling for women in the 1880s was not just a means of exercise and a method of travel; it also let them assert themselves and their rights, thereby establishing a presence in public.

Readers generally appreciated *Wheels and Whims*. Several reviewers thought it would encourage readers, both female and male, to start cycling. The *Congregationalist* predicted that this novel would increase the sale of tricycles and bicycles. The *Literary World*, a Boston weekly, observed, "Such a breezy book as this about the pleasures of this form of locomotion ought to extend the knowledge and the practice of it." The *New York Herald* was less enthusiastic. Though it appreciated McCray's ear for conversation, it found the book "disappointingly silent about tricycling."[12]

The sporting press also reviewed *Wheels and Whims*. *Outing* found that the novel "shows what a nice time young women as well as young men can have in so refined and invigorating a sport as 'cycling." *Outing* was quick to caution readers against using *Wheels and Whims* as a guidebook: "The experienced wheelman will readily see that it is not written by a practical

Fig. 2. Hy Sandham illustrates proper cycling etiquette, depicting the female cyclist riding her tricycle in a decorous riding costume as the men atop their high-wheeled machines allow her the right-of-way (L. Prang and Co., 1887). Library of Congress, Prints and Photographs Division, reproduction number LC-DIG-pga-04039.

'cyclist, and will not rely upon the account of runs over roads, some of which are, in sober fact, too sandy for the excursions which the author's imagination has made over them."[13]

Wheels and Whims proved to be modestly popular. After the first printing sold out, a second appeared. According to one source, *Wheels and Whims* went through its fifth printing by mid-1886.[14] The book made its author's literary reputation. As the *Buffalo Evening News* reported: "Mrs. Florine Thayer McCray of Hartford is becoming quite well known from her book, *Wheels and Whims*, especially to the bicyclers. She is young and stylish, blonde hair, fun loving and full of talent."[15]

McCray spoke at length with one interviewer about the tricycle's possibilities: "Tricycling for women is constantly growing in popularity. And why not? It is the most exhilarating, beneficial, and best worth doing of any sport that ever came to the sex. It is modest and graceful, as all can see. That it is thoroughly healthful, I am convinced from observation and experience. It exercises all the walking muscles while the weight of the body is supported by the saddle and specially tends to expand the lungs and strengthen the stomach."[16]

Florine Thayer McCray's enthusiasm for cycle touring fueled her younger brother's excitement. After riding over a thousand miles the year she published the book, George Thayer formed even more ambitious plans the following year. He received encouragement elsewhere, especially from Prof. Alonzo Williams, who taught German at Brown University. Williams had toured Europe by bicycle in 1883 and returned to tell stories of his adventures. Though Thomas Stevens is typically considered the foremost international cyclist of the high-wheeled era, Williams toured Great Britain and Europe the year before Stevens began his round-the-world cycling tour. Since Williams rode a Columbia Expert on his European tour, the Pope Manufacturing Company secured a testimonial from him upon his return. In an advertisement on the front page of the very first issue of the *LAW Bulletin*—the official organ of the League of American Wheelmen—Williams's words appeared as the first of several testimonials under the heading "Practical Words from Practical Wheelmen": "Having examined somewhat carefully the wheels of England and France, I do not believe that a better roadster is made in the world than your Expert Columbia."[17]

In his own writings, Thayer conveyed his debt to Williams but did not clarify precisely where he heard him speak. He identified the professor as his "tutor," someone whose "delightful account of his European trip first set me wild to be a bicycle traveler there."[18] After learning of the professor's bicycle-touring experience, Thayer pelted him with questions. Williams had an excellent reputation as a public speaker, but Thayer may have heard him speak in a more informal, private setting. Since Williams had married Sarah Phelps, the daughter of the Reverend Benjamin C. Phelps, pastor of the Methodist church in Vernon, Connecticut, he and his wife had reason to visit Vernon frequently.[19]

The profound respect Thayer had for Williams went beyond the professor's bicycle touring. Eleven years Thayer's senior, Williams was just old enough to have served in the Civil War; that is, to do what Thayer had only dreamt of: to have served his country as a soldier in battle. Williams enlisted as a private when he was in his teens and rose to the rank of second lieutenant by the end of the war. He saw action at Savannah and Charleston and participated in General Sherman's March to the Sea. In addition to pursuing his professional career after the war, Williams continued his association with the military, serving as an officer in the Rhode Island militia and joining the Grand Army of the Republic, the national association for Union veterans. Soldier, bicycle tourist, intellectual: Alonzo Williams presented a personal ideal for Thayer to follow.

Through the early months of 1885, Thayer restricted himself to day trips, but in June he took his first extended cycling tour, a five-day, 175-mile excursion paralleling the Long Island Sound. He returned from this tour very pleased with cycling, both as a mode of travel and a way of sightseeing. Afterward he explained: "So intense had become my desire to travel, to visit the places of interest here at home, that I then made business arrangements which would permit a more prolonged absence, and took a three weeks' trip of five hundred miles."[20] This three-week tour took place in September. His precise route is uncertain, but apparently he made a big loop through Connecticut, Rhode Island, and Massachusetts, with a side trip to Martha's Vineyard.

In October and November 1885, he took his longest bicycle tour yet, a six-week, 1,200-mile journey through New England, the highlight being the time he spent in the White Mountains. Little more is known about his first two cycling tours this year, but Thayer wrote up the third for the press. He had tried writing for the *Hartford Courant* before, but the paper was uninterested in his earlier writings. After this adventurous bicycle tour, however, the editor of the *Courant* encouraged him to write a travel essay for the paper.[21] In addition, Thayer published an article about the tour in the LAW *Bulletin*. These newspaper and magazine articles permit a reasonably full reconstruction of his ambitious cycling tour. Thayer's enthusiastic accounts of the trip encouraged cyclists to vacation in the White Mountains.

George Thayer left Vernon, Connecticut, atop his Columbia Expert on Friday, October 9, just as the fall foliage was nearing its peak. He found the beauty of the season overwhelming, especially in Vermont and New Hampshire. He was so overwhelmed he could scarcely describe it. The beautiful foliage, he wrote, "beggars my limited powers of description."[22]

Perhaps his sister can help him out. Putting her tricycle tourists on the road the same time of year in *Wheels and Whims*, she observed, "It was one of October's perfect days. The sun shone brilliantly across the landscape, now resplendent with the gorgeous hues that only a New England climate produces on the dying leaves. Masses of color in a thousand hues, from the deep maroon of the oaks, through the countless shades of crimson to fiery scarlet and orange in the maples, to the pale yellow of the walnuts."[23]

The women in *Wheels and Whims* packed extra clothing in a big trunk, which they expressed ahead of them to assure they would always have appropriate outfits for any occasion that might arise. George Thayer, alternatively, carried his gear on his back in an army knapsack. His choice of baggage was somewhat unusual. Bicycle tourists of his day typically carried their gear in a saddlebag attached to their seat with leather straps. Fred E. Van Meerbeke, who would bicycle back and forth across the United States in 1886, used both a saddlebag and a handlebar bag.[24] Danger and discomfort typically kept cyclists from carrying a backpack, which raised the rider's already high center of gravity and caused the back to sweat profusely. Furthermore, the knapsack had an annoying tendency to fly up and hit the rider in the head during an accident.

Despite its disadvantages, Thayer tolerated the knapsack and used it on future cycling tours. For him, its symbolic value outweighed its inconvenience. The knapsack established a connection between cycling and soldiering. He took great pleasure in meeting veterans of the Civil War while bicycle touring. His knapsack gave him a point of contact with them. For someone born too late to serve in the Civil War, Thayer could do something akin to war by bicycle touring. Bicycling did not involve fighting, of course, but it did let the traveler make himself vulnerable to danger and uncertainty, giving him an opportunity to test himself on the road in strange lands far from home.

Starting his ambitious New England tour, Thayer headed

north to Somers, crossed into Massachusetts, and made it to Springfield the first morning. Paralleling the Connecticut River, he reached Holyoke that afternoon. He had hoped to make Northampton by nightfall, but his passion for all things mechanical delayed him. This time the sight of the railway trains rushing up and down the tracks along the river thrilled him, and he lingered to gaze at them.

As Friday night descended, Thayer found himself four or five miles from the nearest hotel. Faced with the prospect of riding that distance in the dark, he sought an alternative and stopped at a farmhouse. He asked the Massachusetts farmer if he could stay the night, and the kindly farmer welcomed him indoors. The experience proved so delightful that Thayer never hesitated to seek out farmer hospitality through the remainder of his trip. He reported, "At the farm-houses I was always given the best room in the house, and with one exception, these were nicely furnished. The food, almost floating in butter or cream, was most excellently cooked and served very abundantly."[25]

Saturday morning he hiked to the top of Mount Tom. The climb was difficult, the view worth it. Many praised nearby Mount Holyoke for the view it offered, but aficionados found the view from Mount Tom more spectacular. After descending from the mountain, Thayer pedaled the four or five miles to Northampton—"the most beautiful village in America," according to a contemporary British tourist.[26] Outside Northampton, Thayer picked up the pace, and the village limits signs—sprint signs, we cyclists call them—started coming more rapidly: South Deerfield, Greenfield, Bernardston. Just before dark he crossed into Vermont, which presented new challenges.

Strange as it sounds, the idea of Vermont bicycle touring was an unusual concept then. Seeing that Vermonters were unused to bicycle tourists, Thayer took extra precautions when he approached a horse and buggy. Ever courteous, he usually dismounted whenever a horse came into view. The horseman or, as it more frequently seemed, the horsewoman, appreciated his courtesy. C. A. Stephens, a cyclist who had passed through Maine the previous year with some friends who called themselves the Knock-About Club, confirmed Thayer's experience: "Frequently in the country, the farmers' wives and daughters will be met, driving to and from the village store."[27] "Thank you," one would say with a smile. Or, perhaps, "You did not need to get off."[28]

After passing through Brattleboro on his way to Bellows Falls on Sunday morning, Thayer began a long downhill stretch. As he loved to do, he took his feet from the pedals, threw his legs over the handlebars, and coasted downhill. Toward the bottom, the road took a sharp bend. As he rounded the bend he saw a horse hitched to a wagon containing two men, a woman, and a little boy. Staring at Thayer in amazement, the driver neglected the horse. It seemed alright at first, but as Thayer neared, the horse stopped short and started bucking.

With his legs dangling over the handlebars, Thayer may have been in a precarious position, but he had a trick he used when he wanted to dismount while coasting. He would brake rapidly, depressing the brake spoon onto the front tire hard enough to lock up the front wheel, which would lift the back of the bicycle off the ground and thus tilt him forward, letting him land in front of the bicycle in a standing position. It was a tricky maneuver, but Thayer had practiced it enough to make it a reliable move. In this instance, he dismounted as quickly as he could, but he was not quick enough. The skittish horse whirled about, tipping everything from the wagon— people, seats, blankets—and leaving them in a heap by the side of the road.

The driver managed to get the horse by the bit. Thayer

helped the other man upend the wagon before it could be damaged. His help could not dispel the driver's anger, however. He asked Thayer why he had not dismounted sooner. Thayer demonstrated his move to the driver, showing him that he had dismounted as soon as the horse showed fright and chastised the driver for not warning him about the nervous horse. A great talker, Thayer convinced the man that he had done all he could have done. The driver admitted that he had never driven this particular horse before.[29]

As Thayer continued on the road north, beauty gave way to grandeur. At Wells River Junction, he left the Connecticut River, turning east into New Hampshire and following the Ammonoosuc River to North Lisbon. A farmer recommended a short cut to Franconia over Sugar Hill, which turned out to be good advice. The farmer's route was much shorter than the one Thayer had planned: riding north to Littleton and then coming back down the next road over. From Franconia he turned south, hoping to spend the night at Profile House, the finest hotel in the White Mountains.

Profile House took its name from the landmark it overlooked: the Profile or, in other words, the Old Man of the Mountains or, in Nathaniel Hawthorne's words, the Great Stone Face, a huge rock formation that looked amazingly like the profile of an old man. Hawthorne's short story is excellent, but the familiar quotation attributed to Daniel Webster may be more memorable: "Men hang out their signs indicative of their respective trades; shoe-makers hang out a gigantic shoe, jewelers a monster watch, and the dentist hangs out a gold tooth; but up in the Mountains of New Hampshire, God Almighty has hung out a sign to show that there, He makes men."[30]

As Thayer climbed the steep road through Franconia Notch, the weather grew increasingly dark; the wind picked up, and it began to rain. He had traveled in the dark and the rain

Fig. 3. This photograph depicts Old Man of the Mountain, Franconia
Notch, White Mountains, as it appeared to Thayer and other tourists
to the region until May 2003, when it crumbled from the cliff,
effacing New Hampshire's iconic face forever (Detroit Publishing
Co., ca. 1890). Library of Congress, Prints and Photographs
Division, reproduction number LC-D4-11785.

before, but the ominous sound of wind whistling through the notch was unlike anything he had ever experienced. He wrote, "Everything would be as still as death when a faint sound could be heard a mile or two away down somewhere in the dark. This grew louder and louder till the roar sounded like a dozen freight trains coming at full speed. I have been out in wind as strong, but never when it came in such gusts, and was accompanied with the roar of a tornado."[31] He started looking for a farmhouse or any house for shelter but could find nothing.

When he finally saw the lights of the Profile House, they cheered him up immensely. The hotel had a reputation for luxury. Gas lighting was just one of several amenities. It also had a billiard parlor, a bowling alley, a barbershop, and a gift shop. Profile House, which could accommodate over five hundred guests, contained the finest dining hall in New England.[32] Thayer had covered 50 miles that day, 236 in the five days since the start of this cycling tour, and he was ready to pamper himself.

He knocked on the door. The manager answered, gruffly telling him that the hotel was closed or, to be precise, closed to holiday travelers. There were some permanent boarders who lived there year-round. The guidebooks said that Profile House was open to holiday travelers from June 1 to mid-October, but this year, apparently, it had closed a few days shy of October's midpoint.

"No," the man told Thayer. "The hotel is closed and we don't want to be bothered. You can get kept at The Flume and you had better keep right on. You may find some trees blown across the way, but it is a straight road down through the woods."[33]

The man's insensitivity shocked Thayer. By "the Flume," he meant the Flume House, which was located six miles south. Owned by the same people who owned Profile House, the Flume House did remain open through mid-October, but

Thayer had no intention of walking his bicycle six miles in the dark over an unknown road during a raging storm. As he pleaded his case before the proprietor of Profile House, the storm spoke in his defense. In other words, a huge blast of wind whooshed through the notch, stirring up dirt, pelting the hotel windows with gravel and rain, and making the whole structure tremble.

The manager relented.

"Well," he said, "if you will take up with what the others have you can stay."

Thayer was ushered into a warm, comfortable, well-lighted room. He enjoyed the accommodations, but the storm hindered his rest. "There was not much sleep that night for me," he explained, "for the storm increased in violence and the suspense in waiting, half-asleep, for the roaring gusts to strike the house lengthened and intensified. At intervals during the night I heard them nailing up the windows to keep them from blowing in, and some stayed up all night."[34]

The next morning he went to nearby Echo Lake, where he whistled and yelled at considerable length and great volume, but he could coax no response from the surrounding mountains. Afterward he coasted down to the Flume over "as nice a road as there is in New England."[35] During moments like this, Thayer experienced what Jean Bobet would call *la volupté*, the delicate, intimate, ephemeral pleasure that only cycling can give: "It arrives, it takes hold of you, sweeps you up and then leaves you again. It is for you alone. It is a combination of speed and ease, force and grace. It is pure happiness."[36]

Morning was the best time to see the Flume, a stream flowing through a narrow gorge of granite, which it had carved over eons. Partway up, a huge egg-shaped boulder was lodged between the walls of the gorge. The boulder looked as if it could slip at any moment and crush whomever stood within the horrible interspace beneath it. After exploring the Flume,

Thayer returned to the Profile on his way to Fabyan, covering an additional twenty-three miles that afternoon.

Thursday, October 15, marked the high point of Thayer's tour. On this day he climbed Mount Washington, the highest peak in New Hampshire. The cog railway was the usual means up the mountain, but it had stopped regular service for the year. Determined to reach the top, Thayer decided to walk. He spoke with the man in charge of the railway at the bottom, who telephoned the signalman, one of three men who lived atop the mountain year-round, and asked them to be on the lookout for Thayer in case of accident.

Over the telephone, the signalman said that the wind at the peak was blowing fifty miles an hour, the temperature was twenty degrees Fahrenheit, and all was covered in fog. Thayer, who arrived at the railway station in shirt sleeves, was astonished but undaunted. He wanted to climb, and climb he would. He even agreed to bring a bag of mail to the stalwart souls who lived at the peak.

Following the tracks of the cog railway, he began his ascent. About a mile up, clouds closed in on him and the wind blew a gale, but he made it all the way up. The Summit House—the grand hotel on Mount Washington—looked desolate. Closed for the season, the Summit House was not just boarded up, it was also chained down. It, and everything else at the top, was coated with ice, and the fog was so thick Thayer had trouble locating the signal house. He finally found it and tried the front door, but it was locked. He went around to the back door, but that was locked as well. As he wondered what might have happened to the men, Thayer heard a voice from inside.

"Come to the other door!" yelled the voice.

Thayer went back around to the front, and they welcomed him inside. He gave them their mail and lingered long enough to warm up before heading back down.

As he descended, ice coated his beard and his clothes, but

Thayer, by his own account, scarcely noticed because all his attention was focused on placing one foot in front of the other:

> Walking on naked ties on a level track is not an easy task, but to walk on ties that descend one foot in three and have them covered with frost and ice: the track thirty or forty feet in the air, the wind blowing as if it would pick me right up and carry me out into the fog and then every little ways come to an open space three or four feet wide, with no ties at all—to walk down such a track under such circumstances was hard on the nerves, to say the least. The going up was easy compared to the coming down, for in descending, one is obliged to look right down into these open spaces, and can see how easy it would be to slip through onto the rocks below. Once or twice I tried to squat down and crawl on the rail across these openings but my head had become so accustomed to the downward motion that I fell forward on my hands whenever I stopped.[37]

Jacob's Ladder, a stretch of railway constructed from an elaborate trestlework that took the track thirty feet above the rocks, presented a challenge to the pedestrian. Crossing this stretch, Thayer slipped, nearly falling from the track to the rocks below. Happily, he grabbed hold of the rail and saved himself from serious harm. An hour after leaving the peak he was back at the base. He remounted his wheel, road to Fabyan, and continued through Crawford Notch to the Willey House.

The Willey House marked the site of a legendary avalanche that occurred in 1826. One night Samuel Willey Jr. and his family awoke to the rumble of a great avalanche. To save themselves, they left their home: a fatal error. A great rock situated further up the mountain directly behind the house split the avalanche. The house was unscathed, but the avalanche overtook the fleeing family members and swept them to their deaths. The tragic event would inspire another one of Nathaniel Hawthorne's short stories, "The Ambitious Guest."

This legendary house prompted Thayer, as it did most guests, regardless of ambition, to ponder the vagaries of fate. He did not stay long, for Mount Washington called him back. Since the fog had prevented him from getting a good view from the peak on Thursday, he decided to return to the top on Friday. That morning he left his bicycle at Willey House and walked three miles to Crawford House, where an eight-mile bridle path ascended Mount Washington to the summit. Before beginning his ascent, Thayer spoke with the landlord of Crawford House, who warned him about the danger should the clouds descend.[38]

"Don't go another step," the landlord cautioned, speaking about the threat of fog. "You will get lost and perish."

To Thayer, the warning seemed unnecessary. As he started his ascent, the sky was perfectly blue. Rising into the blue above the tree line, he found what he was looking for: "a most magnificent view, of the whole world it almost seemed." Scrambling over the rocky ridge, he was unprepared for the profound feelings of loneliness that suddenly beset him. Such feelings made him a little panicky. "To be alone on the top of a mountain over five thousand feet high, many miles from any one, was something I was not prepared for and so I ran. I was not exactly afraid, for there was nothing to be afraid of but I wanted to get near something that had life, everything was so still and dead," he explained. "A railroad, a deserted shanty, even a guild-board served to keep me company the day before and I longed for something of the kind now, but there was nothing, not even a heap of stones, not a thing made by human hands. Everything was as the glaciers left it."[39]

He looked upward and saw clouds begin to mask the summit. Suddenly, he understood the landlord's warning. Proceeding further was out of the question. Instead, he sat down where he was, ate his lunch, and enjoyed what was left of the view before the clouds obscured it completely. He returned to the Willey House and, after completing this twenty-mile hike, remounted his wheel and rode seventeen miles further, reaching the Saco River by dark.

The dangers of the next day were more of the manmade kind. Walking his bicycle down a sandy road through the woods just north of Madison, New Hampshire, Thayer saw four men walking toward him, singing and hollering and taking up the whole road. To be sure, Ginger-Ale George could recognize drunks when he saw them. The biggest of the four was also the drunkest.[40]

"How much longer does this sand last?" Thayer asked, putting up a bold front.

"By ——," the big drunk replied, "it will last *you* all day if you don't give me some rum. You have got some in your bag there. Give me some rum."

Thayer began backing away from the big drunk, telling him in a friendly way that he had neither rum nor anything else to drink in his knapsack and letting him know that alcohol was about the worst thing a cyclist could drink while riding. Uninterested in picking a fight, his friends continued past Thayer. Eventually Big Drunk let him pass and rejoined his bottle buddies.

Having escaped from Big Drunk's clutches, Thayer made it to West Ossippee that evening and cycled along Lake Winnipesaukee the next day. It may have been around here that he took the one and only header of this tour. A stick about four inches long got caught between some spokes in his front wheel. When that part of the wheel reached the front fork, the stick became wedged in the fork. The wheel instantly seized up, sending Thayer over the handlebars.[41] He must not have been going too fast: the accident caused no serious damage to either his wheel or his noggin. From Lake Winnipesaukee, he continued through Laconia, Concord, and Manchester, and then back into Massachusetts, stopping at Haverhill for an extended visit with an old friend.

He spent two weeks at Haverhill, giving himself plenty of time to explore the city. While staying here, he took day trips to many places in the surrounding region, including Lawrence, Lowell, Newburyport, and Portsmouth, New Hampshire. Similarly, he spent two more weeks in Boston exploring many places of interest within a twenty-mile radius of "The Hub."[42]

One day during his stay in Boston he rode north along Massachusetts Bay. By this time he was thrilled with bicycle touring and confident that his Columbia Expert could transport him wherever he wished to go. He made up his mind to take an even longer and more ambitious trip: to ride across the continent to California. Visiting Nahant, a small town located on a rocky peninsula jutting into the bay, he brought an empty vial with him and filled it full of water from the Atlantic Ocean. He decided to keep that bottle of Atlantic water until he could mix it with Pacific water on the opposite side of the continent.

3

The Road to Omaha

By the time he finished his third cycling tour in 1885, George Thayer had developed a reputation among local wheelmen as one of the leading cyclotourists in Connecticut.[1] But he hankered to break the bounds of New England. His cycling experiences so far gave him the confidence to ride across the continent. Before he set off on his American odyssey, however, he had much to prepare.

Prior to his departure, he contacted the editor of the *Hartford Evening Post*. Together they reached an agreement whereby Thayer would write intermittent letters to the paper, reporting his progress and describing what he saw as he crossed the nation. This arrangement may have provided a modest income. In addition, it gave him press credentials sufficient to open doors along the way. To those he met on the road, he could introduce himself not solely as a holiday traveler, but as a journalist, a representative of the *Hartford Evening Post*, someone seeking information to delight and instruct a community of readers. Thayer's newspaper correspondence offered another advantage. Upon his return, it could be collected to form the basis for a book-length travel narrative.

He thought long and hard about what equipment to take on his journey. He managed to fit a considerable amount of gear inside his army knapsack: a spare shirt, a coat, an extra pair of knickerbockers (blue ones), some undershirts, a nightshirt, a half dozen pair of stockings, a half dozen handkerchiefs, a sewing kit, a first-aid kit, toiletries, a knife and fork for eating and a long rubber tube for drinking, a repair kit with a spare set of pedal bearings and a spare pedal axle, a lock and chain, and maps. He lashed his rainsuit atop the knapsack. It consisted of a raincoat and leggings made from the lightweight, waterproof fabric known as gossamer, plus a rubber cap and rubber overshoes.

Thayer also brought much writing material with him. In addition to the stationery he would use to maintain his newspaper correspondence and write home to family and friends, he also brought along a notebook to record his day-to-day activities, which he came to call "The Log." After the journey, "The Log" would help him recreate his experience as he revised his newspaper correspondence into *Pedal and Path: Across the Continent Awheel and Afoot*.

One item was noticeably absent from Thayer's luggage: a gun. Thomas Stevens had carried a sidearm when he rode across the continent on the first leg of his round-the-world cycling journey. Thayer's friends advised him to pack a pistol, but he disliked the idea. He explained to his readers: "I decided to maintain my habitual faith in the honesty and good will of the average American and to depend upon diplomacy and conciliation in the circumvention of the exceptional villain."[2] Taking a tip from *Wheels and Whims*, he expressed ahead of him a valise packed with more clothes and extra gear, but he found its contents unnecessary and later shipped the valise home to Connecticut.

Thayer carried some other papers in his knapsack, including a list of wheelmen across the country. This item also attests to his meticulous preparation. A few days before his departure, he went through back issues of the LAW *Bulletin* looking for the names of cyclists who lived along his planned route. By the time he finished, he had compiled a sizeable list. He was able to start his journey knowing the names of members of the League of American Wheelmen (LAW) in almost every city he would visit.[3] Thayer's act of slicing up his back issues of the LAW *Bulletin* suggests one reason why so few copies of this magazine survive: it contained practical information about cycling that riders clipped out and carried with them while riding.

Though Thayer devoted considerable attention to the contents of his knapsack, he did not bother training for his transcontinental tour. The day before he left, he took a thirty-mile shakedown ride just to make sure everything worked properly, but otherwise he did not ride his bicycle at all during the four months preceding his departure. Conditioning rides seemed unnecessary, since he would get in shape as his trip progressed. His high-wheeled, nickel-plated Columbia Expert was in good shape, however. Fitted with a reliable Lakin cyclometer, it was ready to cross the continent and record the distance all the way.[4]

Finally just one task remained: saying good-bye. Before leaving, Thayer hesitated to tell people he was planning to ride all the way to San Francisco. Perhaps he did not want to boast too much, or perhaps he did not want to set his expectations too high. Travelers, he understood, could get themselves in trouble by boasting too much about their plans.

Thayer was more cautious as he discussed his planned journey. He told his mother that he was only going to Iowa, afraid that any destination further west would unsettle her already nervous temperament. He told his friends he was going to Omaha.[5] Having lived in Omaha earlier, he knew the city well. It was a familiar, comfortable place. He was confident that he could make it that far. Privately, he planned to go much further. His list of league members contained the names of wheel-men living at least as far west as Salt Lake City.[6] And he also carried that tiny vial of Atlantic Ocean water in his knapsack, intending to tote it all the way to the Pacific.

Adorned in a brown shirt, seal-brown corduroy knicker-bockers, brown stockings, and low canvas shoes, all topped with a blue riding cap, Thayer left Vernon, Connecticut, on his wheel on Saturday, April 10. His four-month cycling hiatus quickly took its toll. Though he had ridden to New Haven and back in one day two years earlier, just getting to the City of Elms this day proved to be a monumental chore. He did not arrive until after dark Saturday night.

He stayed there through Monday, meeting people and seeing the sights. On Sunday, George Kimball, a Yale student and fellow wheelman, showed him around town, but Kimball set a brisk pace that made severe demands on the out-of-shape out-of-towner. Thayer also visited the Peabody Museum. Since opening a decade earlier, the museum had been expanding its collection of dinosaur bones significantly. Here Thayer saw, as he said, some "fine specimens of ancient life."[7] To see some fine specimens of modern life, he acquainted himself with riders from the New Haven Bicycle Club, including one of its most active members, W. H. Thomas. After a sociable Monday, Thayer awoke to rain the next morning, so he did not get back on the road until noon on Tuesday.

The time he spent in New Haven indicates the leisurely pace Thayer had chosen for his transcontinental tour. He would ride when he wanted, stop when he didn't, and take time throughout the trip to see whatever he wished and meet whomever he wanted. Thayer was one cyclotourist who did not feel the need to ride as many miles as possible every day. He had the same philosophy of bicycle touring that Harold Elvin would exemplify in the twentieth century. In *The Ride to Chandigarh*, a narrative of a cycling journey through India that reads

ACCOUTRED FOR THE START. — (*Frontispiece.*)

Fig. 4. This engraving, which forms the frontispiece for Thayer's
Pedal and Path, depicts how he and his bicycle looked upon starting
their transcontinental journey (Moss Engraving Co., New York). From
George B. Thayer, *Pedal and Path: Across the Continent Awheel and
Afoot* (Hartford: Evening Post Association, 1887). Courtesy
Lilly Library, Indiana University, Bloomington IN.

like a prose poem, Elvin observes, "It's not the miles in the life that count but the life in the miles."[8]

The fact that Thayer actively sought out wheelmen across the nation indicates his gregarious nature, but his behavior also reflects how much the League of American Wheelmen had done in its brief history to create a sense of camaraderie and fraternity among members across the nation.

The LAW had been formed in 1880 as a protective league, an organization allowing American cyclists to show their solidarity, to give themselves the political clout to assert their rights to the road in the face of ever-demanding horsemen, some of whom sought to ban cyclists from public highways altogether. Joining the league became a way of supporting the cause of cycling. Karl Kron considered "the act of joining the League of American Wheelmen one of the very first duties which every cycler in this country owes to his fellows."[9] The efforts of the LAW proved highly successful. At the end of the decade, Thayer himself observed: "The day has passed when bicyclers fail, as a rule, to get their just rights upon the roads. These rights have mainly been secured to wheelmen everywhere by the League."[10]

The governmental structure of the LAW paralleled the nation's political structure. The league elected a national president, and every state division had its leader, known as a chief consul. Secretary-treasurer was another statewide office. New Haven cyclist W. H. Thomas, for instance, was secretary-treasurer for the Connecticut division of the LAW.[11] Furthermore, each state was entitled to one league representative for every fifty members. On the recommendation of a state's league representative, the chief consul could appoint league consuls to serve individual communities. It was the responsibility of the league consuls to provide information about roads, hotels, and other local attractions to passing wheelmen. Always a joiner, George B. Thayer became a member of the LAW and served as league consul of Vernon, Connecticut.

The LAW would continue to promote camaraderie among its members well into the twentieth century. Whereas Thayer compiled his own list of wheelmen prior to the start of his cross-country tour in 1886, LAW members a century later could take advantage of the "Hospitality Homes" directory, an annually published list of league members who welcomed touring cyclists into their residences, offering overnight accommodation free of charge.

Pausing at Stamford, Connecticut, on Wednesday, April 14, Thayer enjoyed a pleasant chat with William Hurlbutt, league representative and president of the Stamford Wheel Club. Though *Pedal and Path* begins as a day-by-day account of Thayer's journey, after the first few days he found it unnecessary to say precisely what happened on which days, so it is sometimes difficult, but oftentimes unnecessary to say precisely what he did on a day-by-day basis.

At Greenwich Thayer met a group of three riders. He could tell by their jerseys that two-thirds of the group had spent some time in the dirt that day, but he judiciously refrained from saying which ones wore evidence of their accident. One of the riders was Consul E. W. Reynolds; another was Dr. E. N. Judd, vice president of the Greenwich cycling club. Dr. Judd was one of many professional men who took to the wheel in the early days of cycling. Attorneys, clergymen, dentists, druggists, physicians, professors: all took up cycling as a form of exercise in the 1880s.[12]

Continuing his journey beyond Greenwich, Thayer followed Long Island Sound until he crossed the New York state line, where he turned inland. Pedaling through the region Washington Irving made famous as Sleepy Hollow, Thayer took time to visit a seventeenth-century Dutch church. Though it was growing dark, he dawdled in the adjacent churchyard to indulge a favorite pastime: reading grave markers. With this stop, he turned the day's ride into a tombstone tour. He looked long enough to discover several tombstones nearly as old as the church itself.

Leaving the churchyard after dark, he continued riding through Sleepy Hollow by the light of a full moon. Passing a gypsy camp, he imagined how he must have looked, imbued by the local atmosphere: "Coasting silently down unknown hills in the dark, I really think I must have looked like a genuine goblin astride of a silver broomstick."[13]

Eventually he reached this evening's destination, the American House at Ossining. What had really delayed Thayer so long this day was not the country churchyard, but something else he encountered two miles outside Tarrytown. Spying a cluster of workmen's shanties, he recognized the place as one of the construction sites for the New Croton Aqueduct, the largest public works project the state of New York had ever undertaken, which was built to bring water from upstate reservoirs to New York City. Specifically, it was the site of shaft number eleven. With a Walt Whitman–like penchant for watching construction crews at work, Thayer tried to take a ride on the elevator to the tunnel site, but not even his press credentials could gain him access without official permission.

Turning him away, the foreman told him to get permission from the office in Tarrytown. Thayer remounted his wheel, rode into town, and spent much time tracking down the company official who could help him. His press credentials now came in handy. Once Thayer secured permission, however, he decided not to return to shaft number eleven. Instead, he would visit a site closer to his destination for that day, shaft number one. This shaft was eight miles out of his way but well worth the detour, he reckoned. As he went to bed at the American House in Ossining, he was so excited about the chance to witness the underground construction that he laid awake half the night.

The next morning he pedaled eight miles over a hilly, muddy road to reach that shaft. There, a worker loaned him an old coat and a pair of rubber boots, and Thayer took a place on the elevator car. Only then did he realize that whereas shaft number eleven went sixty feet into the earth, shaft number one was much deeper, six times deeper, in fact. Some good-humored workers who joined him on the elevator joked about a man who had died there recently. Thayer was not amused. Their jokes spooked him so much that he asked to be let out before the elevator got going. Perhaps it was too early in his epic journey for a descent to the underworld.

It does seem strange that Thayer would chicken out after devoting so much effort to gain access, but his behavior on this occasion is characteristic of his personality. Ever the optimist, he never really thought in terms of lost opportunities. If he missed one chance, he felt sure others would come along. He might be a little older before the next opportunity presented itself, but a few extra months or years under his belt scarcely bothered him. He would not let age stop him from doing whatever he wanted to do.

Even on this tour he felt that there was time enough for everything. Staying at the Catskill Mountain House a few days later, he took a seat in the shade of the hotel and spent four hours by himself enjoying the view of the Hudson, the finest from any of the mountain hotels, he concluded. In the Mohawk Valley, the railway trains captured his attention, much as they had on his earlier tour through New England. The drums along the Mohawk may have fallen silent, but the steam whistles of the trains could be heard far and wide. At one point Thayer was astonished to see a passenger train overtake a freight train as a third train scooted between them with a fourth close behind.

All across New York fellow wheelmen welcomed Thayer with friendship, hospitality, and advice. Everyone he met, it seems, was happy to point him in the right direction. When he approached a Poughkeepsie policeman to ask where the city's wheelmen gathered, the officer agreed to escort him there. The sight of a policeman taking Thayer through the streets of Poughkeepsie delighted the local urchins, who assumed the cyclist was under arrest, and they teased him mercilessly.

The "nest of wheelmen" Thayer found in Poughkeepsie was a gathering of the Ariel Wheel Club. J. R. Adriance, club president and league representative, was "a tall, sandy complexioned gentleman of thirty-five or forty, with a full beard."[14] Thayer also met Edward A. King, a clean-shaven man in his early twenties who was captain of the club. Though the offices of president and captain might seem redundant, a key difference separated them. The captain was the leader on the road, the president off the road. Thayer enjoyed the cordiality of President Adriance and Captain King and paid tribute to both in *Pedal and Path*.

Thayer sought out the bicycle clubs in every major city in New York. After visiting the Albany Bicycle Club House, he grumbled that the club had become more of a social than an athletic club. He made an important point. The final third of the nineteenth century was the golden age of the American club. Numerous social clubs were founded across the nation during this period. Membership in these clubs conferred status and prestige. The cycling clubs were no exception. As Thayer's remark suggests, the Albany Bicycle Club had achieved such a level of prestige in the community that many noncyclists wanted to join in order to participate in its social activities.

Thayer was more impressed with the Schenectady Bicycle Club. Jacob W. Clute honed his leadership skills as captain of the club: years later he was elected mayor of Schenectady. Knowing Clute was an attorney by profession, Thayer visited the Schenectady County Courthouse on Union Street to meet him. Erected in 1831, this courthouse was already over a half-century old. Its monumental Greek Doric portico lent it a sense of grandeur. Once inside, Thayer went upstairs to the second floor, where the courtroom was located. Through a crack in the door, he watched Clute cross-examine a witness but was unable to speak with him personally. Thayer's account reveals his nascent interest in courtroom practice and procedure. His behavior at the Schenectady County Courthouse looks forward to his later career in the legal profession.

Though Clute's activities before the bar prevented Thayer from making his acquaintance, Thayer had better luck getting to know a former captain of the Schenectady club, the tricycle-riding Sam R. James, whom he described as "a good-sized man of sixty, with side whiskers and moustache."[15] One contemporary reviewer of *Pedal and Path*, while generally liking the book, complained about its "undue amount of personalities, as regards appearance of people encountered, etc."[16] Apparently this reviewer disliked Thayer's tendency to describe the facial hair of every man he met. All these whisker descriptions have documentary value: they show the significance and variety of facial hair among contemporary athletes, aspects that contribute much to the iconography of the era. James and his mutton chops escorted Thayer to the Erie Canal towpath.

Having imagined that it would be a smooth surface he could navigate at breakneck speed, Thayer was disappointed with the towpath. George Nellis would react to the Erie Canal towpath similarly when he crossed upstate New York at the start of his transcontinental ride the following year.[17] Thayer followed the canal as far as Fonda, where he left it for good. Far superior to the towpath, the roads in upstate New York quickly took him to Utica, where he met a dozen or so members of the Fort Schuyler Wheelmen at their club rooms in the evening. He happily reported: "The members are mostly young men and nearly all riders, and bicycling has certainly taken a firm hold at this place."[18]

Compared to Utica, Syracuse was a disappointment. The Syracuse Bicycle Club seemed to be gasping for breath. Thayer observed, "With equally good roads, a larger population, with club rooms, rent free, in the YMCA building, a beautiful structure in a city of fine buildings, with all things seemingly favorable, the club hardly numbers a dozen lifeless members."[19] Thayer's prediction of the club's demise was premature. The Syracuse Bicycle Club would survive for many years to come.

Speaking with a newspaper reporter in Syracuse, Thayer revealed much about himself. He had started his journey telling people that he was going to Iowa or Omaha. Now he was giving Denver as his destination.[20] The change verifies his growing confidence yet does indicate some lingering doubts. He still refrained from admitting his real goal: San Francisco.

His trek across western New York brought him in contact with other hospitable wheelmen, including Dr. A. G. Coleman, who belonged to the Canandaigua Bicycle Club. Adorned in dark gray knickerbockers and blue stockings, members of this club cut a handsome appearance on the road.[21] Coleman had much advice for him. The doctor had more experience atop his wheel than anyone Thayer had met so far, with the exception of Alonzo Williams.

Short, thickset, and sporting a gray beard, Coleman did not look much like a cyclist, but he had ridden across both Colorado and California. Furthermore, Coleman took an active role in local, national, and international cycling activities. He had previously served as both president and captain of the Canandaigua club.[22] He was also league representative and chief consul for the Cyclists' Touring Club (CTC), the LAW's British equivalent, which used to have an active American branch. Coleman did whatever he could to encourage bicycle touring, and he regaled Thayer with stories of his touring experiences in the West.

The roads, the weather, the scenery: all remained beautiful across New York. Once he reached Buffalo, Thayer encountered C. W. Adams, a bespectacled young man who made him feel perfectly at home. Adams escorted him on a ride around Buffalo, a city containing "fifteen or twenty miles of asphalt as smooth as glass" and "miles and miles of fine park roads."[23] Such beautiful roads greatly encouraged the popularity of cycling in Buffalo. The number of cyclists there had grown so much in recent years that the Buffalo Bicycle Club had outgrown its old clubhouse and was in the process of moving into nicer digs, a large two-story building, which, Thayer foresaw, would "soon be nicely filled up with everything that such a genuine riding, working, racing, hospitable club needs."[24] Adams magnanimously offered to escort Thayer on a side trip to Niagara Falls. Thayer accepted. They took the train to Niagara Falls, but brought their bicycles with them to take a few turns around Goat Island: a favorite ride among contemporary cyclists.

Except for the Erie Canal towpath and one ornery farmer who told him to quit riding his bicycle and get a job, Thayer had a great time riding across upstate New York. The only other thing he found to complain about was the general absence of road signs. This complaint disappeared once he entered Pennsylvania. "The change is like magic," he said. Pennsylvania roads were well marked with easy-to-read signs.[25]

Having crossed the state of New York on his wheel, Thayer was much fitter and more road-hardened than when he began. Dangers and difficulties scarcely bothered him now. He took his first header in Pennsylvania, but he took it with ease. On this instance, he suffered two blows to the head, the first as he hit the ground, the second as his knapsack flew up and hit him. The blows to his head stunned him but also helped him see how far he had come since starting this tour, not just in terms of distance but also in terms of personal growth. He wrote, "If I had been at home I would have bandaged my head, gone into an easy chair, and called the doctor. As it was, I simply remounted, trundled on, and was all right again in an hour."[26]

Despite this header, Thayer made excellent time, covering the two hundred miles from Buffalo to Cleveland in only three days. The road between the two cities was excellent. "I never saw as long a stretch of fine wheeling," he said.[27] He would modify this judgment before he left Ohio. Nearing Cleveland, he visited Lake View Cemetery to see the tomb of President James A. Garfield, who had been assassinated five years earlier. The massive Garfield monument remained unfinished, but Thayer admired the location its planners had chosen, a site, he said, "that commands a fine view of the lake, the city, and the surrounding country for miles, the most beautiful location in that part of the state."[28]

Euclid, Ohio, on the other hand, was "a small village full of rum-holes, and surrounded by mud and water, the most forsaken place I have yet seen."[29] This forlorn place did not give him much hope for Cleveland, but when he came out the other side of Euclid and entered an avenue of the same name, Thayer was surprised and amazed: "Euclid Avenue in Cleveland is as far removed from Euclid as Paradise from Purgatory. Buffalo has streets as beautiful, with better pavements, but none as long. The poplar seems to be the popular tree, long stately rows lining the sides of the street."[30]

After Cleveland, Thayer had a choice to make. Since he was heading for Chicago, the most direct route would take him through northwest Ohio, a route Thomas Stevens had enjoyed very much.[31] The road along the Maumee River was (and is) quite beautiful. But Thayer had a thing for state capitals, so he bypassed the Maumee Valley to take the long way through Ohio. From Cleveland he dropped down to Columbus to see the Ohio Statehouse, an excellent example of Greek Revival architecture. On the way, he passed through Ohio's grape-growing region, which impressed him very much: "This industry, new for this section of the country, is assuming enormous proportions, and I passed acres and acres of land entirely devoted to grapes. In fact the country seemed to be one vast vineyard, and I could easily imagine what a delicious sight it must present in the fall of the year; and my parched mouth seemed to get drier as I rode past the immense cellars that I knew were full of the cool wine."[32] If Ginger-Ale George was tempted to stop for a glass of Ohio wine, he avoided the temptation and kept riding.

Many people Thayer met were astonished with what he was trying to do and pelted him with questions. Take for example the portly, middle-aged man he met in Wellington, Ohio. Seated in a carriage waiting for his wife, the man stopped Thayer, asking him the same questions Thayer had heard countless times already. Where was he from? Where had he been? Where was he headed? Once Thayer had answered all these questions, the man called to his wife, who remained inside their home.

"Wife, wife, come out here and see this boy; this boy from Connecticut," he hollered for the whole city to hear. "Come all the way on a bicycle, goes sixty and seventy miles a day some days; going clear out to Denver on it. There's an Eastern boy for you, that's Eastern grit, that is. That's Eastern." The man smiled a big old smile and wished Thayer all the luck in the world.[33]

Muddy roads often gave cyclists fits, slowing them down and sometimes making it impossible to ride altogether. One Ohio morning, a light drizzle started to fall, making the roads too slick to ride. Thayer dismounted, turned his bicycle upside down, putting the little wheel in the air, and pushed it like a wheelbarrow. Mud continued to accumulate between the

A DRAG THROUGH THE MUD. —(*Page 46.*)]

Fig. 5. Thayer gets a lift from a kindly buggy driver, who saves him from trudging through the muddy road (Moss Engraving Co., New York). From George B. Thayer, *Pedal and Path: Across the Continent Awheel and Afoot* (Hartford: Evening Post Association, 1887). Courtesy Lilly Library, Indiana University, Bloomington IN.

drive wheel and the fork until the wheel stuck fast. He managed to make it through the day, but a heavy downpour the next morning made even walking on the roads impossible. Thayer left the roads and walked on the adjoining lots, but that provided further difficulties because he had to keep hopping fences and lifting his machine over them.

That afternoon, a man in a buggy—the first Thayer had seen all day—offered to help out. Thayer took him up on his offer. Seating himself backward in the buggy with his legs dangling off, he held onto the handlebars and let the large wheel of his machine roll behind.

Before he reached Columbus, the roads improved considerably. Thirty-five miles north of the city, Thayer encountered a type of highway he had never seen before: a double-track road.

Since this term has escaped the attention of the dictionary makers, Thayer's definition is worth quoting: "These double-track or 'summer' roads, as they are called, are made of coarse gravel on one side, and the natural soil, the clay, on the other, the clay being preferred in the summer and the gravel in the winter and spring."[34] A road even better than the one from Buffalo to Cleveland was the pike from Columbus to Indianapolis, which was uniformly good for 180 miles. Speaking with an interviewer toward the end of his journey, Thayer still remembered that road, the greatest he encountered throughout the trip: "I did the best traveling on the national pike in Ohio. It is a hard, level road, and very fast."[35]

Thayer felt so contented at this point in his journey that he indulged in some creative writing. As it does with so many other long-distance bicyclists, food became an obsession, prompting him to draw some clever comparisons with figures from antiquity:

> The appetite such a journey as this gives one is no small part of the pleasure of the trip, everything tastes so good. The truth was never more plainly stated than by a Spartan waiter. Dionysus was taking a "hasty plate of soup," at one of those free lunches they gave there in Greece so often, when, pushing back from the table, he complained that the black broth was not highly seasoned enough for him. The waiter roared it through the hall "Seasoned! We season it by running, sweating, and getting tired, hungry, and thirsty." It is truly wonderful how such exercise does increase a person's digestive ability. I can imagine to a certain degree just how Milo, a Grecian athlete, must have enjoyed himself. Twenty pounds was the amount of his daily bread, and the same quantity of meat, besides fifteen quarts of wine, taken afterwards, no doubt, for his stomach's ache. One day, feeling somewhat faint from lack of nourishment, he knocked a four-year-old [cow] in the

head with his fist, and devoured the whole "beef critter" during the day. To some this may at first appear incredible, but there is one explanation, at least, that is plausible: Milo must undoubtedly have been a wheelman.[36]

Ohio was good to Thayer. He experienced few setbacks beyond tearing a hole in his pants on the road from Cleveland to Columbus. The gaping hole was too big for him to fix with his portable sewing kit, so he had to find some help. Stopping at Cardington, he met Samuel Brown, a wheelman who was also a tailor. Sam Brown soon put Thayer's seal-brown knickerbockers back in riding order and got him on the road again.

A more serious mishap occurred once Thayer crossed into Indiana. The hard rubber tires of a high-wheeled bicycle were generally maintenance free, but in Indiana, Thayer's rear tire broke into pieces and came off the rim. In nearby Richmond, he met a wheelman who generously gave him a secondhand rear tire. This spare tire was made for an eighteen-inch rim, so they had to cut it down to fit. To help secure the tire, Thayer bought a spool of wire for a nickel and wired the makeshift tire onto the rim. I suppose you could say that Thayer had a wired-on tire *avant la lettre*: the wired-on pneumatic tire or "clincher" would not be invented until a few years later. This repair let Thayer make it to Chicago, where he could replace the rear tire. He put the leftover spool of wire into his knapsack. Who knew when that might come in handy again?

He crossed Indiana in a northwest direction to Lafayette. Given the rainy weather and the clayey roads, it took him a long time to reconnoiter the Hoosier State. At times so much mud would accumulate between the wheels and the frame of his bicycle that the wheels would seize up. By the time he reached Lafayette, he had endured three straight days of rain. Before he left home, Thayer had decided to take the train whenever he felt like it. Since he was not trying to set a cycling record, he had no compulsion to pedal all the way across the continent. Thayer took the train from Lafayette to Chicago.

He stayed in the metropolis a week to see the sights, including the stockyards. In *Pedal and Path*, Thayer dwells upon his visit to the stockyards at length, describing what he saw in gruesome detail. His description of the slaughtering process would do Upton Sinclair proud. As George Nellis would the following year, George Thayer also enjoyed riding the super-smooth asphalt pavement of Chicago's major thoroughfares. Here, as everywhere, the local wheelmen proved to be friendly and obliging.

From Thayer's perspective, the only strange thing about the Chicago wheelmen was their reluctance to coast. It was so flat there they never bothered. Tooling around town one day, Thayer and some other cyclists started descending into a tunnel running beneath the Chicago River. Now this was the kind of descent Thayer enjoyed. He lifted his feet from the pedals, threw his legs over the handlebars, and coasted into the darkness of the tunnel.

The Chicago cyclists, alternatively, kept their feet on the pedals and spun faster and faster as they descended into the tunnel. Thayer could hardly believe that the Chicagoans could not coast, but his is not the only testimony to this fact. Other cyclists commented similarly on the Chicagoans' preference for keeping their feet on the rapidly spinning pedals. When some Chicago wheelmen came to St. Louis for a meet, the St. Louis wheelmen chuckled as they watched the Chicago riders pedal down every grade.[37]

Before Thayer left Chicago, he spoke with a reporter, who asked about the difficulties he had encountered. In his reply, Thayer said that the greatest obstructions he had met with so far were the "gaping crowds in country towns and rural dogs that want to test the quality of his socks."[38]

The roads deteriorated quickly west of Chicago. Riding a

Fig. 6. Thayer says he rode atop the rail, which the illustrator at
Moss Engraving Company took literally. More likely, he rode over
the railroad ties. From George B. Thayer, *Pedal and Path: Across the
Continent Awheel and Afoot* (Hartford: Evening Post Association,
1887). Courtesy Lilly Library, Indiana University, Bloomington IN.

bumpy path parallel to some railroad tracks one day, Thayer
decided to try riding on one of the iron rails. And he did—or
so he says. To prove it, an illustration in *Pedal and Path* depicts
him riding atop the rail, as difficult as it might be to believe.
He must have had an extraordinary sense of balance and tremendous concentration to keep his bicycle upright while riding that rail. It was only the threat of an oncoming locomotive,
he says, that made him get down from it.

West of Chicago, Thayer stopped in Minonk, Illinois, to see
his cousin John W. January, who now lived on a comfortable
homestead in the western part of Minonk. Thayer wanted to

Fig. 7. Thayer's cousin John W. January demonstrates how his prosthetic legs work in a promotional brochure for their manufacturer, A. A. Marks. From George Edwin Marks, *A Treatise on Marks' Patent Artificial Limbs with Rubber Hands and Feet* (New York: A. A. Marks, 1888).

meet the cousin who had amputated his own feet to survive as a POW during the Civil War, partly from curiosity but also to thank him for his bravery and his sacrifice. Seeing him for the first time, Thayer could hardly tell his cousin had suffered such debilitating injuries. He looked nothing like his picture in *Harper's Weekly*. He had fleshed out considerably, not only returning to his original weight of 165 but surpassing that by another fifteen pounds. A. A. Marks, a manufacturer of artificial limbs, had fitted January with two prosthetic legs, which allowed him to walk upright.

Since leaving the army, January had been successfully working his farm in Illinois. He had related his experience as a prisoner of war countless times already, but he told it once again to indulge a cousin who had ridden his bicycle from Connecticut to see him. Thayer stayed on January's farm in Minonk for several days, helping out and hearing stories. Seeing with his own eyes the evidence of January's bravery and sacrifice, Thayer reaffirmed his belief in the battlefield as a proving ground for manhood.[39]

From Minonk, Thayer continued to Grinnell, Iowa, where he saw signs of the recent tornado that had ripped through the town and across the campus of Grinnell College. By the time he reached Des Moines, Thayer had run out of money. He did not mention this fact in *Pedal and Path*, but he later enjoyed telling the story of how he rescued himself from poverty in the middle of Iowa, relying on his previous retail experience. He established the first peanut stand Des Moines had ever seen and did such a brisk business that he was able to clear about seven dollars a day, money to help him continue his cross-country journey.[40]

Back in the black, Thayer got back on the road. As he continued his journey, he discovered that the rolling hills of western Iowa got steeper and steeper as he continued west. Coasting down one hill with his legs over the handlebars, Thayer lost control of his bicycle and took a nasty spill, entertaining an Iowa couple standing by the side of the road. To prevent any similar mishaps, he took the train to Omaha.

Thayer reached Omaha seventy days after leaving home. His easy-going pace indicates the leisurely nature of his journey. The following year George Nellis would only take two days longer to ride his Columbia Expert from New York to San Francisco.[41] It was now the third week of June, and Thayer had ridden a total of 1,980 miles. He was pleased with his total mileage but somewhat surprised it had taken him so long.

After a few days in Omaha, his old stomping ground, Thayer considered taking the train to Denver. A strong storm and the promise of further rain helped make up his mind. This thrifty traveler managed to finagle a bargain on his train ticket. As

Fig. 8. Though Thayer was a daredevil, who loved to coast downhill with his legs over the handlebars, this Iowa hill was too steep for him to handle (Moss Engraving Co., New York). From George B. Thayer, *Pedal and Path: Across the Continent Awheel and Afoot* (Hartford: Evening Post Association, 1887). Courtesy Lilly Library, Indiana University, Bloomington IN.

it happened, Charles M. Woodman, the secretary-treasurer of the Omaha Wheel Club, worked as a stenographer for the Union Pacific Railway. Hoping to avoid the expensive fare, Thayer approached him for help. His plea for assistance worked: Woodman spared him that fee.[42]

Waiting on the station platform for the Denver train, Thayer took the opportunity to consider his personal appearance. After being outdoors for so long, his arms and legs were almost as dark as his seal-brown trousers. His fair complexion was not meant for cycle touring. His nose had burned, peeled, and burned again countless times. He had lost between fifteen and eighteen pounds, making his clothes hang loose. And the patch that Samuel Brown had sewn onto his corduroy knickerbockers in Ohio had now worn through. In Omaha, Thayer had his corduroys reseated with thick buckskin and dyed to match. Why did he go to the bother and expense of such an elaborate repair? The answer to that question is simple: He was planning to ride further, much further, once he reached Denver.

4

The Way to San Francisco

Denver weather can be quite pleasant in June. To George Thayer, the Mile-High City felt "as crisp and cool as an October morning in Connecticut."[1] After arriving, he introduced himself to local wheelmen, including the mustachioed George F. Higgins, chief consul of the LAW for Colorado. Higgins led Thayer around Denver, and F. J. Chamard, a member of the Denver Wheel Club and secretary-treasurer of the Colorado division of the LAW, escorted him partway to Colorado Springs. They were accompanied by a third cyclist, J. A. Hasley, a member of the Kansas City Wheelmen who had reached Denver a few days earlier. He, too, was on a westbound cycling tour. Hasley and Thayer were thinking about cycling to California together; they had decided to use this side trip to Pike's Peak to see how they got along. Before Colorado Springs, Chamard peeled off and headed back to Denver. Thayer and Hasley pushed ahead.

The two soon found themselves on a road that threaded through a region of barbed wire. Before passing all the barbed-wire fences, they encountered a vast herd of horses and cattle. At the sight of these cyclists, the horses took fright and stampeded down the road and the cows and calves followed, all stirring up great clouds of dust behind them. Quickly dismounting, Thayer and Hasley scrambled to the closest fence to get out of the way as the angry rancher tried to slow his herds and calm them down. Finally getting the animals under control, the rancher, all eyes and beard, approached the two cyclists.

"By J——s, you fellows will get shot down here before you go very far with them things! If my horses had gone over that wire fence, by J——s, I should have wanted to put a hole through you," he exclaimed.

After Thayer and Hasley apologized, the rancher cooled down somewhat. He admitted that an earlier experience had given him a bad attitude toward cyclists, the sour memory of which prompted him to launch a long story.

"A while ago," he began,

coming from Denver with a load of oats, I met a couple of fellows on their velocipedes and they were yelling, and hollering and did not offer to stop. My horses saw them first, and started down the hill as if nothing was hitched to them. They turned down the railroad track and took that forty hundred of oats over those ties as if they were feathers. I finally stopped them down in the cut, but I was mad, you bet. These dudes were strangers around here or they would not have said what they did to me. They told me to go talk to a dog and to do some other things. They did not know enough to keep their mouths shut after they had got me into that fix. So I just pulled my belt gun and held it up. "Now," says I, "you just come back or I will corral you. While I go out and stick up a couple flags, you just lay down those things and go and pack those bags of oats out here into the road." They wouldn't at first, but finally did, and it did me good to see them New York dudes tugging away at them 300-pound sacks. I unhitched the horses and made them fellows pull the wagon back and load the oats in again, but they emptied both their bottles before they got through.[2]

For *Pedal and Path*, Thayer directly quoted this rancher's story but admitted after the quotation that what he wrote was not exactly a word-for-word transcription of what the rancher said. "To appreciate this story, and the manner in which it was told," Thayer explained, "one needs to hear it highly spiced, as it was with the huge oaths and many of the strange expressions used out here."[3] Regardless, the friendly, apologetic attitude of both Thayer and Hasley gave the rancher a more positive attitude toward cyclists.

Early one morning, they reached Cliff House, the hotel at Manitou Springs. William H. Thomes, who also stayed here in 1886, called it "the most charming spot in Colorado in the summer months." Welsh poet Emily Pfeiffer, who had stayed there during her recent visit to Colorado, noted the hotel's "kind and attentive hostess" and its excellent view of Pike's Peak.[4]

Thayer and Hasley intended to leave their bicycles here and hike to Grand Cavern, but a guide told them they could enjoy some fine coasting on the other side of Ute Pass, so they decided to take their machines with them. The road was okay at first, a smooth carriage road, and they soon reached Grand Cavern, where another guide told them the road was all downhill. Well, not exactly. The first problem: the road was not a road but a trail. The second problem: there was more than one trail. Thayer and Hasley took the wrong one.

The route they followed was a steep, rocky trail impossible to ride. Partway down they realized they had taken the wrong trail, so they had to climb back up, hauling their bicycles with them. One would climb a few feet up as the other stayed below to lift the bicycles, handing them to the man above. Though both cyclists were quite fit, it took every ounce of strength they had to ascend back to the fork.

DESCENT INTO THE CAVE OF THE WINDS. — (*Page 92.*)

Fig. 9. Descending into the Cave of the Winds, Thayer and J. A. Hasley learn the hard way that advice from people who were not cyclists was nearly always well intended but not always useful (Moss Engraving Co., New York). From George B. Thayer, *Pedal and Path: Across the Continent Awheel and Afoot* (Hartford: Evening Post Association, 1887). Courtesy Lilly Library, Indiana University, Bloomington IN.

They finally found the right trail and started toward Williams Canyon. The trail ended at the edge of the canyon, which dropped three or four hundred feet straight down. They also located an immense hole (perhaps twenty-five feet across) that descended into the mountain, two hundred feet down to the Cave of the Winds. Thayer tells the story best:

Rickety ladders and shaky stairs wound down around the inside of this hole, and down these we must go with our wheels! Yes, the guide was right, it was down hill with a vengeance. We took my wheel first, it being the lightest, and Hasley went down a few rounds on the ladder and then took hold of the big wheel and held it firm so that the rubber tire slid down the ladder. I held onto the handlebar with one hand and the ladder with the other, and thus we reached the bottom of the first ladder, step by step, but safely. The next pair of steep stairs went under the shelving rocks so close that there was not room to get the wheel down, and so we lifted it over the edge of the railing, and I let it down as far as I could with one hand, and Hasley ran down to the next stairs underneath and caught the wheel as I let go. The rest of the stairs were not so steep, but a single misstep at any time would have sent us all to the bottom of this hole in unseemly haste. Getting Hasley's wheel down was a repetition of our first experience, only his was heavier, and the stairs creaked more, and it was more difficult to get his machine over the railing and let it down at arm's length, to be caught by the other underneath; but at the entrance of the cave, stairs led down under a boulder, suspended as that one was at the Flume in the White Mountains, and out into the daylight of the cañon, and we were soon down in the road, hardly realizing how we had got there.

The scenery down the cañon was so grand, and the whole trip was so exciting that we did not regret at the end that we had taken our wheels where no other wheels have ever been, and where no other wheels ever ought to be taken again.[5]

They returned to Cliff House by nightfall. Though dog tired after the day's efforts, they started planning a trip to the top of Pike's Peak the following day. This time they would leave their machines at Cliff House and travel by shank's mare. Learning of their plans, a man asked them if they would escort two young ladies to the top of Pike's Peak. Of course, these two bachelors were happy to escort the two young women to the top. At the last moment, however, one of the women refused to go because the adventure would prevent her from attending the first cotillion of the season. The other young woman, who wasn't going to the dance, still wanted to climb the mountain. She was so enthusiastic that she almost forgot her sense of propriety. Eventually she realized it would be improper for a single woman to go off with two men by herself. Her disappointment left her almost inconsolable.[6]

"Now I will go up to my room and have a good cry," she said to the others as her eyes welled up.

The next morning, Thayer and Hasley started up the trail, which proved to be a good foot path, well maintained with many scenic views. After two hours, they had covered five miles, reaching the Halfway House. Afterward, the trail entered a wooded area and suddenly grew much steeper. Just below the timber line, around twelve thousand feet above sea level, they started to meet other hiking parties descending from the top.[7]

"Only four miles farther," one hiker told Thayer and Hasley.

"Keep your strength for the last two miles," said another.

"You will have to leave the trail the last mile and follow the telegraph poles up over the snow," said a third, giving them some bad advice. Thayer and Hasley would have been better off staying on the trail. Taking the third hiker's advice took them off the trail, giving them a shorter route but one that was steep and rugged.

The legs of these two long-distance cyclists held up, but they became more and more thirsty, so they ate some snow to moisten their mouths. About a thousand feet above the tree line, they crossed some deep snow drifts up to two hundred feet wide, and their feet got soaked. Sometimes they sank into the snow up to their hips, and they had to exert more and more effort as they continued up the mountain. Nearly exhausted, Thayer and Hasley soon had to cope with snow from above as well as below. As the two approached the top, it began snowing, and the wind blew a gale. The snowstorm became so heavy they could hardly see from one telegraph pole to the next. Complicating matters, the altitude made them dizzy. When they could see them, the telegraph poles seemed to extend to infinity.

The last mile took them an hour and a half, crawling, staggering, and climbing. Finally, Thayer caught sight of a big stone house through the blowing snow.

"Look at the chimneys," he yelled to Hasley.

The signalmen who lived and worked at the top of Pike's Peak welcomed the two inside, making them feel so much at home that Thayer and Hasley decided to stay on the summit a second night. Their first morning at the summit, they witnessed a glorious sunrise. They spent the day exploring the mountaintop. Thayer especially enjoyed the profusion of multicolored wildflowers.[8]

Their second morning at the top they awoke to a much different scene. Thayer explained:

> As if to give us one more startling effect before we started down, the next morning opened cloudy. The morning before we seemed to be on the edge of some great ocean that stretched out to the east as far as the eye could reach, but now we were

cast away at sea ourselves. The clouds covered the whole earth in all directions and were so solid and motionless that they looked like one great sea of light gray marble, beautifully carved and polished, but we were high above this sea of marble, and were looking down upon it. The sun had just risen above it when I opened my eyes, and I could hardly believe what they told me. The light brought out every line and feature of the glassy clouds, and the peak on which we were was, apparently, only about 2,000 feet above the level of this sea, for it surrounded us on all sides. Occasionally, here and there, other peaks pierced through the clouds like so many rocky islands, but there was not a rift anywhere to indicate that there was a beautiful earth beneath this great ocean of gray, polished marble, solid enough apparently to walk upon. Very soon the sun took the polish off the clouds, and before long they grew fleecy and soon broke up and passed away.[9]

Together Thayer and Hasley descended to Cliff House, where they could look back toward the mountain and marvel at how high they had climbed. They enjoyed a hearty meal before cycling to the Garden of the Gods, a mountain valley filled with red rock formations in a variety of fantastic shapes. The Garden of the Gods was already a huge tourist attraction. Some visitors marveled at the bizarre shapes the red sandstone formed. Others, like Emily Pfeiffer, thought the area did not live up to the hype.

Riding back to Denver, Thayer and Hasley encountered the same rancher they had met on the way there. This time he was all smiles. He recognized them and waved as they passed.

On Wednesday, June 23, they reached Denver, where Thayer had a decision to make. Having told others he was going to Denver, he had met that goal, but he really wanted to continue to the Pacific coast. The decision was easy. "No small consideration would induce me to turn back," he said. "I was in better physical condition than when I left home, and the farther I went the more confidence it gave me to continue the journey across to the Pacific."[10]

The side trip to Pike's Peak convinced him that he and Hasley were compatible; they could travel well together. One cyclist who met the two agreed, calling them both "genial gentlemen."[11] Before continuing westward, Thayer lightened his load. He left behind his gossamer rainsuit, which he assumed would no longer be necessary. He also decided to wear his lightweight trousers instead of the heavy corduroy knickerbockers with the new buckskin-reinforced seat: a possible error. On June 24, the two left Denver together for San Francisco.

Pulling into Salina (pop. 100), Thayer found it quite pleasant. Aware the place was a mining town, he had imagined Salina to be rowdy and rough-edged, but it turned out to be much different than he had expected. Salina was actually more genteel than many factory villages in Connecticut. Thayer saw several well-dressed ladies and gentlemen there, and he learned that nearly the entire population belonged to the local temperance society.

Such information comforted readers in the East, who otherwise accepted the clichés and stereotypes of the day, fearing that men and women faced moral decay in the Wild West. Florine Thayer McCray used what she learned from her brother to emphasize the rising state of American society. In "the most remote regions of the mountainous mining camps of the far west," she wrote, there are "men of culture, men of right feeling and justice under the rough exterior of those pioneers."[12]

The stop in Salina gave the two cyclists the chance to see the First National Mine. Finally, Thayer had the opportunity to descend to the underworld. This time there would be no hesitation on his part. The mine shaft went down to where the miners were, two hundred feet beneath the surface. Unlike in New York, there was no elevator to transport the men below the surface. They would have to climb down the shaft rung by rung. Upon reaching the bottom, Thayer and Hasley watched the miners working mole-like in two low tunnels that extended in opposite directions.

Having seen enough, they started the long climb up the mine shaft, Thayer being the last to ascend. He had to stop and rest once, mainly because of nervous excitement. For a moment, he felt as if he had just enough strength to keep from falling but not enough to ascend any higher. His memory of the experience would sometimes haunt him in the future, but he would forever remain fascinated by what went on beneath the earth's surface.[13]

The time Thayer spent in Colorado helped dispel his own prejudice toward the state and its people: "Denver is noted for having many confidence men and bunco steerers, but there is no class of men I would sooner trust myself with than the ranchmen, guides, and cowboys of Colorado. They like to open one's eyes by telling what they have done in the past, but in the mountains, mines, or on the plains a traveler is as safe in their hands as he would be in any city in the East."[14] As he and Hasley cycled westward, they would continue to rely on the kindness of ranchers.

West of Laramie, Wyoming, they reached a fork in the road. Should they continue to follow the Union Pacific railroad or take the old emigrant trail across the plains? The section houses along the railroad provided a fairly reliable source of shelter and sustenance. On his transcontinental tour two years earlier, Thomas Stevens had taken advantage of the regularly spaced section houses with reasonably good luck. Faced with the same decision the year after Thayer came through, George Nellis left the railroad west of Laramie but soon regretted his decision. Once he rejoined the Union Pacific line, he stuck close to it and sought the hospitality of the railroad workers who lived in the section houses along the way.[15] In light of their Colorado experience, Thayer and Hasley were confident they could depend on rancher hospitality through Wyoming. They left the path paralleling the railroad tracks to follow the old emigrant trail.

Tired and hungry one day, they discovered a ranch about seven o'clock in the evening but found no one home. Instead of trying to make it to the next ranch—eight or ten miles further—they chose to stay here for the night. In the kitchen, Thayer found the coffee grounds moldy: an indication the coffee pot had not been used for a few days at least.[16] They waited as long as they could for someone to return, but their cyclists' appetites could wait only so long. Searching the pantry, they found a can of Dr. Price's Baking Powder, along with some flour, lard, salt, and sugar. Suddenly, they knew they had all the fixin's for griddlecakes, which they made that evening and again the next morning. Though they left the rancher a note of thanks, they did not even do the dishes!

A few days later Thayer and Hasley saw a mysterious cardboard box in the middle of the road ahead of them. As they approached, it did not take long to realize what that box contained. "A wagon wheel had crushed one corner," Thayer explained, "but inside, what a sight for hungry wheelmen! Nicely packed in rows were two dozen fresh, even warm doughnuts, all frosted with sugar, and four dozen cookies, looking equally tempting."[17]

They snatched up the box and headed to the nearby riverbank to hold a feast. Not even these two hungry cyclists could finish all the doughnuts and cookies in one sitting. What they did not eat, they packed in Thayer's knapsack for later. They felt a little sorry for the rancher who had lost his supply of baked goods, but, as Thayer frankly admitted, "Our sorrow did not seriously affect our appetites."[18]

At Rawlins they hopped a freight train but soon got off to ride the next seventy-five miles to Green River, arriving at eleven o'clock Saturday night, July 3. Reluctant to spend four dollars for a hotel, they sought alternate accommodations. Green River had plenty of saloons, all doing a lively business the eve of the Fourth of July, so they popped into one to ask about a place to stay. Their search did not take long. As soon as they entered, a short little man spied them from across the room. By their knee socks and knickerbockers, the man could tell they were cyclists.[19]

"Come over and stay with me," he said. "You are welcome to the best I have."

The man turned out to be Frank H. Van Meerbeke, older brother to transcontinental cyclist Fred E. Van Meerbeke and himself a former member of the Kings County Bicycle Club in Brooklyn. Six weeks before Thayer had left Connecticut on his transcontinental ride, Fred Van Meerbeke had left New York City on his. He was taking the longer southern route. From New York, he dropped down to Atlanta and then turned west, passing through New Orleans to Houston.

The day Thayer reached Green River, Fred Van Meerbeke left El Paso. From there, he would ride across Arizona Territory. A reporter from Yuma, Arizona, found him in amazing condition: "He seems in very good health and spirits, and has only lost but three pounds on the trip." From Yuma, Fred Van Meerbeke would pedal up the California coast to San Francisco. He hoped to return via a more northerly route, which would take him through Green River. Frank Van Meerbeke planned to join his brother on the west-to-east portion of his transcontinental tour.[20]

Frank clearly understood the importance of hospitality to bicycle tourists, but as a bachelor, he was at a loss when it came to feeding Thayer and Hasley. He took his meals at a local establishment that was a combination restaurant and saloon and suggested they do the same. With little choice, they agreed to the arrangement, though Thayer was somewhat leery when he learned the restaurant had only just reopened. So many men had been shot there in recent weeks the sheriff had temporarily closed the joint.[21]

Given their host's kindly treatment, Thayer and Hasley decided to spend the Fourth of July in Green River.[22] During the day they explored the surrounding countryside. That night they were in for a rip-roaring time in town. The saloons were going full blast. Outside bonfires flamed, cannons boomed, and fireworks exploded. Some people fired Roman candles into each other's faces without the slightest warning. One Roman candle whizzed so closely past Thayer that it scorched the flannel shirt he was wearing!

Frank Van Meerbeke persuaded them to stay in Green River yet another night. Glancing at their machines, he saw what looked like a job for Bicycle Repairman. Since he used to manage a cycling rink back in Brooklyn, Van Meerbeke was pretty handy with a wrench, so he offered to tune up their bicycles on Monday. Unable to turn down such a magnanimous offer, the two cyclists decided to stay in Green River through Monday to give him time to work. They got back on the road at four o'clock Tuesday morning. The early start let them avoid the winds that typically picked up later in the day.

Thayer had few expectations for Utah. When he had gone through the back issues of the LAW *Bulletin* looking for names of wheelmen along his route, he had found only a few in Salt Lake City. Consequently, it came as quite a pleasant surprise to be greeted by many local cyclists. He wrote, "Riding into the city about six o'clock, we had passed up Main Street but a little way when, by chance, we met the secretary of the bicycle club. Before we had reached the hotel another member came tearing up the street after us, and in less than fifteen minutes ten or twelve wheelmen came into the hotel to welcome us, all this, too, without a minute's warning from us, or without our knowing a single person in the city by name."[23]

It turned out that A. C. Brixen, the proprietor of the Valley House, the hotel they had chosen, was a wheelman, as were several of his boarders. Thayer honored these local cyclists in *Pedal and Path*: "Although at Buffalo, Denver, and many other places I have been most cordially received, the Salt Lake City wheelmen outdid all other wheelmen in their spontaneous outburst of welcome."[24] The kindly welcome he received from the Salt Lake cyclists helped soften his prejudice toward Mormons. Thayer and his wheel turned out to be curiosities among the Utah cyclists. No one in Salt Lake City had ever seen a forty-six-inch Columbia Expert.[25]

Thayer and Hasley decided to board the night train from Ogden the rest of the way through Utah and all the way through Nevada. It was a tough decision. On one hand, Thayer hated to miss so much scenery, but on the other, taking the train would allow him more time to enjoy the really spectacular scenery of Yosemite. Another factor affected Thayer's decision to take the train at Ogden, though he does not say so in *Pedal and Path*. He had been taking a leisurely journey so far but did not have an unlimited amount of time: he wanted to reach San Francisco in time for the National Encampment of the Grand Army of the Republic, a jamboree of Union veterans from the Civil War, which was scheduled to begin on August 4. If he rode across Nevada, he would not have time to see Yosemite *and* reach San Francisco in time.

After they boarded the train, Thayer did not regret their decision, not a bit. He told his readers, "Once during that Saturday night, after leaving Ogden, I looked out of the car window and in the moonlight saw a perfectly level sea of alkali without so much as a sage bush growing upon it, and then I went to sleep again more contented than ever with the way I was crossing this part of the continent."[26]

Perhaps northwestern Utah and northern Nevada could not offer much in terms of scenic variety, but skipping that section of the country did deprive Thayer of a certain sense of accomplishment—and a sense of the nation as a whole. To achieve those feelings, however, required some personal sacrifice, as S. G. Spier, who also rode across the continent that year, discovered for himself. A reporter who met Spier in Denver characterized him as "a compact, muscular built young man, the picture of ruddy health." It took Spier two weeks longer than he anticipated to ride from Denver to Sacramento, and the heat and desolation of Nevada showed. A Sacramento reporter painted a very different picture than his Denver counterpart. According to this reporter, Spier was a tattered man when he entered Sacramento. His physical appearance suggested that crossing the West on a wheel was "a tedious and toilsome journey."[27]

After entering California on the train, Thayer and Hasley disembarked at Truckee. It was too close to daybreak for them to bother about overnight accommodations. Instead, they found some bales of hay on the freight house platform, where they slept for a couple hours. Around four o'clock that morning they shook the hayseeds from their hair, brushed off their breeches, mounted their bikes, and got back on the road.

Returning to the bicycle after going partway by train, Thayer could compare the two. The noise and soot and speed of the steam locomotive had dulled his senses; the bicycle reawakened them. His feelings resemble what other cyclotourists have experienced. Riaan Manser, after spending two years by himself cycling the circumference of Africa, would express a feeling Thayer had realized over a century earlier: "A cyclist sees and hears more than a traveler using any other form of transport could ever imagine."[28]

Though Thayer generally got along with Hasley, something happened soon after they left Truckee that indicates rising tensions between them. This new episode reignited a disagreement the two men had had when they passed through prairie dog country in Wyoming. Prairie dog towns required extra vigilance on the cyclist's part because the critters would sometimes dig their holes in the middle of the road, holes that could trip up cyclists unawares. Despite the danger, Thayer enjoyed the prairie dogs. He was fascinated by the fact that they lived underground, and he especially liked the way they chirped and chattered as he approached, ducking back into their holes for safety, only to pop up with a shrill squeak, determined to have the last word.[29]

Hasley enjoyed a different kind of fun among the prairie dogs. Unlike Thayer, he rode with a sidearm. To him, a prairie dog town was like one giant shooting gallery, and Hasley enjoyed target practice. Thayer omitted the prairie dog episode from *Pedal and Path*, but he did tell it on a subsequent occasion. In a magazine article he wrote four years later, Thayer told the story, though without mentioning Hasley by name. He said that his "Denver companion" had pulled "the trigger on one of those chattering little things." Four years on, the memory remained vivid—and unsettling: "I can hear the smothered cry of that wounded prairie-dog now from the depths of his underground home."[30]

Their differing attitudes toward gunplay came to a head on that dark and dusty road out of Truckee where they encountered a small herd of cattle. Grazing with the cattle close to the road were two young deer. Thayer decided to befriend them. He dismounted and slowly walked toward the deer with his hand outstretched, hoping to stroke their coat. As Thayer came close to the deer, he glanced back to see Hasley taking aim.[31]

"Don't shoot!" Thayer yelled. "They're tame."

His yell spooked the deer, which ran up the hillside out of sight. Thayer was disappointed that he did not get the chance to pet the deer; Hasley was disappointed that he had lost the fifteen dollars their pelts could have brought. Nowhere else in *Pedal and Path* does Thayer suggest that there was any tension between him and Hasley, but Thayer obviously found Hasley's trigger-happy behavior disconcerting. Before continuing much further, the two wheelmen parted ways.

The road from Truckee to Sacramento was beautiful. C. Theron Gray, a cyclist from East Springfield, New York, who would ride from Chicago to San Francisco the following year, described the scenery to a reporter for the *Sacramento Daily Record-Union*. (Then, as now, Sacramento had some great cycling reporters.) The Sacramento reporter explained: "The balmy mountain air, the streams of sparkling water, the magnificent forests, radiating from the pine on the summit, through spruce, fire, cedar, and hemlock, to the oaks of the foothills and the valley, were to him a panorama of magnificence in nature."[32]

If the name C. Theron Gray sounds familiar, it should. He is none other than the mysterious "C. T. Gray," who accompanied George W. Nellis out of Chicago during his record-breaking transcontinental ride. I call Gray mysterious because Nellis grew so frustrated with him that he almost completely effaced him from the story of his transcontinental journey. When I retold Nellis's story as *An American Cycling Odyssey, 1887*, I had difficulty discovering any further information about Gray. Though he and Nellis had left Chicago together, they soon parted company. I conjectured that Nellis, always intent on establishing a new transcontinental record, grew frustrated with Gray's leisurely pace. This newly discovered article from the *Sacramento Record-Union* verifies my conjecture. Though he and Nellis left Chicago together, it took Gray *two months* longer to reach Sacramento.

George Thayer paused in Sacramento briefly before starting a big loop that would bring him to the Calaveras Big Trees and Yosemite. It took two and a half days to reach Calaveras—not bad considering the temperature hovered around a hundred degrees every afternoon. It got hot enough to soften the cement that held Thayer's tires to the rims: a dangerous situation.

Giant sequoias were like no trees Thayer had ever seen. A hollow tree on the ground, which was known as the "Father of the Forest," was so immense that Thayer could ride into it atop his wheel. The bottom was a little squishy, and it was dark as pitch inside, but by proceeding slowly and feeling his way, he managed to ride inside the hollow tree for a distance of nearly two hundred feet. Not wanting his small stature to minimize the tree's size, Thayer insisted that a man riding a sixty-inch wheel—the largest size Columbia made—could accomplish the same feat. A tree that had been cut down about five feet from the ground left a flat stump twenty-five feet across. Thayer climbed onto the stump, pulled his bike up after him, mounted it, and rode around, cutting figure eights atop the stump.[33]

Yosemite was more than a hundred miles beyond Calaveras Big Trees, a distance that took Thayer another two and a half days. Almost as soon as he entered the park he saw Bridal Veil Falls and then El Capitan. It was dark by the time he reached the hotel, but the next day he hit the trails to do some hiking. He decided to take it fairly easy his first day in Yosemite.

A short route brought him close to Vernal Falls, so close that the mist and spray soaked his clothes and coated the rocky trail, making it dangerously slick. He found a sunny rock where he could rest, where the sun could remedy what the water had done. Once his clothes were dry, he had lunch at Snow's, a small hotel midway between Vernal and Nevada Falls. The meal fortified him, and he climbed to the top of Nevada Falls, where he was treated to a view of the water rushing through the narrow gorge under a bridge over the cliff and down to the base of the falls seven hundred feet below.

At the top of Nevada Falls Thayer found another big sunny

THROUGH THE SEQUOIA'S HEART.— (*Page 141.*)

Fig. 10. This scene from Calaveras Big Trees shows how much fun
Thayer had visiting the park on his bicycle (Moss Engraving Co.,
New York). From George B. Thayer, *Pedal and Path: Across the
Continent Awheel and Afoot* (Hartford: Evening Post Association,
1887). Courtesy Lilly Library, Indiana University, Bloomington IN.

rock suitable for sleeping or writing, whichever he wished. He slept a little while and wrote a little while more. He loved to take writing materials with him when he hiked. Picturesque spots with beautiful views made the best places to write, as he confirmed the next day.

He went back to Snow's Hotel to spend the night. The next morning he started up the trail to the top of Cloud's Rest. After hiking about three miles, he wondered whether he was on the right trail. He stopped at a nearby cabin to ask the way to Cloud's Rest.[34]

"This is not the way," the man replied. "You missed the trail back there a mile and a half."

Thayer turned back to find the right trail. It took more than an hour of scrambling over rocks and boulders and fallen trees before he found the right trail. He now saw why he had missed the trail: recent rains had almost obliterated it. Sometimes he had to ascend the steep, rugged terrain by crawling over the rocks on his hands and knees. Once he reached the peak, he felt rewarded for his effort and endurance. Ten thousand feet above sea level, Cloud's Rest was six thousand feet above the valley. After getting a good look, he found a comfortable place to sit and took out pen and paper to record his impressions: "El Capitan, the Half Dome, the Cap of Liberty, the North Dome, and all the other immense peaks that rise up three or four thousand feet above the valley, I can look down on as a tall man upon a crowd of boys."[35] George Thayer, who had gone through life always a little ashamed and embarrassed about being short, felt tall as he perched atop Cloud's Rest. For Thayer every mountain climb was a personal vindication.

The day after he left Yosemite, his bicycle broke. Specifically, the rim of the little wheel snapped, rendering the bike impossible to ride. Forty-five miles from the railroad and who-knows-how-many miles from the nearest blacksmith, Thayer was stranded—until he remembered that spool of wire he had been carrying since Indiana. He located a piece of hoop iron, bound it to the rim with the wire, and repaired the rear wheel well enough to ride thirty miles further before he finally found a blacksmith, who riveted the rim back together.[36]

The Yosemite detour took twelve days and involved nearly four hundred miles of riding. Back in Sacramento, Thayer felt the stares of local citizens and realized what he must have looked like at this point in his transcontinental tour: "My shoes had become so worn and torn, that the different pieces of canvas had to be tied together with strings in order to keep them on my feet." Continuing his personal description, Thayer indulged his penchant for puns: "My stockings were little better than leggings—feet all gone—and what there was left of the uppers was very holey, in sharp contrast with the almost soleless condition of my shoes."[37]

Though he had left his corduroy trousers with the buckskin seat back in Denver because they were too heavy to wear through a summer in the West, the lightweight knickerbockers he wore lacked durability. He had frequently darned and quilted them with his portable sewing kit. He explained what they looked like at this point in the trip: "Not to mention one knee torn out and the other sewed up in a bunch, the part most intimately acquainted with the saddle would make a very good crazy-quilt pattern. A piece of black silk taken from an old skull cap, a portion of a pair of overalls, and a part of a pair of merino stockings were all sewed into the inside of the trousers to strengthen them, and as the different pieces wore through it left a garment of many colors."[38]

Thayer's efforts with needle and thread indicate his extreme thrift. Fred Van Meerbeke, in contrast, simply bought new shoes and trousers whenever his old ones wore out. On his ride from New York to New Orleans to San Francisco, Van Meerbeke wore out six pair of trousers and five pair of shoes.[39]

Fig. 11. The ever-thrifty Thayer preferred patching worn-out clothing rather than buying new garments. This scene of open-air tailoring was enacted countless times during his trip (Moss Engraving Co., New York). From George B. Thayer, *Pedal and Path: Across the Continent Awheel and Afoot* (Hartford: Evening Post Association, 1887). Courtesy Lilly Library, Indiana University, Bloomington IN.

With his clothing beyond repair, Thayer went shopping in Sacramento, purchasing some new trousers and a new pair of shoes. He also took time to recruit his strength in a hotel dining room. As Tom Kevill-Davies says, "Food and cycling are the perfect partners."[40] Thayer would agree. Cycling across North America 120 years before Kevill-Davies, the self-styled Hungry Cyclist, George Thayer could be considered the Original Hungry Cyclist. His account of this Sacramento hotel dining room looks forward to Kevill-Davies's account of a three-and-a-half-hour pig-out at the Banff Springs Hotel brunch buffet. As soon as Thayer was seated in his hotel dining room, a waiter sidled over to his table.[41]

"Beef-steak, pork-steak, mutton-chop, fried tripe, corned-beef, pork and beans, fried liver and onions, bacon, and potpie," the waiter said, rattling off the various menu items in quick succession.

Once Thayer made his choice, another waiter approached, asking whether he wanted coffee or tea. Thayer chose coffee, but before his sugar cubes had time to dissolve, the first waiter returned with his order—and much else besides. There was hardly enough room on the table to hold everything. The waiter piled the various dishes around him in a semicircle two or three layers high. Thayer was quite pleased with his first meal and continued to eat here throughout his stay in Sacramento:

> I rather liked the way they had of doing business in that dining-room. Once or twice during the first meal I dug a hole through the breastwork, but at a nod the waiters quickly filled it up again, preventing my escape in that direction. I liked the place, first-rate, and so I stayed there two days—not in the dining-room, but close by. I had considerable writing to do, and thus I simply vibrated all the next day between the desk and the dining-room. It was immaterial what I ordered at the table, everything tasted so good, and so much tasted that same way. In short, I ate as never a wheelman ate before, and as this particular wheelman will never eat again, under the same circumstances. I have forgotten just what the various dishes were that surrounded me at the beginning, during the progress, and at the latter part of the supper siege, but I remember distinctly that fried liver and onions were the last to enter the list and that in a few hours, they were, like the "Bloody Sixty-ninth," the last on the field and the first to leave.[42]

Thayer alludes to an old chestnut about an Irish-Catholic regiment from New York that had been retold countless times since the end of the Civil War. As two veterans of the unit were enjoying a wee taste of the creature, one raised his glass to make a toast to their regiment. In so doing, he accidentally transposed the words "first" and "last": "Here's to the gallant ould Sixty-ninth: the last in the field and the first to leave!"[43]

Even this little bit of fun shows how much the Civil War continued to affect Thayer's mindset. Still looking forward to the Grand Army Encampment, he realized in Sacramento that he was behind schedule and would have to take the train to San Francisco. His desire to attend the event violates what Tim Mulliner has called "the cycling tourist's number-one rule: never commit to a rendezvous on a specific date."[44]

Taking the train from Sacramento to San Francisco, Thayer denied himself a beautiful ride with numerous opportunities for coasting, but obviously the Grand Army Encampment meant more to him. Bicycle touring remained Thayer's substitute for going to war. Arriving in San Francisco after an arduous journey across the continent at the same time as thousands of Civil War veterans arrived in San Francisco, he would give himself a sense of camaraderie with the veterans.

By the time he reached San Francisco, he had cycled 3,036 miles, traveled another 1,800 miles on the train, and hiked around a hundred miles at Pike's Peak and Yosemite, making the total distance traveled right around five thousand miles. The trip had taken him 110 days, and he had spent a total of one hundred and twenty dollars, a sum that included the price of a celebratory glass of California wine, the first and only glass of spirits Ginger-Ale George enjoyed during the entire trip.

Once he reached San Francisco, he rode out to Cliff House, where he saw the sea lions swarming over the nearby rocks. He found a convenient place where the water was accessible, took out the tiny vial of Atlantic Ocean water that had miraculously survived all the heat and the headers, and emptied half of it into the Pacific. He then filled the vial with Pacific water, mixed the Atlantic with the Pacific together, recorked the bottle, and packed it away to take back across the continent. Thayer had one more ceremonial duty to perform. He paid homage to his trusty Columbia Expert: "To-day, standing on the extreme western limit of the Great American Continent, I make obeisance to the good wheel by whose aid I have now accomplished the wonderful and laborious yet delectable journey!"

5

Eastbound and Down

Though his trusty Columbia Expert had seen Thayer safely across the continent, the mechanical breakdown he had suffered outside Yosemite reminded him that he needed to keep his machine in good working order to make sure it would last the rest of the trip. Having enjoyed crossing the continent from east to west, Thayer now thought he would see what it looked like from the opposite direction. By no means did he intend to pedal all the way home. Instead, he would ride when he wished and take the train when he didn't. In San Francisco, Thayer brought his machine to the local Columbia dealer, whose shop was located across the street from the Pacific Hotel, where many prominent members of the Grand Army of the Republic were staying. Thayer asked the dealer to give his Columbia the once over. Inspired by the story of his transcontinental journey, the Columbia dealer promised to cement the tires on properly and fix up Thayer's Expert. Though this bicycle repairman was a little vague about what he meant by "fixing up," Thayer trusted him and left his machine at the bike shop to explore San Francisco on foot.

Since Thayer's arrival coincided with the Grand Army

Encampment, the Columbia dealer, naturally enough, adorned the bicycle with Grand Army of the Republic decorations. Furthermore, he hung a big placard on it describing Thayer's transcontinental journey before displaying the bicycle on the sidewalk in front of his shop. Though both General William Tecumseh Sherman and General John A. Logan were in town for the Grand Army Encampment, George Thayer found himself an unwitting celebrity in San Francisco due to the enterprising efforts of the local Columbia dealer. Thayer may have been a little embarrassed that his bicycle could be taking attention away from the generals and majors, but the military-style decorations on his machine confirmed what he had been thinking for a long time, that there was something similar between fighting a war and going on a bicycle tour. The cyclist may not put his life on the line like the soldier, but both cycling and soldiering provided ways for men to test themselves.[1]

Along with many of the Civil War veterans, Thayer took the opportunity to see the sights in San Francisco and the surrounding region. Always fascinated with machinery, he enjoyed the cable cars immensely. He also took a day trip down to Monterey on the train. In addition, he enjoyed a longer trip into Northern California to see its geysers. For this last excursion, he would bring his bike along to experience some of the fine cycling Northern California had to offer.

The morning he left to explore the region north of San Francisco Bay, Thayer retrieved his bicycle from the Columbia dealer and stripped all the variegated gonfalon from its frame and wheels and handlebars. Crossing into Marin County was more complicated in the time before the Golden Gate Bridge. Thayer's journey began with a three-hour boat-and-train trip. He crossed the bay to Oakland, took a short train ride to Vallejo Junction, crossed another part of the bay, and then boarded a train to Napa. He spent the night in Napa and started riding north through Napa Valley the next morning.

Though he had thoroughly enjoyed visiting San Francisco, it felt good to get away from the bustle of the city. The countryside offered calm and quiet: "The roads were excellent and the country pretty thickly settled for California, but very few persons were stirring about, and the quiet and peaceful appearance of everything was in pleasant contrast with the noise and excitement of the past week."[2] Thayer reached Calistoga by noon and then pedaled another twelve or fifteen miles before the road went uphill. After climbing for seven miles without reaching the top, he had had enough for the day. He stopped at Pine Flat, where a hearty meal of venison and eggs set him right. The next morning he easily reached the top of the climb.

A thrilling descent is the reward for a hard climb, so Thayer looked forward to a long coast. But this time the downhill proved extremely treacherous. Built into the side of a mountain, the road was barely wide enough for a stagecoach. It had a perpendicular rock face on one side and a steep precipice on the other. Increasing the danger, the road contained a series of blind curves. For three or four miles, Thayer dreaded the possibility of an oncoming stagecoach.

Approaching one of these blind curves in his typical coasting position—legs dangling over the handlebars—Thayer struck a rock, which caused him to hit his brake, lock up the front wheel, and dismount off the front of the bicycle. Before he could remount and continue downhill, a stage came around the bend, not more than ten feet in front of him. Had he not hit that rock, he would have been coasting around that blind curve just as the stage approached, and either he or the stage, its horses, and all twelve passengers would have tumbled over the precipice. Instead, the stage stopped, and the passengers peppered him with questions.

For five minutes he gratified their curiosity as best he could. When the stage got going, the gentlemen on board waved their hats, the women their handkerchiefs, and all wished

PERILS OF CAÑON COASTING. — (*Page 174.*)

Fig. 12. This engraving from Thayer's *Pedal and Path: Across the Continent Awheel and Afoot* (Hartford: Evening Post Association, 1887) illustrates the dangers the cyclist faced while coasting down narrow mountain roads (Moss Engraving Co., New York). Courtesy Lilly Library, Indiana University, Bloomington IN.

him well. The life-threatening danger had become a convivial encounter. Toward Cloverdale, the curves straightened out, the grade lessening enough to let him enjoy some fine coasting. The California geysers proved a big disappointment, but the pleasant cycling there and back more than made up for the lackluster geysers.

Thayer's next major destination was Portland. He could have, perhaps should have, kept riding north through California, but he had already bought a ticket on another mode of transportation named *Columbia*, a steamship lit with electricity that plied its way between San Francisco and Portland. Having bought the ticket from an agent in Salt Lake City, Thayer had been imagining the voyage ever since. Consequently, he turned south and rode back to San Francisco. Since he had ridden through Napa Valley going north, he took Sonoma Valley going south.

The road through Sonoma was excellent, but Thayer found the countryside dry and dusty. Save for the trees and grapevines, he saw little else that was green through this valley. The warm sunshine helped him imagine his forthcoming ocean voyage—or so he thought. He began to daydream how he would sun himself on the deck of the *Columbia* as he enjoyed the beautiful scenery of the Pacific coast. Little did Thayer realize that California temperatures varied wildly between the inland valleys and the coast. The sun that smiles on Sonoma lurks behind the clouds at Bodega Bay. Dense fog and cold rain would prevent Thayer from seeing either the sun or the coast throughout the passage to Portland.

Unable to secure a stateroom for the voyage, Thayer had managed to get a lower berth, which he would share with another man in a large bunk room. Once Thayer entered the room he spied a round box of sawdust on the floor near his bunk: an ominous sight. Thayer's bunkmate, an old man from Kansas, had already turned in for the evening, but a slowly building nausea kept him awake. They introduced themselves, but as the seas rocked the ship, the old man felt worse and worse.[3]

"I can't stand this any longer," the old man said. "Oh, I stayed here too long, I guess."

Before he could say another word, the old man turned his head toward the box of sawdust, which would have been okay except for the fact that the man in the upper berth happened to lean toward the box of sawdust at the identical moment. Thayer explained, "My friend's head, which was the lower of the two suspended over the box, and which was scantily clothed with gray hair, received a shampoo of a variety of ingredients."

Sounds of sickness echoed across the bunk room all night: "The place was full of men apparently tearing themselves all to pieces during most of the night." Thayer held out as long as he could, but toward morning he, too, found himself bending over the now soggy box of sawdust.

The next day Thayer ventured to the upper deck. Regardless of the cold raw wind, he had to fill his lungs with some fresh air. On deck he met a young man with blue eyes and a smoothly shaven face who looked just like Bartley Hubbard from *A Modern Instance*, the novel by William Dean Howells. Against ship's rules, Thayer had brought a blanket to the deck, but Bartley was shivering so much Thayer gave his blanket to him. Afterward he snuck back to the bunkrooms to appropriate a couple more blankets for himself.

When he returned to the upper deck who should he find there but Alonzo Williams, the professor who had inspired him to start bicycle touring in the first place. Senior vice commander of the Rhode Island chapter of the Grand Army of the Republic, Professor Williams had been in San Francisco for the National Encampment and was now heading to Portland to see a little more of the wide-open spaces of the West before returning to the East Coast stuffiness of Brown University. Williams wore an overcoat and heavy underclothing, but he, too, could not stop shivering. Thayer forced both his blankets on the professor, happy to do something for a man who had meant so much to him. Thayer went downstairs again to abscond with another blanket. Back on the upper deck, the steward accosted Thayer, asking him if he knew who was taking all the blankets.

Eventually—it seemed an eternity—the ship steamed up the Columbia River to Astoria and then to Portland, where Thayer left water for rail, taking the train across Oregon into Idaho. At three-thirty the next morning, the train reached Shoshone, where Thayer disembarked with plans to bicycle to Shoshone Falls, about twenty-five miles distant. Dawdling around the station until daybreak, Thayer chatted up a stage driver, who told him there was nowhere to get water before the falls and advised him to carry his own. Thayer took the advice and brought a bottle of water with him, something he had rarely, if ever, done before. The bottle wasn't big enough: he drained it long before he reached the falls.

Thayer marveled that molten lava once covered the northwestern corner of the United States. Riding across a lava bed triggered his powers of contemplation: "The thought that I had been allowed to ride over a portion, a very small portion of this lava that ages ago burst out through some immense fissure or great vent in the earth's surface, this thought alone paid me for the hours of thirst endured."[4] Volcanic and geothermal activity continued to fascinate Thayer. The idea that beneath the earth's surface there was another world, a world of intense heat and molten rock that could burst through the crust at any moment was something that would intrigue him during future travels.

Unlike the California geysers, Shoshone Falls did not disappoint Thayer. He found them much more impressive than any of the other waterfalls he had seen in the West. Why, they were almost as grand as Niagara. Adding to the picturesque quality of Shoshone Falls, eagles soared overhead, circling above the falls again and again.

The eastbound trains were on a regular schedule, so Thayer knew another one would stop at Shoshone at three-thirty the next morning. He left the falls in the late afternoon, allowing himself plenty of time to reach the station. As darkness loomed, he remained short of his goal. It was too dangerous after dark to ride this road, which was really nothing more than a wagon rut. Once he could no longer see the rut, Thayer dismounted and walked the rest of the way. He got lost once and did not reach the station until after ten o'clock. Tired and thirsty, he nonetheless finished his scenic detour to Shoshone Falls with a great feeling of accomplishment. No one before him, he learned, had ever cycled from the railway station to the falls.

Thayer took the train to Beaver Canyon, reaching it on August 22. He cycled from Beaver Canyon to Yellowstone National Park, a two-day ride along the stagecoach route. A fifty-five mile stretch brought him to the Halfway Hotel, a log hut with a line of tents on either side, which formed the sleeping quarters for the stage passengers, men on one side, women on the other. The stage passengers filled all the tents this evening, so Thayer slept on the floor of the bar. One night in a barroom was enough for him. The next morning he got an early start, leaving before the stagecoaches.

The biggest obstacle he faced on the road to Yellowstone was the Snake River. Thigh high and two hundred feet wide, the ford was too deep and too wide for Thayer to cross without removing his shoes, stockings, and knickerbockers. It would take two trips to transport everything across the river, one to take his knapsack and his clothing, a second to take his bicycle. After carrying his pack and clothing over, he returned through the icy water to retrieve his machine.

About halfway across, he heard a stagecoach coming. Uh-oh! Standing in the river in his skivvies, he suddenly imagined how he would look to a stagecoach full of women. He considered submerging himself in the river and remaining there until the stage passed, but the water was much too cold for that. Instead, he dashed through the water as quickly as he could, ducking behind some scrub brush once he reached the riverbank. "But as good fortune would have it," he explained, "the lady passengers waited to ride in the second stage, and the men in this one laughed well at what appeared to them uncalled-for modesty on my part in retiring so expeditiously behind so slight a shelter."[5]

On this, his second day out of Beaver Canyon, Thayer reached Firehole, the first stopping place in Yellowstone Park. The two-day, 105-mile stretch had proven to be "as fine riding as any wheelman could desire."[6] In Fire Hole, Thayer stayed with one of the stage drivers, waking early the next day to pedal through the park and see the sights. For other tourists, Thayer himself was a sight to see. They appreciated both his daring and his athleticism and invited him to join them.

One group of campers asked him to dine on ham that had been boiled in one of the park's hot springs. After dinner, another group invited him to join them that evening. This group included John B. Patterson and Joseph M. Thomas, two Philadelphia wheelmen who enjoyed swapping bicycle stories with him. After supper, Thayer accompanied the group over to Fountain Geyser, where several young women appeared. Once the men built a fire, one woman recited a poem. The men responded by singing some Gilbert and Sullivan songs from *The Mikado*. This opera was currently responsible for the Japanese craze sweeping the nation. (George's sister, Florine, attributed the popularity of Oriental costumes and the furor for flowered silks and jeweled hairpins directly to *The*

Mikado.) Soon the men and women found themselves waltzing on the coarse gravel surface surrounding Fountain Geyser.

All merriment ended as the geyser burst into the air, rising thirty or forty feet. Thayer's description of the scene creates a vivid word picture: "It was certainly a queer sight, the white spray and steam rising high up into the starry heavens, the bright camp fire making the surroundings all the blacker, and a dozen or fifteen persons looking on with bright eyes and red faces, and their forms standing out so distinctly against the black background."[8]

He stayed overnight with the campers and the next day began riding toward the Upper Geysers to the most famous one of all: Old Faithful. Less than a mile into the day's ride, Thayer's Columbia suffered a potentially crippling breakdown: his handlebars broke. Whereas today's one-piece handlebars are held fast by the handlebar stem, on Thayer's Columbia Expert, the handlebars consisted of two separate pieces that threaded into the stem. The left handlebar on Thayer's bicycle cracked at the threads and broke off.

There was no way he was going to let a broken handlebar stop him from seeing Old Faithful. He jammed the left handlebar back into the stem and somehow managed to fix it there using some of his Indiana wire. It wasn't a perfect fix, but if he rode gingerly, he could make forward progress. Ten slow miles later he reached Old Faithful, which he watched shoot water into the sky in all its glory.

The next morning he rode his broken bicycle back to Firehole, hoping to find the only blacksmith's shop in a hundred miles. He found the shop, but he also discovered that the blacksmith was off on a drunk. Thayer had no choice but to fix the bicycle himself. He located a suitable die, ran a new thread on his handlebar, removed the small broken piece from the socket of his stem, screwed the shortened, yet newly threaded handlebar into its place, and rode away tickled by his own ingenuity.

Leaving Firehole on the road back to Beaver Canyon, he saw an Indian on horseback galloping across a meadow. Conditioned by dime-novel depictions of cowboys and Indians, Thayer felt a twinge of fear, which quickly dissipated. The man asked him in broken English if he had seen an Indian hunting party. Thayer had not, but his wheel prompted further questions on the Indian's part. Where did he come from? How many miles a day could he ride? In other words, he posed the same questions everyone else had asked all the way across the continent.[9]

"You know my name?" the Indian suddenly asked.

"No," Thayer replied.

"My name is Major Jim. *Major*," he replied with emphasis.

Thayer told the story of his encounter with Major Jim in *Pedal and Path* and retold it countless times afterward.[10] It's a simple story, really, but quite a sweet one, especially compared with Thomas Stevens's Indian encounters. Stevens basically saw Indians as playthings he could manipulate for his own personal amusement.[11] Thayer, alternately, recognized the Indian's essential humanity. Recording how Major Jim asserted his identity, Thayer captured his dignity.

After Yellowstone, Thayer returned to Salt Lake City, intending to take the scenic train east across the Rocky Mountains to Denver. A destructive rainstorm temporarily quashed his plans. After boarding the Denver and Rio Grande passenger train, he traveled about a hundred miles east, when the train encountered a bridge damaged by recent floods. The train had to backtrack to Salt Lake City, where Thayer was stuck for a week until repairs to the bridge could be made. Finding himself stranded in Salt Lake City with no cash, he was grateful to D. L. Davis for cashing a personal check. Captain of the Salt Lake Bicycle Club and chief consul of the Utah division of the LAW, Davis was also a purveyor of Columbia bicycles, one of many items he sold at his retail store on Main Street.[12] This unplanned stop in Salt Lake City soured Thayer on the Mormon Church, but it did let him make one of the best friends of his entire trip: he and Davis became quite close during their time together.

The train to Denver came equipped with an observation car, which let Thayer enjoy his passage through the Rockies with ease and awe. After a few days in Denver lounging around the club rooms of the Colorado Wheel Club, Thayer boarded a train for Kansas on a mission: to meet the famous Connecticut abolitionist Prudence Crandall Philleo, a schoolteacher who had dared to teach African American girls to read and write. She now lived in Elk Falls, Kansas.

Thayer took the train as far as he could, but no train went all the way to Elk Falls, less than thirty miles from the border between Kansas and Indian Territory. Though Elk Falls was a small town with a population of only seven or eight hundred, Thayer had some difficulty locating the woman he sought. One man told him she lived on a farm outside of town. Before he reached the farm, another man told him she lived in town, right next door to the Methodist Church. The man's words spun Thayer around, sending him scurrying back into Elk Falls, where he found both the Methodist Church and Mrs. Philleo's house next to it. Mr. Williams, her caretaker, answered the door and told him she was at church. Williams volunteered much more information about her, as well.[13]

"She enjoys excellent health, and it is wonderful how much she, a woman of eighty-four years, can endure," Williams said.

"Yesterday she wanted to ride over to the farm and see about some things, and before I was ready to come home she started on foot and got clear home before I overtook her, and she didn't seem tired either." As Williams and Thayer spoke, she came home, and Williams introduced her.

"I am glad to see anyone from good old Connecticut," she said, welcoming Thayer inside.

He took a good look at her, observing, "As she removed her bonnet, it showed a good growth of sandy gray hair, smoothed back with a common round comb, and cut straight around, the ends curling around under and in front of her ears; of medium height, but somewhat bent and spare, and with blue eyes, and a face very wrinkled, and rather long; her chin quite prominent, and a solitary tooth on her upper jaw, the only one seen in her mouth."

"Come, you must be hungry, coming so far," she said. Though Thayer had told her he had ridden from Connecticut, he modestly left out the part about coming by way of California. She offered him apple pie, ginger snaps, johnny-cakes, potatoes, ham, bread and butter, and tea. Once Thayer finished one cup of tea, he asked for a little more. "No," she replied. "As my grandmother used to say, I never break a cup, you must take another full one. Now do you make yourself at home; I know you must be tired."

Afterward, she invited him into the sitting room. They each took a rocking chair, and she showed him her collection of photographs of famous men.

"I am going to have these photographs of these noble men all put into a frame together," she said. "I don't want them in an album, for I have to turn and turn the leaves so much. I want them in a frame, so I can get the inspiration from them at a glance."

Mrs. Philleo showed Thayer the first two photographs and identified the men they pictured. As she showed him the third, he recognized it as a photograph of Samuel Clemens. She had received a kind letter from him in which he complimented her work as an abolitionist and offered to send her a set of his books. She kept his letter with the photograph and read it to Thayer as they talked. But, she added, Clemens never did send the books: "Probably so busy he forgot it. I do wish I could see them, for I had a chance once to read part of *Innocents Abroad*, and I do like his beautiful style of expression." She showed Thayer several more photographs, including one of fellow abolitionist, William Lloyd Garrison, whose image decorated more than one room of her house.[14]

She invited Thayer to stay overnight. He accepted. After breakfast the next morning, he returned to the sitting room and glanced through a book she had been reading, William Denton's *Is Darwin Right?* As soon as she entered the room, she said, "Now you must stop reading, for I want to talk." And they talked and talked and talked. Thayer devoted a whole chapter of *Pedal and Path* to his encounter with Prudence Crandall Philleo, which is considered the finest firsthand account of her ever written.[15] His eye for detail and ear for dialogue have helped preserve the personality of this renowned abolitionist.

As Thayer rode from Elk Falls back to Emporia, his Columbia Expert failed him: the head tube of his frame cracked. He says "head tube" in *Pedal and Path*, but he may have meant the steering column, that is, the top part of the fork which fits inside the head tube: a likelier tube to fail. Regardless, this was one breakdown that no amount of Indiana wire could fix. He took the train to St. Louis, where he hoped to get the tube replaced.

Soon after he reached St. Louis, Thayer looked up his old school chum A. W. Sumner, now proprietor of the St. Louis Stoneware Company. Thayer had only intended to stay in town a few days, but Sumner invited him to stay as long as he wished. A good thing: Thayer's bicycle ended up taking much longer to fix than he had anticipated. Shortly before he reached St. Louis, the Simmons Hardware Company—the local agent for Columbia bicycles—had opened a lavish new retail outlet, six stories tall. One Sunday night the top floor collapsed, bringing down all the floors beneath it and destroying over a hundred bicycles and a huge stock of parts. To fix Thayer's bicycle, the company had to send to Hartford for spare parts.[16]

He stayed in St. Louis for nearly two weeks, time enough to enjoy some important festivities, including the triennial conclave of the Knights of Columbus. Summing up local conditions during the event, Thayer observed, "It was beer, beer everywhere." Visiting the fairgrounds one day, Ginger-Ale George looked for a glass of water in vain: "I went from one end of the fairgrounds to the other in search of it, and finally was obliged to drink from the end of an iron pipe where they water horses. Water, evidently, is not used here as a beverage."[17]

Thayer elaborated his point by telling a joke that was going around St. Louis. While taking a ferry boat across the Mississippi, a Missourian was accidentally knocked overboard into the water. His life was in great peril, but he was finally rescued and brought back on deck.

"Are you hurt much?" one person asked.

"No," the Missourian replied. "Thank God, I don't think a drop of water got into my mouth."

Another exciting event in St. Louis, the Wheelman's Illuminated Parade, took place the evening of October 1. Around dark, two hundred wheelmen gathered at the natatorium, where many of them changed into outrageous costumes. After watching several men in street clothes walk into the dressing rooms at the natatorium, Thayer was astonished to see what walked out: "an immense green frog nearly six feet high, walking on his hind legs," a gorilla "with an unusual appendage in the shape of a tail long enough for several 'missing links,'" and a towering white rooster.[18]

The frog, the gorilla, and the rooster formed part of the Animal Squad, along with a hog, a baboon, and an ostrich.

Thayer also noticed a devil in red tights with wings so wide he had to go sideways through the doors: one of several members of the Demon Squad. Another squad of cyclists dressed up as cowboys and Indians. Two riders wore Asian garb to pedal their tandem tricycle, which was decorated as an Oriental palanquin with over a hundred Chinese lanterns. One of the riders was dressed as Yum-Yum, the other as Nanki-Poo: further evidence of *The Mikado*'s influence.[19]

The wheelman wearing the white tights and tiny wings of Cupid was one of the most renowned cyclists of the bunch; it was none other than George W. Baker of the St. Louis Ramblers. Thayer had heard about this St. Louis Rambler. The previous summer Baker, then only twenty years old, had ridden his forty-eight-inch Victor from St. Louis to Boston in nineteen and a half days. Many members of the League of American Wheelmen decorated themselves to celebrate their membership, covering their faces in clown white and painting the letters "LAW" in red across their noses and cheeks. Members of the Missouri Bicycle Club, which hosted the event, wore white suits with spiked helmets.[20]

The bicycles in the parade were decorated as lavishly as their riders. A reporter for the *St. Louis Post-Dispatch* wrote up a detailed account titled "Weird Wheelmen." Multicolored Chinese lanterns festooned many bicycles, hanging not only from the handlebars, but also from the pedals. Some cyclists erected great superstructures above their machines. Given the sturdy platform of three wheels, the tricyclists could be more extravagant in their display of lights than the bicyclists. To compete, three wheelmen connected their bicycles together side by side and erected a canopy above them, from which they hung nearly a hundred lanterns. A squad of mounted police began the parade, followed by a brass band in a circus chariot. The grand marshal followed on his bicycle, accompanied by his staff and some special assistants. The two hundred bedaubed and bedecked cyclists followed. The parade took a four-mile route through the city, nearly all asphalt. Accompanying the grand marshal as a special guest was a cross-country Connecticut cyclist named George B. Thayer.[21]

Though proud to ride at the head of the parade as assistant to the grand marshal, Thayer's position denied him a good view of the other cyclists until after he had reached the end of the route. Once he stopped riding and looked back, he saw a fantastic sight, the likes of which neither he nor St. Louis had ever seen. It was crucial that Thayer get a good look at all the riders in the parade because the local wheelmen had chosen him as one of the judges for the event. He and the other two judges had the responsibility to select the best decorated and illuminated bicycle and tricycle.[22]

The following night the St. Louis wheelmen hosted a banquet at the Lindell Hotel, welcoming all of the visiting wheelmen who had joined in the parade. Thayer, as an honored guest, was called upon to give a speech. In *Pedal and Path*, Thayer said he was embarrassed to speak in public, but other evidence verifies that he generally loved to talk. At the banquet, he retold some of his favorite stories from his transcontinental trip so far and acquitted himself admirably.

Once the new tube arrived from Hartford and was securely welded into place, Thayer could leave St. Louis. Instead of riding directly from the city, he decided to take the train a little further. Since he had already ridden through parts of Illinois and Indiana, he took the train from St. Louis to Louisville and resumed his ride there. Kentucky turned out to be a mixed bag. The state's African American residents were quite friendly. Instead of teasing Thayer or making fun of him, as so many other people did elsewhere, they greeted him politely.[23]

"Good mornin'," one would say. Or, perhaps, "How de do?"

Kentucky horsemen were less obliging. Riding past a country saloon, Thayer unintentionally spooked the one horse hitched out front. The horse broke its bridle and ran down the road. As soon as the horse started off, a tall, big-boned man with a long face, red cheeks, and, of course, a moustache and goatee reeled out of the saloon with a rawhide whip in his hand.[24]

"Now you jest take that bridle, and ketch that horse, and bring him back here again, or you'll get a pounden," the man said, brandishing his whip. "I am a peaceable man, but I ain't afraid of Christ, damnation, or high water. Now you do as I say."

Thayer did.

Passing through Georgetown, Kentucky, he headed north, crossed the Ohio River to Cincinnati, and rode through southern Ohio to Marietta, where he crossed the river once again to enter West Virginia. The West Virginia folk could not get enough of Thayer and his wheel. He told one interviewer, "My mode of traveling seemed to surprise the country people of West Virginia more than in any other state. In the mountains of West Virginia the women and children stared at and followed me—in some instances, for a mile or more."[25]

When they could catch him, they had an endless stream of questions. Though their questions became annoying, Thayer found much to like about West Virginia: "The beauty of the changing foliage was at its prime, the air cool, and the wind blew the rustling leaves about with a pleasing noise."[26] There were plenty of apples for nourishment and plenty of squirrels for entertainment. Thayer often stopped to enjoy the rugged scenery, using rest periods to catch up on "The Log."

West Virginia farmers welcomed him into their homes and to their tables. As always, this hungry cyclist was fascinated with local foodways. He learned that West Virginians kept several different types of sauce on the table but called them all butter: apple butter, grape butter, peach butter.[27]

WORK ON "THE LOG."

Fig. 13. Capturing a contemplative moment, this engraving depicts Thayer catching up on his journal during a rest break (Moss Engraving Co., New York). From George B. Thayer, *Pedal and Path: Across the Continent Awheel and Afoot* (Hartford: Evening Post Association, 1887). Courtesy Lilly Library, Indiana University, Bloomington IN.

"Pass the butter," he heard someone say at dinner. Given the numerous pots of sauce covering the table, this request was ambiguous. The requestor clarified, "Pass the cow butter."

Crossing the Maryland border to Cumberland, Thayer put the mountains of West Virginia behind him. The trip through Maryland along the Chesapeake and Ohio Canal proved one of the most beautiful stretches of the whole trip. He enjoyed "the fine mountain scenery, the beautiful foliage, the cool, bracing air, a broad river, a winding canal, and an almost perfect bicycle path for nearly two hundred miles."[28]

Thayer was pleased to be in a region of the country where so many important battles of the Civil War had been fought. He left the towpath at Williamsport, taking the road toward Sharpsburg, just in the rear of General Lee's line of battle at Antietam. After a solemn visit to the national cemetery there, he rode to Burnside Bridge, which he recognized from a picture he had seen in *Harper's Weekly*. As a boy, he had studied that picture so intently that the sight of the real thing almost made him shiver. He explained: "When I passed a bend in the road, and the three-arched stone bridge came in sight, I felt as if I was walking on sacred ground. More lives were laid down in other parts of the field, I did not know just where, but this spot I recognized instantly, and remembered reading at the time of how much importance it was, and I left it with greater respect than I ever had for the brave Connecticut men who faced death in that battle."[29]

He took the train the rest of the way to Baltimore, where he stayed a day and a half with his uncle and namesake, George W. Burton, who was general manager of the National Protective Union, a cooperative life insurance company. During his time in Baltimore, Thayer spoke with a local reporter, whose interview appeared in the *Baltimore American* and the Washington *Evening Star*. The reporter conveyed Thayer's accomplishment, noting that in his back and forth journey across the continent, he had covered 11,000 miles in seven months, 4,224 of them by bicycle. The Baltimore reporter also described Thayer's physical appearance. Predictably, he was as brown as a nut and fit as a fiddle.[30]

Thayer intended to bicycle back to Connecticut, but a sudden twinge of homesickness compelled him to board the train to Hartford. Once it reached the city, Thayer lingered long enough to speak with a reporter from the *Courant*, after which he mounted his wheel and took the pike from Hartford to Vernon Depot, adding another fourteen miles to his journey, making his total distance by bicycle 4,238 miles.[31] Though he had not dawdled in Hartford unnecessarily, he had stayed long enough to leave a lasting impression on the *Courant* reporter, who noticed Thayer's army knapsack, his magnificent tan, and, best of all, "the twinkle of a pair of very blue eyes."

—•6•—

From New England to Old

Announcements of George Thayer's safe return to Vernon, Connecticut, appeared in newspapers and cycling magazines across North America, earning him a reputation among his Connecticut neighbors and across the nationwide network of cyclists.[1] It felt good to be home, but several follow-up tasks demanded his attention. He had formed strong bonds with many cyclists from Connecticut to California. And the bonds of brotherhood among wheelmen, he decided, were stronger than those of any fraternal organization or secret order.[2] He expressed his gratitude once he got home by writing thank-you letters to wheelmen he had met.

One letter went to D. L. Davis to thank him for his hospitality in Salt Lake City and also to inform him how the trip had gone once he left Utah: "I enjoyed the return trip fully as much as I did going and shall not soon forget your kindness. Should be glad to hear from you."[3] Not only did Thayer want to thank the cyclists he befriended, he also hoped to perpetuate the friendships he had made. Davis, well aware he was not the only friend Thayer had made in Salt Lake City, passed his thank-you letter to the editor of the "Wheel Notes" column for the *Salt Lake Herald*, who quoted it to remind readers about the "little bald-headed man from Connecticut."[4]

Thayer also reached out to cyclists contemplating their own cross-country bicycle tours. In a letter to the editor of the LAW *Bulletin*, he provided an outline of his trip, which he concluded with an offer of help: "If any wheelman should desire any information about any part of the trip I should be only too glad to give him all that I possess."[5] Thayer's behavior in this instance established a pattern he would frequently repeat. He would travel to many faraway places in the future, but he would always make a point to share his personal experiences with others upon his return.

George Nellis was one person who asked for more information. Busy planning a solo transcontinental cycling tour of his own, Nellis wished to learn as much as he could beforehand, so he wrote for advice. Thayer reassured him that cycling across the continent involved much less danger than might be supposed. The Rocky Mountains may seem intimidating, but ascending them was less difficult than climbing many New England hills. The climbs were longer but not nearly as steep. The biggest difficulty is finding water on the Plains. Thayer advised Nellis to be ready to endure long periods of thirst. The wind presented another problem. On the plus side, the western ranchers are friendly and hospitable, willing to go out of their way to assist passing cyclists. In short, Thayer's reassurance helped fuel Nellis's confidence, a confidence that would propel him across the nation in record time.[6]

Karl Kron also wrote Thayer for more information about transcontinental cycling, which he would incorporate in his forthcoming book, *Ten Thousand Miles on a Bicycle*. Thayer provided a few additional details but informed Kron that he would retell the whole story in a book of his own, which he planned to call "From Ocean to Ocean on a Bicycle."[7] For this book, Thayer assembled the letters he had written for the *Hartford Evening Post* and revised them considerably, as he explained in his preface: "I have been able when seated quietly at my own desk to give fuller details at certain interesting points, and to round out a narrative which was sometimes rather meagre."[8]

Before finishing the revision, Thayer also changed his title to make it a little catchier. He trimmed the number of prepositions by two-thirds and enhanced the alliteration: *Pedal and Path: Across the Continent Awheel and Afoot.* Thayer arranged with the prestigious Moss Engraving Company in New York to illustrate the book. The engravings Moss produced were excellent—with one exception. Depicting Thayer crossing the Snake River, the engraver made the river much too narrow and decorously portrayed Thayer fully clothed. Having published Thayer's original travel letters, the *Hartford Evening Post* agreed to publish *Pedal and Path.*

Cost of the book's publication was subsidized by the insurance companies for which the city of Hartford is famous. Travelers Insurance Company placed an advertisement inside the front of the book emphasizing that its policies would cover the cost of bicycle riding at no extra charge. An advertisement for Aetna appeared on the back cover. Inside the back cover Connecticut Mutual Life addressed its advertisement to "Young Men Who Contemplate Life Insurance." The insurance companies clearly sought to broaden their customer base and attract nontraditional insurance buyers, that is, young, single men. The advertisements in *Pedal and Path* specifically appealed to cyclists and other lovers of outdoor adventure.

Though handsomely printed and illustrated, *Pedal and Path*, George Thayer's first book, was issued in an inexpensive paperback format. Furthermore, it received almost no publicity and, consequently, little attention in the press. *Wheels and Whims*, his sister's first book, received much more attention. The few national magazines that reviewed *Pedal and*

Path did not publish their reviews until two years after the book appeared.

Outing generally liked *Pedal and Path*: "Mr. Thayer tells his story in a pleasant, chatty style, well adapted to the original form his writings took—newspaper letters—and furnishing pleasant light literature in book-form." The reviewer was not totally positive, suggesting that some passages savored of a naïveté that could prove to be embarrassing to female readers.[9] No doubt the reviewer had in mind Thayer's story about crossing the Snake River in his skivvies.

Wildwood's Magazine, another national publication that reviewed *Pedal and Path*, had nothing but good things to say about the book. *Wildwood's* called Thayer a "plucky wheelman" and found his book "an entertaining account of an adventurous cycling trip, through a rugged and picturesque region." Overall, Thayer described "the country, the people, and customs in a pleasant style."[10]

Though he had returned to Vernon after his transcontinental cycling tour, it was not long before Thayer realized the village held little for him beyond memories. Having sold his grocery store before leaving on his long-distance tour, he had no means of employment in Vernon and no more ties to the town. Hartford, alternatively, had much to offer, including several daily papers. The newspaper business fascinated Thayer. Since boyhood he had read every paper he could get his hands on. Having written for the *Hartford Evening Post* throughout his trip across the nation, he now approached its editor for a job. The *Evening Post* editor offered Thayer an apprenticeship as a reporter at four dollars a week.[11]

Thirty-three and bald, George Thayer looked a little old to be a cub reporter, but he did not care a whit whether he looked the part. Neither did he care about the meager salary. Four dollars a week was less than he could make working at one of the local factories, but his needs were few. He knew he could get by on this wage—as long as it would eventually lead to steady work. What he really wanted was a permanent, full-time job at the *Evening Post* or one of Hartford's other daily newspapers. He accepted the position and moved to Hartford.

As the capital of Connecticut, Hartford had much going for it in the 1880s. It contained many handsome buildings, including the Connecticut State House, City Hall, the Opera House, and Union Station. Furthermore, it was the home of several important cultural institutions, such as the Connecticut Historical Society, the Hartford Public Library, the Wadsworth Athenaeum, and the Young Men's Institute. Long known for its numerous insurance companies, Hartford more recently fostered the growth of many new industries. In addition to being home to several printing plants, the city had become the center of American bicycle manufacture. Hartford also had a reputation as the home of some distinguished literary figures, the most prominent being Mark Twain and Harriet Beecher Stowe.

Hartford became a center for bicycle manufacture during the final third of the nineteenth century. Colonel Albert A. Pope was more responsible for bringing bicycle manufacture to Hartford than anyone. After encountering the English-made penny-farthing bicycle at the Centennial Exhibition in Philadelphia, he became intrigued with its commercial possibilities. He subsequently visited England, where he learned about bicycle manufacture. Pope began importing English bicycles in 1877. The following year he arranged for them to be made in America, contracting with the Weed Sewing Machine Company in Hartford to manufacture his own brand of bicycles, which he shrewdly named Columbia, thus giving the machine patriotic associations.[12]

Columbia bicycles proved to be quite successful, partly because they were well built, but mainly because Pope was a master manipulator when it came to patenting his product and a marketing genius when it came to promotion. Colonel Pope marketed Columbia bicycles in many different ways. He sponsored some riders. Both Fred Van Meerbeke and S. G. Spier had signed contracts with Pope prior to their transcontinental tours in 1886. Pope supplied each with equipment and a stipend. He presented Spier with a custom-made Columbia Expert manufactured specially for his transcontinental ride. Pope's support of Van Meerbeke and Spier gave him the privilege of using their names in his advertising.[13] He could thus puff the speed and sturdiness of Columbia bicycles by showing how they could endure rough riding across America.

Thayer made no such agreement with Pope, but he did agree to let Pope use his name in Columbia advertisements after he had crossed the continent. The cover of the April 1887 issue of *The Wheelmen's Gazette*, for example, contains an advertisement headed "Some Records on Columbia Bicycles." Besides listing Thomas Stevens's round-the-world journey, it also listed two riders who cycled across North America: F. E. Van Meerbeke and George B. Thayer.

In addition to being home to Columbia Bicycles and numerous other manufacturers of bicycles and bicycle componentry, Hartford also had a lively cycling culture. The city had its own cycling club as early as 1879, when the Connecticut Bicycle Club was founded. Many of Pope's employees belonged to the factory-sponsored Columbia Cycle Club. And members of Hartford's high society had a club of their own: the Asylum Hill Club.[14] At the time of his transcontinental ride, Thayer was a member of the Connecticut Bicycle Club and proudly identifies himself as such on the title page of *Pedal and Path*. Once the Hartford Wheel Club was founded, he joined that club. He would remain an active member for years to come.

When it came to Hartford's literary scene, Thayer greatly respected Harriet Beecher Stowe. His attitude toward Mark Twain was more tentative.[15] But there was one Hartford author who meant the world to him: his sister. Living in Hartford meant living close to her.

Since publishing *Wheels and Whims* in 1884, Florine Thayer McCray had continued to contribute to the newspapers and periodicals. She had also started writing a new novel. In 1887 she published *Environment*, a society novel with a temperance theme set in New York. Living in the same neighborhood, she and Harriet Beecher Stowe became friends. McCray frequently spoke with Stowe and accompanied her on neighborhood walks. She would use what she learned in conversation to write her most ambitious book, a biography she titled *The Life-Work of the Author of "Uncle Tom's Cabin,"* which Funk and Wagnalls would publish in 1889. Florine was shrewder than her brother when it came to placing her work with publishers. Whereas he published his writings with whatever publisher who would issue them expeditiously, she sought well-established firms that stood behind their publications and suitably promoted them.

George Thayer learned the newspaper business during his apprenticeship, but he remained restless throughout his time with the *Evening Post*. Taken together, two comments he made after crossing North America indicate his mood. Speaking of his transcontinental tour in the letter to the editor of the LAW *Bulletin*, he said, "As a trip, intended from the first to be one of pleasure, it was a great success, so much so that I would like to take another one."[16] Mentioning Alonzo Williams in *Pedal and Path*, Thayer remembered how the professor's delightful account of his European bicycle tour had inspired him.[17] After a year and a half of sedentary newspaper work, Thayer was wild for a European cycling tour.

As he imagined the trip, he would cycle lengthwise through Great Britain and then cross into Europe, taking a zigzag course through France, Belgium, Germany, and Italy. From Italy his plans were less certain. Perhaps he would cross the

Mediterranean to Egypt. He told the reporter from the *Brooklyn Daily Eagle* that he would travel through Greece and ride overland to Constantinople.[18] His remarks indicate the confidence Thayer had gained during his trip across North America. Whereas he had been reluctant to tell others how far he planned to go in 1886, now he did not hesitate to share his ambitious goals with reporters.

To prepare for the first leg of his trip, he read all he could about the history of Great Britain. He explained, "Hoping to appear at ease, to the manner born, when among English people, I at once loaded up with all there was to know about English history, English architecture, English writers, English painters, English birth places later made famous and all that kind of stuff. It was quite a load."[19]

He arranged with the *New York World* to write letters home from Europe reporting his adventures. Since his sister wrote for the *World*, presumably she helped arrange for George to contribute travel letters to the paper. The fact that the *New York Times* announced his trip may indicate Thayer's growing reputation as a traveler, but the article tempered his fame as it ended by identifying him as "a brother of the novelist, Mrs. Florine Thayer McCray."[20] The *Washington Post* provided a surer indication of his reputation as a bicycle tourist, announcing, "George B. Thayer, of Hartford, Conn., who crossed the continent to California on a bicycle two years ago, is crossing the ocean now to do Europe in the same way."[21]

Friday evening, June 8, 1888, Thayer found himself in New York boarding the *Anchoria* bound for Glasgow. Scarcely one hour past sunrise Saturday morning, the *Anchoria* was underway, as were five other transatlantic steamships, carrying many distinguished tourists to Europe for the summer. As they passed through the Narrows, the French steamer *Gascogne* led the procession, followed by the *Edam*, bound for Amsterdam. Third in line, the *Anchoria* caught the swash of the *Edam*. By ten that morning, Thayer's ship had already passed Sandy Hook.[22]

The next morning he awoke to a sea of fog, but once the wind shifted from the north a few days later, it brought some cool, beautiful, sunny weather. His fellow passengers included two men of the cloth, the Reverend Omar W. Folsom, a Congregationalist minister from Maine, and the Reverend T. S. Wynkoop, a Presbyterian missionary. Wynkoop may have interested Thayer more. For years Wynkoop had worked as a missionary in India, and his experience there provided the kind of details that fired Thayer's imagination. The *Anchoria* made good time: it reached Glasgow nine days after leaving New York.[23]

Having crated his Columbia before leaving home, Thayer decided to have it and his fully loaded knapsack carted to his hotel instead of uncrating the machine and reassembling it at the pier. His bicycle and his gear, along with luggage from other passengers going to the same hotel, were loaded into a roadside cart. The cartload amounted to around three hundred pounds. Thayer was astonished to discover that this heavy load would be pulled by neither horse nor ox nor man. Rather, a boy, scarcely twelve years old and barely a hundred pounds himself, would pull the cart. A man standing nearby had the responsibility of driving the cart, but he usually just walked beside it, pulling only when the grade was steep.

Once the cart was full, the man ordered the boy to step between its handles and strap himself in. It looked to Thayer like it took every muscle in the boy's tiny body to overcome inertia and get the cart moving. The insensitive driver did nothing to help. Knowing well the driver's habits, the boy automatically stopped in front of one particular tavern along the way. The driver went inside for a drink as the boy waited outside. It took one more tavern stop before they reached the hotel. This episode was no isolated incident. Thayer witnessed other abusive child labor practices during his time in Glasgow. One day he saw two young girls with barrels strapped to their backs going house to house collecting swill.

After assembling his bicycle, Thayer spent a few days doing the town. It was no problem finding plenty of healthful, inexpensive things to eat. Another bicycle tourist observed that in Glasgow "almost every other shop seems to be a fruitseller's."[24] Once Thayer left the city, he headed for Loch Lomond, the Queen of the Scottish Lakes.

At Balloch, a village on Loch Lomond's southwest shore, he checked into the Colquhoun Arms Hotel. In its advertisements, the Colquhoun Arms puffed its billiard room, smoking room, and hot baths. Traveling through Scotland around the same time as Thayer, Joseph and Elizabeth Pennell stopped at the Colquhoun Arms for lunch. The experience left them in a "mood for lounging." Lunch was so relaxing they had a difficult time resuming their journey.[25]

Thayer liked the smoking room at the Colquhoun Arms the best. He was not a smoker, of course, but the hotel's smoking room contained a plentiful sideboard. He marveled at the vast amount of food. Ever hungry and ever thrifty, Thayer enjoyed the concept of a self-serve buffet. He could eat all he wanted without having to squander money on a waiter's tip. He visited Loch Lomond the next morning before continuing to Loch Katrine and stopping for the night at Stirling. Owen Seaman, who had taken a lengthy tricycling tour through Scotland a few years earlier, called Stirling "a curious town, having a mixture of ancient and quite modern buildings."[26]

From Stirling, Thayer rode to Edinburgh, where he lingered for a few days. As he had on previous tours, he used each major city as a base and took day trips to nearby sights. One day while staying in Edinburgh, he rode to Porto Bello, a fashionable resort for sea bathing, about three miles east of the city. Porto Bello contained a marine promenade, an elegant iron pier, and a spacious dance hall. The sea bathing facilities were its primary attraction.

A series of small, wheeled bathing shelters lined the beach. For a modest fee, Thayer rented one of these huts. He mounted the steps and closed the door behind him. Just as he began to undress, the hut started rocking. Peeking out, he noticed a man hitching a horse to the hut. Once it was hitched, the man straddled the horse and towed the portable hut into the sea. As soon as they reached the proper depth, the man unhitched the horse and rode back to the shore, leaving Thayer inside the hut.

Having undressed and put on his bathing suit, Thayer opened the door. As soon as he did, water rushed in. He stepped from the hut and instantly felt a cold wind—"a Bleak House east wind," he called it. The breeze passed right through his bathing suit, making him feel as blue all over as Mr. Jarndyce used to feel in the Dickens novel. Slowly stepping into the water, Thayer got so cold he decided it would be better to jump in and immerse himself all at once. He normally loved to swim, but the water at Porto Bello was too cold to tolerate. He turned around and scrambled back into the hut. The man on horseback observed—no doubt with a grin—how quickly the American had ended his swim. He pointed his horse toward the water, returned to the hut, hitched it to the horse, and pulled it ashore.[27]

Cycling through Scotland in June, Thayer could use the long days to indulge his love of sightseeing. G. W. Burston and H. R. Stokes, two intrepid Australian riders from the Melbourne Bicycle Club who followed a similar route through Great Britain during their round-the-world tour, also came through Scotland in June. Like Thayer they, too, marveled over the long summer days, which let them put some long miles in the saddle.[28]

From Edinburgh, Thayer headed south toward Abbotsford, the renowned home of Sir Walter Scott. Abbotsford did not appeal to everyone: Burston and Stokes blew right past without stopping. Thayer, on the other hand, found it well worth the stop. In his road guide to Scotland, James Lennox, chief consul of the Cyclists' Touring Club (CTC), noted that the public is admitted to Abbotsford during the summer months between ten and six. Typically, visitors were shown only five rooms: Sir Walter's study with his old desk and overstuffed armchair; the library, some twenty-thousand volumes strong; the drawing room where Sir Walter died; the armory; and the grand entrance hall.[29]

After Abbotsford, Thayer rode through Melrose to the ruins of Dryburgh Abbey, the twelfth-century monastery where Sir Walter Scott is buried. Located on a wooded peninsula almost surrounded by the Tweed River, encircled by orchards, and covered in ivy, the abbey made a picturesque sight. Lennox rose to poetry as he described it: "The ruins on the banks of the Tweed peer out here and there from a thick covering of ivy, which is always green, like the memory of the minstrel buried within the walls."[30]

Riding up and down the Cheviot Hills, Thayer crossed into England. He spent one night in the tiny village of Kirkwhelpington. It was pouring as he awoke the next day, but he was prepared for the weather, having packed his rainsuit, which was even more elaborate than the one he took to Denver two years earlier. He had the same long gossamer coat and hood, but this time he brought along some bright yellow oil-cloth knee protectors, rubber leggings, and large rubber overshoes. The overshoes were so big that, as Thayer told the story, one English farmer punningly asked him if he was "performing some big feat."[31]

Wearing the whole getup in the rain, Thayer made a bizarre appearance. To keep the rest of his gear dry, he would carry his army knapsack beneath his raincoat, which thus gave him a hunchbacked, Richard the Third kind of look. Atop his head,

Fig. 14. Joseph Pennell depicts a "danger board," a type of sign erected
throughout England by the Cyclists' Touring Club in conjunction
with the National Cyclists' Union to warn passing cyclists. From
William Coutts Keppel, Earl of Albemarle; and G. Lacy Hillier,
Cycling (London: Longmans, Green, 1887). Courtesy Lilly
Library, Indiana University, Bloomington IN.

the gossamer hood covered so much of his face that only his
eyes and nose showed.[32]

Thayer should have given the road as much attention as his
rainwear. A long, steep hill led from Kirkwhelpington. Since
the early 1880s, the CTC, in conjunction with the National
Cyclists' Union (NCU), had been placing danger boards at the
top of treacherous descents. The warnings on these cast-iron
signs could not be clearer:

TO

CYCLISTS

THIS HILL

IS

DANGEROUS

Though Thayer saw no sign when he left Kirkwhelpington, he could have read about the hill beforehand in James Lennox's road guide. Lennox cautioned cyclists about the "steep and loose descent" on the road from Kirkwhelpington.[33] Whenever Thayer threw his legs over the handlebars, he threw caution to the wind. With his feet sticking out front, he let those big floppy overshoes flutter in the wind. Word of this strange sight went through the village even faster than Thayer could ride. Despite the wet weather, Kirkwhelpingtonians came out from their homes to watch him leave town.

As his speed increased, so did his concern. To moderate his speed, he feathered the brake only to find that the brake spoon would not hold against the front tire, now covered with a thin film of mud. He knew he would have to dismount quickly or else he would crash, so he tried his old trick of hitting the brake hard enough to lock up the front wheel, tipping the rear end of the bike and allowing him to step off the front feet first. He had performed this maneuver with considerable dexterity many times before. Having never done it wearing big floppy rubber overshoes, he neglected to factor them in. As soon as those overshoes came in contact with the wet, muddy road surface, they slipped out from under him, and he plopped down on his backside.

Thayer did not stop moving once he hit the ground. Rather, he rolled off the road and into a muddy ditch filled with nettles—face first! The bike did not stop moving, either. It followed him into the ditch, where it came to a standstill upside down next to him. Its rear wheel, now pointed skyward, kept spinning. The citizens of Kirkwhelpington applauded with glee.

To his credit, Thayer could laugh at himself, so he did not mind too much that the English had a good laugh at his expense this morning. Other times the English seemed more diffident. He couldn't understand why until he realized that they took offense at the Baedeker guidebook he carried with him. Its red covers were instantly recognizable, and its presence in his hands marked him as a tourist.

In the 1830s German publisher Karl Baedeker had published the first of many guidebooks his firm would publish. Over the next half-century, Baedekers, as travelers called them, became essential for European travel. The greatest contribution Baedeker made to the guidebook format was the star system. In 1844 he began marking with an asterisk important sights that busy travelers should not miss. Later he extended his star system to denote the quality of hotels and restaurants.[34]

Though a German-language Baedeker to Great Britain and English-language Baedekers to the Continent had been available for decades before George Thayer's European tour, English-language Baedekers to Great Britain were more recent. The first, J. F. Muirhead's *London and Its Environs*, appeared in 1878, and the next, *Great Britain, England, Wales, and Scotland*, also prepared by Muirhead, appeared the year before Thayer's tour. Perhaps the idea of a guide to England in English is what unsettled the British the most. Why should English speakers need a guidebook to England? Shouldn't they already know everything a portable, one-volume guide could tell them?

Recalling his tour of Great Britain many years later, Thayer recorded the English dislike of Baedekers: "Everywhere I showed the little red book the act was a confession on my part there was something I did not know or knew only in part, which conduct, don't you know, is not English." He came to realize that the British saw the red covers of a Baedeker as "a sort of cautionary signal of the approach of a disagreeable presence."[35]

The day he left Kirkwhelpington would be Thayer's first full day in England. His Baedeker, which contained a brief section on cycle touring by E. R. Shipton, the secretary of the CTC, offered encouragement. Shipton noted the good quality

Fig. 15. This photograph depicts Durham Cathedral as it would have looked to Thayer during his bicycle tour of England (Detroit Publishing Co., ca. 1910). Library of Congress, Prints and Photographs Division, reproduction number LC-D4-73178.

of English roads, though his description does sound a little jingoistic: "The American cyclist will probably find them far better adapted to his requirements than the ordinary highways of the United States."[36]

Durham, the first cathedral city Thayer visited in England, gave him a taste of what he would experience in the days to come as he approached other cathedral towns: Ely, Lincoln, Peterborough, and York. Upon seeing the Durham Cathedral ahead, he thought he was almost there, but the distance to the city turned out to be much further then he imagined. It took at least an hour from the time he saw Durham Cathedral to the time he entered the city. Consolation came in the form of excellent lodgings at the Three Tuns Hotel. Baedeker gave the Three Tuns a star. Reinforcing its suitability for cyclists,

Durham City Cycling Club had its headquarters at the Three Tuns. But what really made the establishment memorable was Mrs. Brown, the hotel's cheerful hostess and proprietor.[37]

In an account of his cycle tour across England, Alfred Nixon of the London Tricycle Club found that the Three Tuns provided the best accommodation of his entire trip. "The kindness of everyone was great," he observed, "and I hope other wheelmen will make a point of stopping at the same house." They did. Joseph and Elizabeth Pennell stopped here when they passed through Durham. "A jolly little inn," she called it.[38]

"Come and have a glass of cherry brandy," Mrs. Brown would say to guests upon their arrival. For those who initially refused the complimentary glass of ardent spirits, she would insist: "It is a custom of the house." It was almost impossible to resist Mrs. Brown's kindly, yet insistent offer. Elizabeth Pennell could not. Out of all the travelers who stopped at the Three Tuns in the late nineteenth century whose accounts I have located, only one successfully resisted Mrs. Brown's cherry brandy: a prim and proper schoolmarm-turned-journalist named Eliza Archard Conner. Capturing Mrs. Brown's reaction, Mrs. Conner wrote: "I think she was a little hurt at my declining the 'custom of the house,' but, on learning that I was an American, she put me down at once, *prima facie*, as a teetotaler, and the sunshine of her rubicund countenance was only temporarily obscured."[39]

Thayer's account mentions the Three Tuns but says nothing about Mrs. Brown or her cherry brandy, so we are left to guess whether he partook. Though Ginger-Ale George was against the consumption of alcohol in principle, he could seldom refuse such generous hospitality. One word may have swayed him: "complimentary." Thayer almost never turned down anything free. His account does mention that he enjoyed the bountiful sideboard at the Three Tuns. Did he drink the cherry brandy or didn't he? As he had on other special occasions, George Thayer, I believe, made an exception to his rule against drinking and enjoyed a snifter of Mrs. Brown's cherry brandy the night he stayed at the Three Tuns.

It was raining as Thayer entered Peterborough. He left his bicycle and his knapsack and, presumably, his big floppy overshoes in a covered alleyway out of the rain to enter Peterborough Cathedral. Baedeker gave the cathedral a star, describing it as "one of the most important Norman churches left in England, though the first glance at the exterior does not seem to bear out this assertion."[40] Baedeker gave the interior of Peterborough Cathedral a star of its own, but it, too, scarcely seemed to deserve the distinction.

Thayer really wanted to see the grave of Catherine of Aragon. After climbing over heaps of lumber and piles of stone that filled the choir, which was being renovated, he still could not find her burial place, so he asked a workman. The man led him to the north aisle, where he brushed away a considerable amount of rubble to uncover a small brass plate imbedded in a large paving stone. Only one word on the plate had not been completely worn off: "Katherine."[41]

The fondness for Shakespeare that Thayer had acquired as a child compelled him to stop at Stratford-on-Avon to see the birthplace of the greatest playwright in the history of English literature. From there it was not too far to London. He found a good place to stay on Euston Road, just a mile and a half from Fleet Street, for $7.50 a week, which included room and attendance, a meat breakfast, and a five-course dinner.[42] That Thayer situated himself in relation to Fleet Street—the center of British newspaper publishing—may indicate how important newspapers continued to be to him. He planned to spend four weeks in London to enjoy what the city had to offer.

Not everything he saw in London pleased his eyes. As in Glasgow, he witnessed many children put to work in the mean streets of the big city. The London boys had to do a job that was both dirty and dangerous: to clean the streets of horse manure. Their size, speed, and agility made them ideal for darting around the moving wheels of horse-drawn vehicles. As he watched them dash behind, beneath, and between the moving vehicles, Thayer feared for the boys' well-being. He called the job "a peril put upon the boys that cost many of them their lives."[43]

On the plus side, London was making great strides to improve the quality of its street pavement. Thayer concluded that the asphalt streets of London provided the best argument for paving more city streets with asphalt in the United States: "No city in the world, probably, has a greater carrying traffic in the streets than London, yet the crowds of heavy teams and lumbering buses roll over the asphalt pavement with a pleasing absence of noise. If asphalt was ever put to a severe test, it is in London: but instead of breaking up and becoming uneven, as it is claimed it would in the busy American cities, asphalt in London is fast supplanting all other kinds of pavement."[44]

Given the smooth asphalt streets, Thayer enjoyed cycling around London. He developed a regular routine the month he stayed there. After breakfast at his boarding house, he would explore the city until lunchtime, when he would enjoy a light lunch wherever he happened to be. He explained, "Plenty of nice places were to be found where a cup of coffee and a sandwich or bun could be had for twelve or fifteen cents." Admittance to many of the tourist destinations, this thrifty traveler discovered, was free. Thayer especially enjoyed the British Museum.[45]

He also witnessed the House of Commons in session. In one account of his trip, he mentioned being in the spectators' gallery at the House of Commons, in July 1888, when "Parnell was triumphantly acquitted in the eyes of the whole world."[46] Thayer was referring to the matter of the Phoenix

Park murders. After Chief Secretary Lord Frederick Cavendish and Under Secretary Thomas Henry Burke were assassinated in Dublin, in 1882, Charles Stewart Parnell, the leader of the Irish party, wrote a letter condemning the murders. The issue resurfaced in 1888 as the *Times* suggested Parnell's complicity in the murders and even printed a facsimile of another letter, purportedly by Parnell, retracting his condemnation. Thayer watched from the gallery as debate in the House of Commons grew heated. The *Times* letter ultimately proved to be a forgery, and Parnell was exonerated.

Thayer visited the National Gallery, as well. He specifically mentions seeing several paintings by J. M. W. Turner, whose works had gone to the National Gallery by bequest and were displayed in its West Room. Baedeker lists several of the paintings by name, placing stars by three of them: *Crossing the Brook*, *The "Fighting Temeraire" Towed to the Last Berth to Be Broken Up*, and *Richmond Hill*.[47]

By the 1880s Turner was recognized as the greatest landscape painter in the history of British art. Thayer had mixed feelings about his work, observing that Turner "drew not from nature but from his own crazy notions as to colors." Calling Turner "crazy," Thayer may seem derogatory, but what he said next clarifies that he was simply overwhelmed by Turner's palette: "Like the shout before the walls of Jericho, the colors were so loud they knocked you flat. No wonder, in Baedeker's, the very name of Turner makes you see stars."[48]

Thayer's difficulty with Turner's colors is partly understandable in light of his current mindset. By the time he reached the National Gallery, he was already starting to anticipate the next leg of his European cycling tour, which would take him through Germany and the Swiss Alps. As Thayer imagined the real, yet spectacular landscapes he would soon see for himself, he had difficulty accepting the unreal though spectacular landscapes Turner imagined.

7

The Grand Tour

Crossing the English Channel to begin his tour of the Continent, George Thayer decided to do something in Europe similar to what he had done in Great Britain. Having spent four weeks in London at the end of his British tour, he wished to take the same amount of time to see Paris. But he did not want to do Paris right away. After his London sojourn, he was anxious to get some more miles under his belt, so he decided to zigzag across Europe in a roughly north-south direction before settling in Paris. This trek would take him through Belgium, Germany, Switzerland, and northern Italy. Baedekers would guide his way.

His journey across Belgium brought him to Waterloo one Saturday in August 1888. Baedeker recommended two hours to tour the famous battlefield.[1] Thayer may have taken longer. He would often dawdle in places that suited his contemplative nature. After strolling around the slightly undulating battlefield, he climbed the two-hundred-foot mound atop which stood the Belgian Lion, a twenty-eight-ton statue cast from the metal of captured French cannon. The man-made mound provided a good vantage point to survey the battlefield; the massive lion statue was something to see in itself. He approached for a better look but flinched as he got close.[2] Like Victor Hugo before him, Thayer startled some birds nesting in the lion's mouth.

Though the Belgian Lion was impressive, Thayer's most memorable experience in Belgium came the following day. That Sunday morning he entered Liège in a drizzling rain. The city was nearly silent. The only sound disturbing the quiet was the clatter of wooden shoes as children ran across the pavé. He passed through the city center, crossed a bridge over the Vesdre, and turned toward Cologne. Before he cleared the outskirts of Liège, it started to pour. Spying a woodshed behind a cobbler's house, he sought shelter there. Once Thayer reached the shed, he dismounted, removed his gossamer coat, and spread it on the woodpile. As he was about to take a seat on the woodpile himself to wait out the storm, the cobbler stepped from his home and motioned him to come inside. Thayer entered the house but left his raincoat outdoors.

The cobbler's wife rushed into the rain to retrieve the coat. She brought it inside and draped it over a chair near their stove. She put Thayer in another chair and had him prop his wet stocking feet on the edge of the stove's open doorway. Soon Thayer was munching on bread and butter, which he washed down with some steaming hot Belgian coffee.

He stayed until the rain stopped and his gear was dry. He was so grateful that he took out some money and tried to pay the cobbler and his wife, but they frowned upon his gesture. They had helped him from the goodness of their hearts: they expected nothing in return. Thayer thanked them profusely and got back on the road. The simple kindness of the Belgian people meant more to him than any Belgian Lion could.[3]

The border between Belgium and Germany was quite permeable. John Foster Fraser—a British cyclist who pedaled through the region on a round-the-world tour with a couple of mates a few years later—rode from Belgium to Germany at night without realizing his group had crossed the border until they were several miles into Germany.[4] Similarly, Thayer crossed the border without incident. Not all border crossings went so smoothly, as he would later come to learn.

In Germany Thayer received a much different impression of the people than the one Thomas Stevens had received three years earlier. Stevens's time there did not lessen his prejudice toward Germans. He observed that most bicycle tourists in Germany came from England. The average German, according to Stevens, "would much rather loll around, sipping wine or beer, and smoking cigarettes than impel a bicycle across a continent." More open-minded than Stevens, Thayer encountered several German cyclists as he passed through their lovely countryside.[5]

He became good friends with one in particular, a German student who was taking a bicycle tour through his homeland during the school holidays. Though Thayer could not speak German and this student could not speak English, the two shared a love of fresh air and fresh fruit. They got along well. The German cyclist—Thayer does not mention his name, so he must remain anonymous—taught him the local customs when it came to foraging for food in nearby orchards. The ever-hungry Thayer appreciated the knowledge. Passing the German orchards, travelers were welcome to eat individual pieces of fruit but forbidden to carry any away with them. Thayer consequently avoided the temptation to load up his knapsack, contenting himself to enjoy the apples, pears, and plums he found here and there. Thayer and the German cyclist rode together for a few days. By the time they parted, they had become good friends. They exchanged addresses and hoped to write one another.[6]

Thayer reached his first major European mountain pass before leaving Germany. As he crested the top, he anticipated a glorious seven-mile coast downhill. The tight bends and seemingly endless horseshoe curves were intimidating at first. Going around some of the sharp turns, he could only see the road for twenty or thirty feet ahead of him. But after a mile or two, he recognized how smooth the roads were and gained more confidence. He whizzed past some English cyclists, leaving them in his dust. Eventually, he let up on the brake, going faster and faster. To be safe, he kept one finger on the brake lever. Once that digit cramped up, he started using two. The brake spoon overheated long before he reached the bottom of the hill.

This day Thayer was the fastest thing on the road. He encountered a team of oxen but whooshed by them so rapidly they did not have time to react. He scared some children who were crossing the road, but they jumped out of the way just in time. Cyclists, oxen, children: nothing, it seems, could slow the downward progress of this coasting Connecticut daredevil. Thayer described the exhilarating experience: "I went like the wind over the same steep grade and smooth road down from top to bottom, without mishap, but with a feeling I never before experienced in coasting that I was glad I was at the bottom."[7]

How fast did he travel? It's impossible to say for sure, but his account provides a relative gauge of his speed. He stopped at the bottom to wait for the English cyclists he had passed on the way down. They did not arrive until six minutes later! The fastest descenders in the Tour de France today cannot gain that much time over their rivals on a long descent.

Thayer's route through Switzerland brought him to Lucerne, but apparently he did not dawdle there. He was anxious to tackle more mountain passes. During his time in Switzerland he climbed at least a half dozen Alpine passes and enjoyed several more hair-raising descents.[8] South of Lucerne he crossed the 7,100-foot Grimsel Pass. From the bottom, the pass looked quite intimidating: a "zigzag road up into the clouds."[9] Thayer had to dismount and push his bike uphill most of the way. As he did so, a rough-looking man started following him. Not only did Thayer have to push his wheel uphill, he also had to push it through slush and over snow drifts. Regardless of the obstacles, the mystery man kept following him. The climb tired Thayer so much that he worried whether he would have the strength to defend himself should the man attack.

Grimsel Pass, according to British cyclist W. Rees Jeffreys, was the most picturesque of all the Swiss passes.[10] The day Thayer crossed, dense fog obscured the top of the pass, preventing him from enjoying its scenic grandeur and exacerbating his paranoia. He now worried that the mystery man was using the fog as cover to sneak ahead and lie in wait. After cresting the pass, Thayer remounted and began coasting downhill. No one on foot could catch him now. He could have finished his descent by nightfall but decided to stop about six miles down, where the hotel at the base of the Rhône Glacier was located. Who should arrive at the hotel that night but the rough-looking mystery man who had followed Thayer through the fog. As Thayer sheepishly realized, the man was neither cutpurse nor cutthroat. Instead, he was an Alpine guide who chased after tourists hoping they would hire him to lead them through the Alps.[11]

Thayer stayed in the vicinity the next day to see the Rhône Glacier and tour the Ice Grotto, a spacious room hewn from the heart of the glacier. Interior spaces within the earth continued to fascinate Thayer. On a trip to Hawaii years later he would visit The Bubble, a hotel formed from a giant bubble of lava inside the extinct Haleakala volcano.[12] Though Thayer's accounts of his European cycling tour do not describe the inside of the Ice Grotto, American novelist Frank R. Stockton, who visited around the same time, left a detailed account. Sensitive to the interests of cyclists, Stockton would later write a cyclotouring novel titled *A Bicycle of Cathay*.

To reach the Ice Grotto, visitors had to pass through a long tunnel with a tall but drippy ceiling. Baedeker recommended carrying an umbrella into the grotto.[13] In the tunnel's early section, sunlight penetrated its roof, making the bluish ice nearly transparent. The tunnel got darker as it penetrated deeper into the ice, but dim lamps helped light the way. At the tunnel's end, travelers ascended a few steps before entering the grotto, which was illumined by a single lamp. As soon as Stockton entered, he heard music. Two old women played zithers for the benefit of the tourists. The doleful sound echoed throughout the chamber. When Thayer revisited this region twenty-six years later, he was saddened to see how the glacier had receded. So much ice had melted that the grotto was gone.[14]

Emerging from the grotto, Thayer got back on his bike to finish his descent. On this and other passes in Switzerland, he descended so quickly and quietly that he often had trouble with pedestrians stepping into the road in front of him. In both England and Germany, wheelmen fastened sleigh bells to their handlebars as a civil way of warning pedestrians. Throughout the Alps, the sound of rushing water drowned out the tinkle of sleigh bells, so more obnoxious methods of warning were necessary. Thayer carried a shrill whistle, but sometimes in Switzerland it proved insufficient. He concluded, "Nothing but the most throat splitting yell would clear the road of the numerous pedestrians."[15]

G. W. Burston and H. R. Stokes, the globe-girdling Australian cyclists, just loved Switzerland. Like Thayer, they enjoyed throwing their legs over the handlebars and coasting downhill atop their high-wheeled bicycles. Speaking of their experience, they said, "Switzerland, instead of being a bad place for cycling, is the finest place to wheel imaginable; the only thing absolutely necessary is a cool head and firm hand and foot, for the roads are narrow, the turns sharp, with oftentimes an unprotected side many hundreds of feet deep."[16]

Before entering Italy, Thayer had to cross St. Gotthard Pass, which was almost as high as Grimsel Pass. The carriage way was the traditional route, but since the nine-mile-long St. Gotthard Tunnel had opened in 1882, travelers had an alternative. The carriage way was more picturesque, but it made for some rugged cycling, not only because of the steepness of the climb but also because of the poor quality of its surface. Ascending the pass by bicycle required frequent dismounts and much walking. Burston and Stokes crossed every pass through Switzerland by bicycle—every one, that is, except St. Gotthard, over which they took the train.[17]

Thayer, too, decided that instead of pushing his wheel uphill, he would take the train to the top and then coast down the other side. The top of the pass offered travelers a beautiful view, featuring several mountain peaks, massive glaciers, and many sparkling lakes. Thayer left the train at its highest point to coast down St. Gotthard Pass on the road to Italy. Descending twisty roads filled with hairpin turns and switchbacks, he enjoyed himself much more than if he had stayed on the train, going "round and round inside the mountain in the dark."[18] On the descent, the view of Lake Maggiore was "inexpressibly beautiful."[19]

The road ended at the lake. Italy awaited on the opposite side. Sailing across Lake Maggiore was delightful, but as Thayer approached the Italian side, he faced a decision: where should he disembark? He had heard rumors that Italian customs often placed steep duties on any bicycle brought into the country. If possible, he hoped to avoid paying a duty. A fellow passenger with a modest command of the English language told him that if he went ashore at Intra, instead of continuing around to Pallanza, he would not have to pay any customs duty.

Thayer followed the advice, got off at Intra, and started riding to Pallanza. Before he had ridden too far, he found a shady spot overlooking the lake. He dismounted and sat

Fig. 16. Lake Maggiore as it looked around the time that Thayer sailed across it (Detroit Publishing Company, ca. 1890). Library of Congress, Prints and Photographs Division, reproduction number LC-DIG-ppmsc-06539.

on the ground to enjoy the lunch he had packed. From his secluded spot, he witnessed two Italian carabinieri running along the road past where he was sitting. For the time being, Thayer thought nothing more about them.

After he finished lunch, he remounted his wheel and continued riding. Before long he saw a division of Italian troops blocking the road. The two running men stood in their midst. Thayer slowed considerably. As he approached the soldiers, a woman walking along the road whispered a warning to him in a hoarse voice. Thayer slowed further, preparing to dismount, but before he could do so, the carabinieri rushed toward him, grabbed his handlebars, threw him off the machine onto the dusty road, and took away his bicycle.

Thayer stood up, dusted himself off, and removed his U.S. passport from his breast pocket, brandishing it like a weapon before the soldiers. He tried to wrest his bike away from them, but they would not let go of its handlebars. They started to wheel it back toward Intra but had a difficult time doing so. It was not as easy to push a high-wheeled bicycle as they had imagined. After much red tape and rigmarole, Thayer freed himself from the carabinieri, but not before paying a sizeable duty for the privilege of riding his wheel on Italian soil.[20]

Pedaling across northern Italy without further incident, Thayer entered Switzerland again over Simplon Pass. Napoleon had originally built the road through the pass as a military route into Italy, and it was impressive. The matronly American journalist Eliza Archard Conner came over the pass a few years before him (before Thayer, not Napoleon). She left a good description: "The fine road across the Simplon seems very nearly an accomplishment of the impossible. In many places it is cut through the solid rock of a precipice a thousand feet high. It scuds along under tremendous overhanging bowlders that seem as if they must roll down upon you, and crush you, and past cliffs so awful that they make you hold your breath."[21] Inclement weather prevented Thayer from enjoying the road through the pass as much as had Mrs. Conner. A hailstorm slowed him down, and he did not reach the top of the pass until after nightfall.

Simplon Hospice, located at the top of the pass, offered overnight accommodations for travelers. The hospice was run by an order of monks who kept St. Bernard dogs to rescue wintertime travelers from the snow. The St. Bernards warmed Thayer's heart, reminding him of Bruiser, his boyhood pet. So far this trip, he had had some awful experiences with dogs— "miserable curs," he called them—but the beautiful creatures at the Simplon Hospice more than made up for the others. Thayer reflected, "When I thought how these great dogs go out into the storm and rescue tired travelers buried in the snow, and when I remembered how I myself had reached the hospice late the night before in a blinding hail and rain-storm, cold and wet, I felt more than ever with Byron those noble brutes, and others like them, were too often 'denied in heaven the souls they held on earth.'"[22]

Thayer quickly crossed into France and headed for Paris, where he found even better accommodations than he had found in London. He rented a corner room with a view of the two intersecting streets, one of which was the shady Avenue Victor Hugo.[23] Centrally located, the room Thayer rented was in walking distance of many of the city's major tourist destinations. The comfortable lodgings ideally suited his plan to stay in Paris for a month to see what the city had to offer. Thayer's published accounts of Paris are a little sketchy. He found the city beautiful but did not say what impressed him most.[24] Thomas Stevens, who spent only two days in Paris during his round-the-world cycling tour, described one beautiful sight Thayer must have seen as well: "Wheeling down the famous Champs Elysées at eleven at night, when the concert gardens are in full blast and everything in a blaze of glory, with myriads of electric lights festooned and in long brilliant rows among the trees, is something to be remembered for a lifetime."[25]

Thayer did record one detail about cycling in Paris that impressed him: the French bicycle horn. These horns delivered a sharp, clear, unmistakable sound. Thayer observed, "Here in Paris the wheelmen have adopted the tram car horn, an instrument with a rubber bulb for forcing the air through, and, really, one blast from those pneumatic levers is enough to lift a whole regiment out of the road."[26]

His most memorable Parisian experience came while riding through the Bois de Boulogne, the large park east of the city that provides an escape from its noise and crowds. He had heard that Frenchmen liked Americans better than other foreigners, which this ride proved. He pedaled softly as he listened to the music of the Grand Opera orchestra, which was

Fig. 17. Riding down the Champs-Élysées at night, Thomas Stevens enjoys an experience Thayer would enjoy a few years after him. From Thomas Stevens, *Around the World on a Bicycle* (New York: Scribner's, 1887–88). Courtesy Lilly Library, Indiana University, Bloomington IN.

performing in the park. He was unaware that cyclists were forbidden from riding some of the roads in the Bois de Boulogne. A policeman stopped him and ordered Thayer to go a different way.

With little grasp of the French language, Thayer did not understand fully what the officer said, so he stayed in the park, riding slowly and listening intently to the music. A half hour later, he met the same policeman, now quite angry. The officer yelled at him, gesticulating wildly to make himself understood. When the policeman paused for a moment, Thayer told him that he did not understand French and could speak only English. The officer switched languages.

"You are an Englishman?" he asked him.

"No," Thayer replied. "I am an American."

"Oh," the officer replied. "Pass on." He stepped aside and pleasantly waved Thayer through.[27]

After a month in Paris, Thayer began a tour of southern France. He headed east to St. Cloud before turning south on the road to Meudon. He said nothing about St. Cloud, but Baedeker recommended the local park as the town's greatest attraction, and Thayer usually took Baedeker's advice. A pretty town originally situated on the slope of the hill crowned by a chateau, Meudon was gradually expanding. The new quarter near the railway station contained a number of handsome villas.[28]

Then as now, the French countryside provided great opportunities for bicycle touring. The people were generally quite friendly, but, as one British cyclist observed, "The fair sex in the country villages are rather fond of giggling at the passing 'cyclist."[29] Thayer did not get too far on his first day out of Paris before one of the hooks that attached the straps to his knapsack broke. Happily, he still carried what was left of that coil of wire he had bought in Indiana two years earlier. It was useful then, and it was useful now. He reattached the strap with some of the Indiana wire and got back on the road in no time.[30]

By this point in his travels, Thayer had learned enough rudimentary French to ask directions as he went—but not enough to understand what the French said to him in response. Fortunately for him, they often gestured as they talked, so he could discern which way to go. In addition, he found milestones along all the main roads. Thayer could not bring himself to call them "milestones," since they gave the distance in kilometers instead of miles, but they were known as milestones nonetheless. Inglis Sheldon-Williams, a Canadian artist who took to bicycle touring in the 1920s, best describes how these milestones appeared to the passing cyclist. In *A Dawdle in France*, he calls them "those whimsical red-headed mushrooms that stand so close together in the crisp of the early morning and such a long way apart at the end of the day."[31] Supplementing the red-headed milestones, blue signboards posted at every crossroads told travelers which direction to turn. Finding his way across France proved to be no problem for Thayer.

He had hoped to reach Fontainebleau his first day out of Paris, but apparently he dawdled too long in St. Cloud and Meudon. As night fell he found himself twenty miles distant. The cobbles slowed him down, as well. Thayer had ridden pavé earlier in Belgium, but he still disliked its bumpy surface. The road to Fontainebleau alternated between dirt and cobbles. The pavé, lighter in color, could be seen from a distance. The sight gave Thayer a sense of foreboding. He explained: "After gliding along a mile or more over the beautifully smooth dirt road it was quite disquieting to ride up over the brow of a low hill and, in the dark distance, see the light colored pavement rising up before me, like Banquo's ghost, between the long lines of tall shade trees, giving me a premonition of the pounding I must endure before the next town."[32]

As he continued south, Thayer reached Essonne, but not before the sun had set. Cresting the last hill before the town, he could see the city lights in the valley below. There would be no downhill coast this evening: it was too dark to ride safely. He walked his bicycle into town and stopped the first man he met.

"Monsieur, the hotel or boarding house?" Thayer, speaking in broken French, asked. The man could not understand the question, so Thayer truncated it. "Le hôtel?" Or, perhaps, "Le hotel?" Surely, Thayer did not speak with a circumflex accent.

The man understood the abbreviated form of the question. This encounter taught Thayer an important lesson: the shorter the question the better. He would continue to use this same question as he headed toward the Mediterranean coast. In Essonne the local man pointed him toward a lamp that marked a building down the street. Once Thayer reached the lamp, he knocked on the hotel door. He had no trouble making the innkeeper understand him as he said, in French, "I am hungry, I sleep." Of all the words in the French language the two most important ones to Thayer were the ones that meant "hungry" and "sleepy."[33]

For breakfast the next morning he had a large bowl of hot milk, bread, and hot coffee. The milk curdled when he poured it into the coffee, but he salvaged it by adding plenty of sugar. The bill for bed and breakfast amounted to $1.20, which Thayer found reasonable, but the next night he found equivalent hotel accommodations for only eighty cents for everything: dinner, room, breakfast, and service.[34]

Montargis was another stop on Thayer's route through France. He said nothing more about this town or several others he visited, but Joseph and Elizabeth Pennell had ridden their tandem tricycle along the same basic route the year before, and her account of their tour brings the experience alive. Elizabeth Pennell called Montargis "one of the prettiest towns in all of France." She especially enjoyed the way the river "wandered around and through the town, as if bent on seeing as much of city life as possible;—now flowing between stone embankments, from which men and boys for ever fished and caught nothing, while the castle frowned down upon it; now, tired already of city ways and sights, running peacefully between green banks and trees whose branches met above; again, crossing the street and making its way by old ruinous houses."[35]

After Montargis, Thayer had a treat in store. The Comte and Comtesse de Montsaulnin had invited him to stay at the Château de Fontenay. Thayer was not normally one to rub elbows with nobility, but the comtesse was none other than New York socialite Anna Zborowski (pronounced Zabriskie). Though she had adjusted to life in France, she always enjoyed speaking with visiting American travelers and welcomed Thayer to her handsome château.

The comtesse may have spoiled Thayer; his accommodations the next night were not nearly so luxurious. When it started raining that afternoon, he sought shelter in a roadside shed on the outskirts of a dense forest. The rain continued into the night. Dissatisfied with the prospect of spending a cold, dinnerless night in this shed, Thayer decided to risk the rain to seek more comfortable shelter. He hoped a kind family would take him in. Around nine that evening he reached a stone house, which initially seemed deserted.

As he stood at the doorway, a peasant woman suddenly rushed from inside the house holding a huge bellows pointed right toward him. She rapidly pumped the bellows into Thayer's face, yelling, "Shoo, shoo!" Her defensive efforts were apparently intended for a stray donkey that had been lounging around her front door. Once she overcame her surprise at Thayer's mysterious appearance, he asked if he could stay the night.

Seeing this bedraggled cyclist as not much better than a scrounging donkey, she refused at first but then relented to invite him inside. Thayer took a seat by the fire to warm himself and dry his clothes. A dog limped up to him. Thayer petted it until two other men entered, one of which kicked the dog into the rain. After the men entered, the woman set the table for two. The hungry cyclist grew concerned that the woman had not set a place for him. Once the two men had eaten, she cleared the table and then reset it for Thayer, much to his relief. He was flattered that she had saved a ham bone for him. After dinner, she showed him to her spare bedroom, where he enjoyed a good night's sleep.[36]

Thayer's route also took him through Moulins and Roanne. He did not record his impressions of these two towns either, but Elizabeth Pennell's account again comes in handy. She called Moulins "a stupid town with a very poor hotel and an American bar."[37] Mrs. Pennell was much blunter than Thayer, who seldom expressed himself so negatively. She did have something good to say about Roanne, sort of. She found Roanne "remarkable for nothing but dust and delicious peaches and grapes." When Sheldon-Williams cycled through Roanne a few decades afterward, he had little else to add. To his eyes, Roanne "seemed to be made up of all the more commonplace elements of a French town."[38]

South of Roanne, the road became much hillier, staying that way to Lyons. For a twenty-mile stretch from Roanne to Lyons, the terrain was downright mountainous. Near the top of one climb, Thayer got caught in a snowstorm. While wearing a heavy coat on the climb, he still found it difficult to keep warm. Though the clouds and snow somewhat obscured the view toward the north, he could see handsome vistas in the other directions. He noticed "smooth, rounded hills, capped with clusters of tiled roofed houses," which harmonized well with the "reddish, upturned patches of soil."[39]

On the other side of the hill the road was clear, so Thayer had another great coast ahead of him: "The first five miles down along the broad, smooth road which wound about the sides of the hill were made in fifteen minutes, and after that there were several other coasts of a mile or two in length, one especially fine one, I thought, at a town called Bully." Thayer's trusty Lakin cyclometer still worked well. By the time he reached Lyons, he had ridden 156 miles in two days, 343 miles since leaving Paris, and 2,233 miles since Glasgow.[40]

The roads in southern France helped make riding fast and comfortable. Thomas G. Allen and William L. Sachtleben, two young American college graduates who would embark on a round-the-world cycling tour two years later, were similarly impressed by the road quality: "The French roads are macadamized with rock and gravel mixed together, which is packed tighter and tighter by every rain, so that they are thus kept as solid and smooth as asphalt. They are made in many places as straight as an arrow stretching for miles in one continuous line of the undulating country."[41]

Two days past Lyons, Thayer pedaled eighty-eight miles in one day. He observed, "Such a ride, straight away, over the average American roads, would be simply impossible; but in Southern France, where the government highways are not only macadamized but are covered with a coating of cement that dries as hard and smooth as asphalt, a ride of seventy-five or eighty miles is an ordinary pleasant day's journey, and a short day's ride at that."[42] After the snow of a few days earlier, the weather had improved considerably. It was a warm, sunny day, and Thayer just felt like riding. On days like these, he experienced the true magic of cycling, which happens when, as Laurent Fignon said, "the simple forward motion from the power in your legs treats you to great bursts of freedom."[43]

Thayer's ride on this beautiful day was not without adversity. Dogs had been a general nuisance throughout Europe, but they were especially annoying in southern France, "a section of country where dogs are a great deal plentier than blackberries."[44] Just a few days earlier, a bulldog snapped at Thayer's heel. As it turned out, the dog did more than snap. Thayer had not exactly felt the bulldog's teeth sink into his flesh, but when he was safely away from the beast, he noticed a tear in his left stocking. He dismounted to examine the tear only to find blood and teeth marks beneath his stocking.

Interrupting the magic of cycling on his eighty-eight-mile day, another dog, a straggly haired mutt this time, took a bead on Thayer and darted into the road after him. It barked and howled and yelped and growled for over a quarter of a mile. After matching Thayer's speed and running parallel to his bicycle, the cur accelerated, spurting ahead and turning right in front of him. He could not avoid hitting the beast. The collision propelled Thayer over the handlebars. He landed ten feet ahead of the bicycle. Since he put his hands out to break his fall, both palms ended up bruised and bloody.

Despite his injuries, Thayer picked himself up, remounted his wheel, got back into his rhythm, and rode another twenty-three miles, stopping at a small roadside inn. The combination of the long ride and the fall did more damage than Thayer initially realized. He checked into the inn, sat down at the table for supper, and promptly fainted. When he came to, he was famished and consequently did justice to the meal the innkeeper set before him. The next day Thayer remounted his wheel and continued like nothing had happened.[45]

Mule teams presented another potential hazard for cyclists touring the French countryside. Riding from Marseilles to Cannes, Thayer crested a hill one evening "just in time to see one of those beautiful sunsets which the clearer atmosphere of the Mediterranean region makes so lovely."[46] He looked forward to coasting downhill after reaching the top. Though the sun had set, the moonlight let him see the road well enough to throw his legs over the handlebars and coast safely downhill. As he came around one bend, however, he saw a mule team ahead of him. The driver did not see Thayer, who yelled to warn him. The driver seized the front mule by the bit and stopped him so suddenly that the rear mule began backing the long cart around directly across the road. Thayer turned toward the side of the road to make his way around the back of the cart, but as he approached he noticed a long pole projecting from the back of the wagon. That pole forced Thayer off the road up an embankment onto a ridge. He feared the pole would force him down the mountainside several hundred feet below, but he cleared the pole with an inch to spare.

From Cannes, he continued along the Mediterranean coast, deciding to stop for the night at a small town near Nice. On the outskirts of town, he met a woman walking toward him.

"Le hotel?" he asked.

The woman understood his words, turned around, and escorted him into town. She led him to a substantial building and left him at the door. Pushing his bicycle through the entry, Thayer found himself in a large hall with a kitchen at the further end. A baby sat crying on the kitchen floor, but its mother was too busy to attend the baby or, for that matter, to notice the bicycle tourist who had just entered her door. After waiting a long time, Thayer motioned to the mother that he would like to wash his face and hands, so she set a large bowl on the stone floor, poured some water into it, and tossed a towel and a hunk of soap onto the floor next to the bowl.

Soon, a tough-looking character with a bag of rags on his back entered the hall and walked upstairs. A few minutes later, the raggedy man came downstairs and stood around the hall waiting for something else. Another scruffy-looking man came in next. He, too, went upstairs and came back down to wait. Before long the line contained about a dozen men. A strange way to run a hotel, Thayer thought, before concluding that he had best get in line himself.

Eventually, a young man with an air of business about him entered. He proceeded to a small desk, where he made some entries in a ledger and then gave the waiting men some slips of paper. Last in line, Thayer gestured that he wanted to sleep there for the night, but the young man refused. Thayer slowly realized his mistake. When he'd asked the first woman he met for "le hotel," she understood his words but misunderstood their meaning. She had escorted him to the Hôtel de Ville; that is, the town poorhouse!

Thayer explained his mistake to the young man, who laughed and laughed but who also agreed to help him find a room. The young man escorted him to a nearby hotel, where he told Thayer's story to a group of men. They laughed in turn and welcomed Thayer to the hotel. All became great friends that evening.[47]

The rest of Thayer's European cycling tour is shrouded in mystery. He may have looked like he belonged to the poorhouse, but he still had enough money left to continue his trip. Traveling through Europe had proven to be much cheaper than he had imagined. When he left Paris, he had intended to ride the length of Italy.[48] He had even made significant preparations for the trip. The Baedeker guide to Italy was a three-volume set, which Thayer studied avidly in Paris. He carried his copy of the first volume—Baedeker's *Northern Italy*—since it also covered the southeast corner of France. He sent his copy of the second volume, *Central Italy and Rome*, to Florence, and the third volume, *Southern Italy and Sicily*, he sent to Rome.[49]

Reports of his visit that appeared in the American press as late as October suggest that he still intended to ride to Rome, visit Greece, and sail to Egypt. Given his ambitious journey, Thayer was starting to be compared with Thomas Stevens. The *Boston Globe*, for instance, observed, "The trip will not be so long, but will be quite as interesting in its way as Thomas Stevens'."[50] For some unknown reason, Thayer cut his trip short. Nice is the southernmost destination his various accounts mention. After the French Riviera, he decided it was time to return to Connecticut.

8

The Rise of the Dwarf

George Thayer's dual ability to turn a pedal and turn a phrase appealed to his readers. The reports he wrote from Europe for the *New York World* were disseminated across the nation, reappearing in newspapers from North Dakota to Arizona Territory.[1] Coming home from Europe, he returned to Hartford to try his hand as a freelance journalist. His decision put him on the cutting edge in the world of journalism. Freelancing was a new concept. The earliest usage of the term may have appeared in *Athletic Sports in America, England and Australia*, a sports encyclopedia published in 1889. In an entry devoted to baseball writers, W. I. Harris included a section about Peter J. Donohue, who wrote under the penname "P. Jay": "Mr. Donohue is now what is known in journalism as a 'free lance,' and his articles on baseball and other sports are always entertaining."[2] If P. Jay could do it, so could G. Bee. Thayer wrote up additional episodes from his American and European travels for the national magazines and actively sought newsworthy subjects related to cycling. His most prestigious assignment was an article for *Frank Leslie's Illustrated Newspaper* or, as it was usually called, *Les-*

lie's Weekly. Thayer would report the 1889 Hartford Bicycle Tournament.

From 1884—the first year it was held—the Hartford Bicycle Tournament had proven to be a great success. Describing the crowd that turned out for the very first tournament, Thayer recalled, "The grand stand and adjoining seats were crowded then as they never were before, with as select a company as it was possible to bring together, and it was then seen that the new sport drew out a class of ladies and gentlemen such as no other out-of-door amusement ever had done."[3]

Thayer's description reveals that the spectators for early bicycle races differed remarkably from the typical sports fans of the period, who were often from the lower classes and almost exclusively male. Many sporting events attracted unsavory characters, those who saw athletic contests solely as opportunities for gambling. Emphasizing both the "select" and mixed nature of the attendance to the Hartford Bicycle Tournament, Thayer indicated the social quality of the spectators. Attending a bicycle race was good, clean fun for everyone.

In its first five years, the Hartford Bicycle Tournament had become one of the most prestigious cycling competitions in the United States. The Connecticut Bicycle Club first organized the event, but the recently formed Hartford Wheel Club took it over in 1887. For 1889 the two-day competition would take advantage of a new holiday on the state calendar, which the Connecticut legislature had approved earlier in the year. The first Monday in September would now be Labor Day in Connecticut. In 1889 Labor Day fell on Monday, September 2. Special trains came into Hartford that day, bringing huge crowds of spectators as well as some of the finest cyclists in the nation. The races would continue the following day.

As he planned his article for *Leslie's Weekly*, Thayer decided to do more than report the Hartford tournament. He would use the event to provide a retrospective of cycling and articulate his thoughts on its current state. Titling his essay "The Evolution of the Bicycle," Thayer demonstrated the ongoing influence of Darwin's thought, which affected how he understood cycling history.

In the first half of the article, Thayer stressed how the bicycle had evolved from its beginnings as a popular fad into a multiuse vehicle. For one thing, it could be used as a mode of holiday travel. Bicycle touring offered a pleasurable way to see the country. Thayer cited his own experience to prove his argument. In addition, the bicycle was far superior to all other modes of urban transportation and methods of locomotion. It was faster than walking, cheaper and cleaner than riding a horse, and more convenient than the streetcar.

Bicycles were so well suited for negotiating the modern city that many people were using them to commute: "Business men and bank clerks, merchants and mechanics alike, go to and from their work on their machines in all the principal cities of the country." In addition, many professional men used the bicycle in their work. Physicians made house calls atop their wheels, and clergymen used the bicycle to carry out their pastoral duties. Thayer's remarks reiterate what other magazine contributors had recently said. When parishioners complained about their bicycle-riding preachers, many reverend gentlemen published articles in both the outdoor magazines and religious weeklies to advocate cycling as an efficient and economical form of transportation.[4]

Thayer also stressed the value of cycling as a form of exercise. "Americans scarcely go a block without taking a car," he observed. He was talking about streetcars, of course, but his observation prefigures the age of the automobile. Thayer's choice of words to describe the bicycle's worth imbues it with an almost God-given sense of purpose: "Perhaps the bicycle has a special mission to work out in this country in persuading people to use their muscles more in traveling." Bringing his discussion of cycling as exercise to a close, Thayer stated, "Of all the sports which Americans indulge in there is none more conducive to good health than bicycling, and the healthy circulation, the perfect digestion, and the ravenous appetites with which wheelmen are blest is sufficient evidence of the fact without further argument."[5]

As a transition from this general discussion to his account of the Hartford tournament, Thayer next considered the value of cycling as a spectator sport. It was one of only a few sports that allowed people to be both spectator and participant. Those unwilling to race could still participate in the noncompetitive rides held in conjunction with a cycling meet. And nonriders could enjoy watching both the races and the fun rides. Who knows? Perhaps the sight of so many cyclists might encourage spectators to take up the sport in the future.

On Labor Day morning, a gala parade started from the capitol steps in Hartford. All the local and visiting cyclists were welcome to participate. This parade looked much different from the one Thayer enjoyed in St. Louis three years earlier. Whereas that one was an illuminated candlelight parade, this one took place in daylight. But there was another crucial difference. The St. Louis parade had been dominated by high-wheeled bicycles and large-wheeled tricycles, but the safety bicycle was now a major presence. Thayer's statistics are telling: "The safety has but recently appeared upon the market, yet it is fast becoming the favorite of many for all-round day and night riding. Of the two kinds, the ordinaries and the safeties, nearly half of those in the parade were safeties, and of the 389 wheels in line, 264 were made in Hartford and were Columbias."[6]

During the 1880s cyclists had several different types of pedal-powered vehicles available. The high-wheeled bicycle was the most common type, hence the name "ordinary." The Star bicycle, another type of high wheeler, had a small wheel

Fig. 18. In this engraving, Joseph Pennell depicts the American Star Machine, a high wheeler that put the smaller wheel in front and supposedly made the bicycle easier to steer. From William Coutts Keppel, Earl of Albemarle; and G. Lacy Hillier, *Cycling* (London: Longmans, Green, 1887). Courtesy Lilly Library, Indiana University, Bloomington IN.

in front and a large, lever-driven rear wheel. Tricycles came in many different configurations. A report that appeared in the July 1886 issue of *Outing* notes that twenty-two men from the Hartford Wheel Club participated in a recent Boston meet. Their numbers provide a good indication of the relative popularity of different cycles. Three of the Hartford cyclists rode Star bicycles, and two rode tricycles; the other seventeen rode ordinaries. Though safety bicycles had come on the market by then, none of the Hartford cyclists rode them at this meet.[7] Slow to catch on, the safety would eventually revolutionize the bicycle industry.

The term "safety" is usually associated with chain-driven bicycles with wheels of the same size, but it was not so specific initially. In 1887 Gormully and Jeffrey, a Chicago manufacturer, marketed a high-wheeled safety model named the

American Safety. That same year, Columbia also produced a high-wheeled safety, though its styling was not as elegant as the Gormully and Jeffrey model.[8]

The drive system separated the high-wheeled safety from the ordinary model. Whereas the ordinary used a direct-drive mechanism, meaning that the crank arms were affixed to the axle of the front wheel, the high-wheeled safety was lever driven. Instead of crank arms, it had levers attached to the axle of the front wheel with pedals mounted on the levers. It could be called a safety because it was much less prone to headers than the ordinary. Though the front wheel was still comparatively large, it was smaller than the front wheel of most ordinaries because it no longer depended on the rider's inseam. Furthermore, the lever-drive system allowed riders to sit further back on the machine, distributing their weight more evenly.

When the chain-driven safety or "dwarf bicycle," as it was sometimes called in its early days, came on the market in the mid-1880s, serious cyclists resisted it. Instead, they found the high-wheeled safety more attractive. The 1887 Gormully and Jeffrey catalogue describes the appeal of the high-wheeled safety over the dwarf bicycle in a blunt, yet oddly vague manner, explaining that "its appearance, which is the nearest approach to the ordinary, of any of the safeties" lets it avoid "that comment so disagreeable to the sensitive."[9] What was the comment that sensitive cyclists found so disagreeable? I suspect it had something to do with impugning the manhood of the safety rider. In the era of the ordinary, size mattered. Cyclists who rode dwarf bicycles were looked down upon by their high-wheeled brethren.

By 1889 the safety bicycle had achieved a much greater degree of acceptance than it had two years earlier. The trade catalogues provide additional evidence to support Thayer's statistics from the Hartford tournament. The organization of the 1889 Columbia catalogue suggests that the ordinary remained on top. The catalogue begins with the two models that had been mainstays of the Columbia line for years, the Light Roadster and the Expert. The first safety listed in the catalogue, the Light Roadster Safety, did not appear until page 24. The catalogue's text does emphasize the growing demand for safeties:

> The rear-driving type of "Safety" bicycle has met with unquestionable favor and a rapidly-growing demand among a large class of riders, who recognize the wheel as a valuable means to health and recreation, or as a business convenience, but incline neither to the enjoyment of the regular bicycle with its contingent possibilities, nor, on the other hand, to the staid reliability of the tricycle. Composed as this class chiefly is, of active men of all ages, whose vocations or natural inclinations make even a slight chance of accident an undesireable thing, the element of special security against falls must be embodied in a machine to fill their wants, without detracting from that satisfaction which the mastery of a well-constructed bicycle can afford to any man in the full possession of his powers.[10]

Like the catalogue itself, this language places the ordinary above the safety. The "regular bicycle," as the ordinary is called here, possesses the greatest potential, but the safety is ideal for people unwilling to take the kinds of risks that those who rode ordinaries took. Ordinaries, the paragraph implies, are for daring men, young and unattached. The safety, on the other hand, would be ideal for family men and businessmen, teachers and preachers, all those who need and want exercise and transportation, yet dare not risk the dangers of the high wheeler.

Other contemporaries testify to the rise of the safety. F. P. Prial, editor of *Cycle Trade Review*, wrote the article on cycling for *Athletic Sports in America, England and Australia*. He went further than the copywriter for Columbia, suggesting that young men, those who would have ridden ordinaries in the past, now opted for safeties. Summing up the new attitude toward safeties, Prial observed, "By far the larger number of young male riders prefer the safety bicycle. Indeed, the popularity of the dwarf wheel has amounted to the proportions of a 'craze,' not only in this country but in England, France, and Germany. The makers are turning out ordinaries, but their greatest ingenuity and capacity are devoted to making safeties. During some months of the spring of 1889 it was impossible to obtain safeties of certain popular styles."[11]

The chain-driven safety bicycle had numerous advantages. To state the obvious, the safety was safer than the ordinary. It had a lower center of gravity; the rider could easily put a foot down at a stop; and it was much less likely to tilt forward during an abrupt stop and send the rider flying over the handlebars. In addition, the chain-driven safety provided a more comfortable riding position, evenly distributing the rider's weight between two same-sized wheels and making it easier to pedal. It was also easier to steer. With the ordinary, the rider used the same wheel to drive and steer the bicycle: the two functions worked against one another. The safety separated the functions, making the rear wheel the drive wheel. Finally, the chain drive allowed riders to gear their bicycles to suit themselves. Though multispeed bikes had yet to emerge, riders could choose how to gear their machines. Competitive riders could gear them higher to achieve greater top-end speed; leisurely riders could gear them lower for easier pedaling.[12]

A game board that survives at the Library Company of Philadelphia shows that by no means did the safety bicycle eliminate accidents. Released in the mid-1890s, when the bicycle craze that the safety helped inaugurate had reached its peak, this bicycle board game indicates that people were still taking spills. Landing on one particular space, a player would take a

"Header." As the players moved their game pieces around the board, they could land on spaces representing other accidents. One said "Collision," another "Wreck." Additional spaces indicated postaccident destinations: "Blacksmith's Forge" and "Doctor's Office."[13]

By 1896 the Prudential Insurance Company became concerned enough about the number and severity of bicycle accidents that its statistics department began keeping a scrapbook of newspaper clippings to indicate their extent.[14] According to this scrapbook, which now survives at the Lilly Library at Indiana University, the accidents reported in the newspapers could be quite gory. Railroad trains would run down cyclists. Streetcars would run down cyclists. Horse-drawn wagons would run down cyclists. Cyclists, in turn, would run down pedestrians. In Jersey City, a gang of street toughs lassoed cyclists and pulled them from their bicycles. One of the most gruesome and deadly kinds of accidents occurred much too frequently. This particular accident represents another clash between the bicycle and horse-drawn vehicles. A cyclist could be killed from being impaled on the shaft of a carriage pole. One article reports four cyclists killed in this manner within a span of seventeen days!

Not all the accidents that the newspapers reported were so gory. Some headlines have a slapstick quality that makes them quite humorous:

Drunken Bicyclist Fined

An Adirondack Bicyclist Who Ran into a Deer

A Bicyclist Knocked Out by a Small Rooster

Bug Got in His Eye: Mr. Staples Thereupon Lost Control of His Wheel and Was Injured

Banana Peel Threw Her: Her Bicycle Slid on It and Her Arm Was Badly Injured

With his article for *Leslie's Weekly*, Thayer captured a crucial moment in the shift from ordinary to safety. The races held at Hartford that year provide another indication of the safety's acceptance. Though safeties were not allowed to race against ordinaries, the organizers did schedule several safety races. All the races would take place on the one-mile trotting track at Charter Oak Park. Having been rolled smooth after the recent horse races, the track was in good condition for some fast times. Over five thousand spectators showed up for the excitement on Labor Day.

The first two races were for ordinaries. After an opening novice race, the one-mile LAW state championship ended in an exciting bunch sprint, which Henry G. Cornell won at the wire. Reporting Cornell's success, the *New York Times* said, "He is a plucky contestant on the track, pushing ahead with a dogged determination up to the very moment of victory."[15] A one-mile safety race came next, followed by a two-mile tandem safety race, which constituted the national LAW tandem safety championship.

Before the invention of the safety, tandems were solely pleasure vehicles. They were usually tricycles; some were side-by-side tricycles or even quadricycles. Safety tandems, alternatively, were sleek vehicles ideal for fast-paced competition. The Banker brothers, W. D. and A. C., of the Berkeley Athletic Club won the race. W. D. Banker also won the three-mile national safety championship on Monday, but the winning time was so slow the referee declared that it was "no race."[16] The event was rescheduled for the following day.

Some of the races at the Hartford tournament were handicapped. The rider with the best personal reputation would start from scratch, and the others would receive head starts of varying distances. After the three-mile safety race came a two-mile handicap race. F. F. Ives of Meriden, Connecticut, started from scratch. The other competitors were given dif-

Fig. 19. This photograph depicts the start of a bicycle race, which closely resembles what Thayer would have seen at Charter Oak Park. Library of Congress, Prints and Photographs Division, reproduction number LC-USZ62-10722.

ferent head starts. P. J. Birlo started seventy-five yards ahead. A young and relatively inexperienced rider from Freehold, New Jersey, named Arthur A. Zimmerman, received a 150-yard head start. Zimmerman rode a Star bicycle.

Though he would go on to become one of the most successful riders in the history of American cycling, Zimmerman had yet to be recognized for his prowess on the bicycle. Had his talent been recognized, he surely would not have received such an insurmountable head start. Zimmie, as he became known, did not win the Hartford handicap race without a fight. Ives was in top form that day. Partway through the two-mile event, Ives made up the seventy-five yards that had separated him from Birlo. As the finish line approached, Ives almost caught Zimmerman, who held him off—but just barely. Zimmerman finished in 5:26¼. Ives, having ridden 150 yards further, finished only one second behind. His time, 5:27¼, was the best two-mile time ever recorded at Charter Oak Park.

The second day of the Hartford Bicycle Tournament began with an organized ride to Wethersfield, where the Connecticut State Prison was located.[17] The short ride, about ten miles round trip, gave the cyclists plenty of time to tour the prison. First constructed in 1827, the state prison had been expanded significantly since then. The oldest buildings were brick. More recent structures were built from brownstone. Visitors could see the inmates as well as the buildings that housed them. Through the nineteenth century, prisons remained popular tourist destinations, but the idea of bicycle-riding tourists visiting a prison seems incongruous. Surely, forcing prison inmates to watch someone riding a bicycle—a great symbol of freedom—is cruel and unusual punishment.

The races continued Tuesday afternoon. The standout rider of the day was George M. Hendee. A native of Springfield, Massachusetts, Hendee had started riding in 1881 when he was in his teens. The following year, at sixteen, he won his first national championship. For the next five years, Hendee dominated national competitions in various distances from sprints to twenty-mile grinds. He was almost unbeatable. He won hundreds of races atop his ordinary, capturing five consecutive national championships.

Hoping to make it six in a row, Hendee had looked forward to the 1887 national championship, but he crashed two weeks before the race and broke his collarbone. He decided to retire from competition. Once safety races became part of the cycling calendar, Hendee returned to competition. Earlier than many other riders who established their reputation racing high-wheeled bicycles, Hendee recognized the possibilities of the chain-driven safety. His return to competition came with great success.[18]

For the one-mile handicap safety race at the Hartford Bicycle Tournament, George Hendee and W. D. Banker started from scratch, but both made up the distance given the other riders. Hendee himself outdistanced Banker by twenty yards, setting a new record, 2:41½. The *New York Times* reported: "George Hendee, the old time champion, spread-eagled the field, which included the fastest men in the country."[19]

Hendee and Banker had an opportunity for a rematch when the three-mile LAW safety championship was repeated Tuesday afternoon. The race started slowly but finished rapidly. Hendee and Banker covered the last quarter mile in only 35¼ seconds. Banker edged out Hendee at the line, winning by a foot. The fast finish could not compensate for the slow start, so the referee again declared it "no race."[20]

With George Hendee, the star of one generation in the twilight of his cycling career, and Arthur Zimmerman, the star of the next generation at the dawn of his, the 1889 Hartford Tournament formed a kind of anthology of American bicycle racing. In "The Evolution of the Bicycle," Thayer did not devote his attention to either Hendee or Zimmie. Instead, he featured Henry Cornell (Corny?), the winner of the one-mile LAW state championship. Thayer's emphasis may reflect his preference for the ordinary over the safety, or it may let him honor a fellow club member: Cornell was also a member of the Hartford Wheel Club. Regardless, the example of Cornell served the implicit purpose of the article: to encourage more people to take up the sport of cycling.

Fig. 20. Though highly stylized, this lithograph depicts the look of a bike race once the ordinary had given way to the safety bicycle, with pneumatic tires (Calvert Lithographing Co., ca. 1895). Library of Congress, Prints and Photographs Division, reproduction number LC-DIG-ppmsca-08935.

Cornell, Thayer explained, did not have much previous cycling experience, but he was accomplished in other sports. As a member of the New York Athletic Club, he had established several running and swimming records. Not until he moved to Hartford to take a position with the National Insurance Company did he start riding a bicycle. His athletic background obviously contributed to his cycling success.[21]

Once Cornell started racing his bicycle that July, he quickly won several events. The emphasis on Cornell's background in other competitive sports reveals much about Thayer, as well. Though best known as a cyclist, he, too, loved to swim and hike. Thayer clearly appreciated such athletic versatility. The example of Cornell effectively encouraged athletes from other sports to give cycling a try.

The organizers of the Hartford Bicycle Tournament invited

champion trick rider D. J. Canary to display his talents as part of the festivities. Fresh from a European tour, Canary demonstrated his fancy bicycle riding on both days of the Hartford tournament. His performance culminated with a daring feat. He had three tables placed one atop another and two chairs on the top table. He climbed onto the chairs, and then a helper handed him his Columbia bicycle. Canary placed the bicycle on the chairs and climbed on top of it, balancing himself on the pedals over twenty feet in the air. After Canary's exhibition, Thayer approached him for an interview.

"You must have considerable confidence in your machine to do that," Thayer said.

"Yes, I do," Canary replied with a smile. "But then, like an old friend, I know how to trust the Columbia. I have never had any other, and this machine has stood as strong a strain as it is possible to put upon a machine."[22]

"The Evolution of the Bicycle" is not exactly objective journalism. With Thayer's interview of D. J. Canary, the essay shades into a promotional piece for Columbia bicycles. As Thayer continued the essay, he would celebrate Columbia machines even further.

The Hartford Bicycle Tournament ended Tuesday evening, but some of the participants seemed unwilling to let it go. Many out-of-town wheelmen wanted to see where Columbia bicycles were built, so Colonel Albert A. Pope made arrangements for them to tour the factory. Pope agreed to conduct the tour himself, which greatly enhanced the experience. His enthusiasm was infectious, and his voice—"deep, strong, modulated and vibrant"—was ideal for a tour guide.[23] The facility contained many different rooms, each devoted to a different function in the bicycle construction process: milling and drilling, tube bending, brazing, polishing, case-hardening, enameling, wheel building, and assembly.

Thayer marveled over the modern welding process: "One

of the most interesting [operations] was the welding by electricity. The welding and brazing of the different parts of the frame as well as the joints in the rim, is now largely done by the new electric process invented by Professor Elihu Thomson. By this process two pieces of steel tubing are joined in from fifteen seconds to twenty seconds, and the place of juncture will be as strong and as homogenous in texture as any other part. As the electric current heats the two pieces of steel at their juncture to the welding temperature, a slight pressure follows up the softening surface until a complete union is effected."[24]

Thayer also described the amenities the Columbia factory provided its employees, including a large, airy reading room stocked with the latest magazines, newspapers, and trade publications.[25] The factory also had a collection of books in its reading room, including a copy of that great compendium of cycling, Karl Kron's *Ten Thousand Miles on a Bicycle*.[26] According to Thayer, the factory served its workers complimentary coffee at noon and, for those working overtime, in the evening, as well.

His feature article in *Leslie's Weekly* extended Thayer's reputation as a cycling journalist. In an aggressive effort to promote the paper, its publisher distributed free copies of the issue containing Thayer's article to bicycle clubs and club members across the nation. Copies reached as far as the new clubhouse of the Los Angeles Wheelmen. In Minnesota, every member of the St. Paul Wheelmen received a copy of the issue gratis.[27]

The literary reputation of George Thayer's sister, Florine Thayer McCray, also continued to grow in 1889, the year she published her most important book, *The Life-Work of the Author of "Uncle Tom's Cabin."* Though critically acclaimed, this biography of Harriet Beecher Stowe created a schism between its author and her subject. Stowe was furious that McCray, her friend and neighbor, had violated her confidence by incorporating elements of their personal conversations in this biography. Despite the contemporary controversy, *Life-Work* is now recognized as one of the foremost firsthand accounts of Harriet Beecher Stowe.[28]

With her newfound celebrity, interviewers sought Florine Thayer McCray's opinion on a variety of topics, including the bicycle. In an interview with Eliza Putnam Heaton, she had much to say about safety tandems, which were lighter, more maneuverable, and more affordable than previous tandems. Though McCray remained an avid tricyclist, she had to admit that the weight of the tricycle, which could make cycling cumbersome, discouraged some women from riding. The safety tandem offered a great new opportunity for women to start cycling. Heaton paraphrased what McCray told her:

> The tandem bicycle runs much more easily and is less bothered by a bit of bad road. The double bicycle has two wheels of moderate size and between them the bar dips quite low so that the bifurcation of garments is wholly unnecessary, and the seat is as seemly as on a tricycle. One or two have appeared among the three wheelers and the women's safety bicycles in the parks, and when the adjournment to the country takes place the chances are that for the young man and his best summer girl they will prove quite popular.[29]

While mentioning women's safety bicycles, McCray hesitated to recommend them, apparently because they did require the "bifurcation of garments." Her new attitude is disappointing. The tandem may have been faster and more comfortable, but women who chose tandems over tricycles sacrificed their independence, giving men control of the handlebars.

Though 1889 is the fulcrum year in the history of cycling—that is, the year the popularity scale tilted in favor of the chain-driven safety—some longtime wheelmen still hesitated to relinquish their ordinaries for safeties. Among the cyclists at the Hartford tournament, D. J. Canary was one who still rode an ordinary. The idea of a trick rider using a so-called safety bicycle does seem ludicrous. Canary would continue to ride his high wheeler. When he notoriously rode down the steps of the U.S. Capitol in 1890, he did so on a high wheeler. And when he came to Sacramento, California, in February 1891 to put on a demonstration of trick riding, he again rode his ordinary. By the time he returned to Sacramento nine months later, however, he had switched to a safety.[30]

Since Canary depended on sponsorships for his livelihood, he simply had to start riding the kind of bicycles that manufacturers were selling, not an increasingly old-fashioned machine that people were increasingly reluctant to purchase. Manufacturers were still making ordinaries, but by 1891 the safety had taken precedence. The Columbia catalogues track the shift. Whereas the 1889 Columbia catalogue had begun with its ordinaries, the 1891 catalogue begins with its safeties. It still included the Light Roadster and the Expert, but these two ordinaries were not listed until nearly halfway through the catalogue. To survive as a trick rider, Canary invented some new tricks for the safety bicycle.

Having hitched his wagon to a Star, so to speak, Arthur Zimmerman continued riding his high-wheeled Star bicycle through 1890, his first full season of racing. He won dozens of races on the machine, catapulting himself into one of the leading competitors in the nation. He rode his Star into the following year, but he also started riding a safety bicycle in competition.[31] After 1891 ordinary races disappeared from the American racing calendar altogether. They almost completely disappeared from the roadways, as well. Karl Kron continued to tour on his high wheeler into the next century, but he was almost alone. In the twentieth century, the ordinary became a symbol for all things old-fashioned.

Following his successful article for *Leslie's Weekly*, Thayer reached an agreement with *Youth's Companion*, a long-running children's magazine, to write a series of cycling articles. "Bicy-cling Accidents in Europe," as he titled his first essay, appeared in the May 15, 1890, issue of *Youth's Companion*. In this arti-cle, Thayer related the most thrilling misadventures from his travels through Great Britain and Europe: the Kirkwhelping-ton ditch dive, the dogs that hounded him throughout France, and the mule cart that almost tipped him over a cliff.[32]

His next article for *Youth's Companion* appeared two weeks later. In this essay, Thayer related his encounter with many different kinds of critters while bicycle touring: prairie dogs, deer, gophers, cattle, horses, goats, pigs, St. Bernards. In his third essay for *Youth's Companion*, Thayer argued against bringing a handgun on a bicycle tour, using as examples sev-eral volatile situations from his bicycle-touring experience, situations that could have erupted into violence had he been carrying a gun. He retold stories of the Colorado rancher, the drunk Kentuckian, and the carabinieri at Lake Maggiore in Italy.[33] This third article is the weakest of the three essays he wrote for *Youth's Companion*. Had Thayer been carrying a lightweight handgun—say, a two-shot derringer—he would hardly have stood a chance against the carabinieri!

Thayer's contributions to *Youth's Companion* appeared in the spring and summer of 1890. It did not take long for him to recognize the difficulties involved with writing for the mag-azines. Journalists who freelance, then as now, must hustle all the time. They must pitch stories to many different maga-zines, write on a variety of subjects, and accept projects that perhaps they would not willingly undertake if they did not depend on journalistic piecework to survive. George's sister, Florine, had much success writing for the newspapers and magazines, but, as the wife of a wealthy insurance executive, she did not rely on her pen to survive.

Clearly, George was running out of ideas for magazine arti-cles. He could not keep recirculating old bicycle-touring stories, especially stories relating adventures from the top of a high wheeler, a now unfashionable style of bicycle. All three of his articles in *Youth's Companion* have a sense of nostalgia, a feeling that its author is relating tales of old times. As Thayer completed his third and final assignment for *Youth's Companion*, he could tell his freelance days were numbered.

9

The Swish of the Fat Pneumatics

Putting his brief career as a freelance cycling journalist behind him, George Thayer found steady work in 1890 as a reporter for the *Hartford Courant*. He tackled a number of topics, but the police court became his favorite beat. Whereas the signed articles he published in the magazines gave him personal recognition, the role of newspaper reporter cloaked his authorship in anonymity. But the promise of a regular salary from the *Hartford Courant* offered a significant advantage over the tenuous existence of a freelancer.

By no means did his newspaper work exhaust Thayer's almost limitless energies. He also became superintendent of the Charity Organization Society, a newly formed group designed to coordinate the efforts of Hartford's various charity organizations, to make sure one was not duplicating the efforts of another and therefore minimize the opportunities for fraud that local con artists had been exploiting. By feigning injury, illness, or hardship, swindlers could bilk several organizations simultaneously. Thayer took it upon himself to investigate individual cases, helping the truly needy and exposing the unscrupulous.[1] His efforts for the Charity Organization Society worked well with his job as a courtroom reporter, which gave him an insider's knowledge of fraud as it was perpetrated across the city.

Though his journalism and charity work occupied much time, physical fitness remained an important aspect of Thayer's life. He volunteered at the Hartford Young Men's Christian Association (YMCA) as a gym teacher. In the summer of 1889, he took a training school course at the YMCA, which gave him the skills to assist the regular gym teacher.[2] The following year he rose to the position of physical director of the Hartford YMCA. The YMCA would remain a vital part of Thayer's life for decades.

He also stayed active with the Hartford Wheel Club. His time with the YMCA taught him the value of a gymnasium, and he took pains to help his cycling club establish a gym of its own. Thayer served on a special committee established for the purpose. In March 1893, the Hartford Wheel Club formally opened its gymnasium. Located on the second floor of the clubhouse, the roomy gym had a spruce floor and contained such apparatus as barbells, dumbbells, a high bar, Indian clubs, a medicine ball, parallel bars, and several elaborate weight-lifting machines.[3] The accounts of the gymnasium do not say for sure, but it may have also had a special training machine for cyclists. Columbia marketed an indoor trainer, which, according to its advertising copy, was "an indispensable adjunct to gymnasiums, and forms a very attractive feature in bicycle club-rooms, affording members opportunities for training, time races, etc."[4] State-of-the-art lockers and shower facilities adjoined the gymnasium of the Hartford Wheel Club. Through Thayer's efforts, his fellow club members could work on strength training when they were not out riding.

Thayer himself continued cycling. During his summer vacation in 1892, he began an extensive personal project: researching his family's genealogy. Reading grave markers had long been a leisurely pastime for him, but now he read headstones with purpose and reason. His genealogical research gave him a perfect excuse to ride his bicycle into the surrounding countryside and seek out old cemeteries, which contained a rich store of biographical and genealogical information. Before he completed his research, Thayer would take many tombstone tours.

He presented his genealogical research in a book-length work, *Ancestors of Adelbert P. Thayer, Florine Thayer McCray and Geo. Burton Thayer, Children of John W. Thayer and Adaline Burton* (1894). He published the book himself in a tiny print run of fifty copies. A few copies reached public collections, but, as his title indicates, George Thayer wrote the work mainly for his family.[5]

That he wrote this highly personal book in his spare time while employed as a reporter for the *Courant* reveals much about Thayer's attitude toward writing. Though his reportage for the *Courant* forced him to subsume his personality within the character of the paper, *Ancestors* was a liberating outlet, a way for him to put some personality back into his writing. The comparative security of a regular reporter's salary gave him the freedom to embark on this highly personal research project. Had he been relying on freelance work for his livelihood, he could not have undertaken such a noncommercial project.

Ancestors is an idiosyncratic work. In addition to the genealogy narrative, it contains two personal essays, "Christmas at Windermere" and "Sunday at Windermere." The first vividly recreates Thayer's childhood. The second relates the story of a sentimental journey, a Sunday bicycle ride from Hartford to Windermere. The essay begins, "One Sunday in July, I visited Windermere, the home of my boyhood. Purposely I took a route through a section of country entirely new to me, but there was little risk of my getting lost, for, like a carrier pigeon,

I was a homing boy once more, let loose from a trap of busy newspaper life, and could easily find my way back. How happy I was, gliding along through the woods on my pneumatic!"[6]

My pneumatic? Sure enough, George Thayer had traded his high-wheeled Columbia Expert for a safety with inflatable tires. The pneumatic tire represents the next, and possibly the most important, development in the evolution of the bicycle. Though many who became avid cyclists during the 1880s hesitated to give up their ordinaries for safeties, the invention of the pneumatic tire finally convinced them that the safety, once equipped with inflatable tires, was a far superior machine, not only in terms of safety but also in terms of comfort and speed.

Before the pneumatic tire overtook the industry, bicycle manufacturers experimented with a different form of air-filled tire, something in between the hard rubber tires of the earlier bicycles and the pneumatic tires of the future. The "cushion tire," as it was known, was constructed from a slightly softer rubber and it had a hollow center. It gave cyclists a more forgiving ride than the hard rubber tires. Though slower and less efficient than the pneumatic tire, the cushion tire was invulnerable to punctures. It would continue to be used through the 1890s for heavy-duty, puncture-proof bicycles, but once the pneumatic tire came on the market, it nudged the cushion tire from the mainstream marketplace.

Invented by Irish veterinarian John Boyd Dunlop in the late 1880s, the pneumatic tire began being used in competition in 1889. When some Irish riders showed up for a race in Liverpool that year riding bicycles equipped with pneumatic tires, the spectators roared with laughter.[7] Compared with the narrow, hard rubber tires, the bulbous tires did look comical. How fat were they? They were so fat that some called them "steamrollers."[8] They sounded funny, too. H. G. Wells, an avid cyclist himself, commented on both the look and the sound of bicycles equipped with pneumatic tires. As many different kinds of cyclists and cycles come together in the madcap chase scene that climaxes his hilarious bicycle-touring novel, *Wheels of Chance*, Wells speaks of "the swish of the fat pneumatics."[9] It did not take long for pneumatics to catch on. Once all those pneumatic-riding Irish cyclists started taking top honors and setting new cycling records, English and American cyclists soon followed their Irish brethren.

Pneumatic tires were introduced to the United States in 1891 and quickly captured the American market. Once again, the Columbia catalogues help track the trends. Whereas the high wheelers went from the front of the catalogue to the middle in the two years from 1889 to 1891, they completely disappeared from the Columbia catalogue over the next two years. The 1893 catalogue lists no ordinaries whatsoever. The Expert, the queen of the Columbia line, had finally met its demise.

Other catalogues of the period follow the trend. The 1893 catalogue for Kenwood bicycles lists no high wheelers, either. The 1894 catalogue of Rouse, Hazard, and Company, a Peoria, Illinois, firm specializing in close-out bicycles at discount prices, included an insert advertising second-hand machines for sale. The insert lists over forty used bicycles, only one of which is an ordinary, a Columbia Light Roadster. Though in splendid condition, this Columbia high wheeler is the cheapest bicycle on the entire list. It originally retailed for $125, but Rouse, Hazard, and Company offered it for only $15.[10]

More than any other aspect of the bicycle, the pneumatic tire initiated the bike boom of the 1890s. As more and more bicycles sold, marketing became increasingly sophisticated, and consumers became quite savvy. Like automobiles nowadays, new models with new features came out every year. The catalogues and the advertisements in newspapers and magazines stressed many aspects of the latest machines, which, according to the advertising copy, made them the lightest, fastest, most comfortable, most reliable, and most beautiful machines ever.

One curious document to survive from the era of the bike boom is a slim promotional pamphlet published by Morgan and Wright, a Chicago tire manufacturer. After it began making tires in 1891, Morgan and Wright emerged as the world's leading manufacturer of pneumatic tires. Titled *Cyclists' Dictionary*, the pamphlet consists of a series of cartoons. A different cycling term appears on each page, and a humorous illustration defines what it means. More strange than humorous, the cartoons nonetheless reflect the high level of technical knowledge the American bicycle consumer had achieved by the mid 1890s.

In the late-nineteenth-century cycling world, the term "scorcher" meant either a recklessly fast rider who put pedestrians in danger or a bicycle designed for fast city riding. *Cyclists' Dictionary* defines scorcher by depicting a short-order cook, who is burning a big pot of slumgullion. To get the joke, one must know the true meaning of the word scorcher, that it does not mean a bad cook who scorches food. Scorchers were the butt of other jokes. Discussing the nature of reckless riding, one contemporary moralist quipped that whoever scorches in this life will not escape scorching in the next.[11]

Other visual jokes in *Cyclists' Dictionary* depend upon a fairly sophisticated technical knowledge of bicycle manufacture. A picture of a horse-drawn ice wagon illustrates the term "cold drawn." Then as now, cold-drawn seamless tubing characterizes the finest-quality bicycle frames. The cartoon is funny only to those who know that cold drawn is a type of bicycle tubing.

One particularly racy illustration in *Cyclists' Dictionary* suggests that the pamphlet was not being distributed through neighborhood bike shops. It may have been a promotional giveaway for the 1895 industry show in Chicago. Beneath the caption "'95 Model" appears an artist painting a picture of a nude model, who stands in the background for all to see. That the image constitutes a literary allusion to *Trilby*, the sensational George du Maurier novel that was currently being serialized in *Harper's*, makes it no less racy.

Comparatively few of the illustrations in *Cyclists' Dictionary* depict bicycles. My favorite is "Good Joint." The phrase literally means a high-quality brazed or welded joint that holds one bicycle tube to another. The illustration depicts a different connotation of the word joint, meaning an eatery or a hangout. In this case, the good joint is a bakery popular with cyclists. The illustration portrays a scene still familiar to cyclists today as it depicts several bicycles parked outside the bakery, obviously a favorite stop for local riders.

It did not take long for George Thayer to get hooked on his pneumatic. His ongoing research into family history gave him a perfect excuse to take a bicycle tour through the region where his ancestors had lived. In June 1892 he toured eastern Connecticut, Rhode Island, and Massachusetts, the longest trip he had taken so far on his pneumatic. Though Thayer's genealogical research kept him busy during this cycling tour, he had another reason to justify the trip. He wanted to test out his pneumatic to see how it would do for "a trip around the world."[12] George Thayer, it seems, was getting itchy feet again. He was thinking about chucking his job as a court reporter for the *Courant* altogether and embarking on a round-the-world bicycle tour.

After Thomas Stevens completed his round-the-world bicycle tour, some people concluded that such an arduous journey need never be taken again. For adventuresome cyclists, Stevens's ride was not an end but a beginning. It provided a pattern for others to follow. G. W. Burston and H. R. Stokes, the two Australian cyclists who circumnavigated the globe on high-wheeled machines in the late 1880s, chronicled their

Fig. 21. *Good Joint*, as this illustration is titled, depicts a scene that has been enacted countless times since the invention of the bicycle, capturing the look of a bakery once a group of riders have stepped inside to refresh themselves during a club ride. From *Cyclists' Dictionary* (Chicago: Morgan and Wright, 1894). Courtesy Lilly Library, Indiana University, Bloomington IN.

journey in a privately published travelogue *Round about the World on Bicycles*. They deserve to be better known. Thomas G. Allen and William L. Sachtleben were the first to circle the globe on cushion-tired safeties, completing their journey in 1893.[13] Considering a round-the-world journey of his own before Allen and Sachtleben finished theirs, Thayer may have wondered if he could be the first one to cycle a safety around the world, but setting records was not his style. Still, the idea of circling the globe fired his imagination.

The pneumatic tires that might take him around the world took him around a little corner of New England in June 1892. On this trip, Thayer's safety bicycle carried him across the Connecticut River to East Hartford and then through Burnside and Manchester in surprisingly rapid time. Not until he reached the hills of Bolton Notch did he have to dismount and walk his bike. Now thirty-nine, he had lost none of the daredevil qualities that had characterized his high-wheeled riding style. Upon cresting a hill after a hard climb, he deserved the reward of a fast descent down the opposite side. After a few too many close calls during this cycling tour, however, Thayer decided to moderate his speed. He began using his brake spoon a little more. When that overheated, he used his pedals to control his downhill speed.

Though pneumatic tires had been invented by the time Thayer started riding a safety, the freewheel—the part of the bicycle that lets riders keep their feet on the pedals while coasting—would not be invented for several more years. Thayer's safety, like all the early safeties, was a fixed-gear machine, meaning that as long as the wheels went around so did the pedals. On this tour, Thayer discovered that riding "Chicago style" was not all bad. Keeping his feet on the pedals, he could finely manage his downhill speed by applying back pressure. Spinning downhill on a fixed gear was not as thrilling as sitting atop an ordinary with his legs thrown over the handlebars, but what Thayer lost in thrills he made up for in a sense of control. And he had to admit that the pneumatic tires did provide a much more comfortable ride than the hard rubber tires of his Columbia Expert.

One of Thayer's main goals for this journey was to find the home where his father had been born. But he wanted to do more than just find it, he wanted to sleep there for a night and thus symbolically take possession of it, to experience something his father had experienced. Though aware his grandfather's farm was near the village of Sterling, Connecticut, Thayer knew little else about it. Once he reached Sterling, he asked an old woman if she knew the whereabouts of Caleb Thayer's old farm. She didn't know but thought that Tom Winsor, who lived across the street, might. A "short, thick set, rough looking old man," Winsor hobbled out to the fence where Thayer stood with his bicycle.

"What under God's heaven you got there?" Winsor shouted. Apparently, the sight of a pneumatic bicycle remained something of a novelty in rural Connecticut in 1892.

After telling the old-timer all about his bicycle, Thayer asked if he knew any of the Thayers who used to live nearby. Winsor remembered several members of the Thayer clan but danged if he could remember where Caleb Thayer used to live. Frustrated with the gaps in his own memory, the old man "swore a blue streak for about five minutes." Thayer wryly observed, "Much as he had forgotten, swearing was not one of his lost arts."[14]

With persistence, Thayer finally located what he thought might be Caleb Thayer's old homestead. He knocked on the door of the farmhouse and explained his purpose. The family living there informed him that this was indeed Caleb Thayer's old farm and invited him to stay the night. To his chagrin, he learned the next day that this farm house was not the original one. Thayer was a little disappointed: "It punctured the poetry of the trip a little to learn that the old house had been torn down years ago, and the present one was built a few feet away from the old foundation."[15] Thayer's verb— "punctured"—is delightful: it shows that the language of the pneumatic bicycle tire had already entered the vernacular. His disappointment did not prevent him from spending another night with the kindly people who now owned the old Caleb Thayer place before returning to Hartford.

By all accounts, George Thayer did an excellent job as a reporter for the *Hartford Courant* after the paper hired him in 1890. His position was stable enough for him to move into fancier digs the following year. When the Linden opened in 1891, the developers advertised it as the finest, most modern, most convenient residential hotel in Hartford. Located on the corner of Main Street and Linden Place, the Linden would be Thayer's home for many years to come.

In "The Evolution of the Bicycle," Thayer had observed that more and more people were using bicycles for urban transportation. Nowhere in his writings does he mention that he commuted by bicycle. He did not need his pneumatic for day-to-day transportation. The Linden was close enough to the courthouse and the *Courant* building that he could simply walk between home and work. Though he had successfully made the transition from ordinary to safety, the bicycle gradually became less important to him, less integral to his daily life. He stopped dreaming of a round-the-world bicycle tour, as well. He kept longing to travel around the world, and would eventually do so, but not by bicycle.

Thayer's experience as a court reporter gave him an idea for a new career: he could earn a law degree and enter the legal profession. It did not bother him that he had already entered his forties by the time he decided to attend law school. Never before had he let his age stop him—and neither had his mother. He remembered how she had begun a Chautauqua course in her old age. If Mom could become a student again in her sixties, surely he could do so in his forties.[16] Yale College, with one of the finest law schools in the nation, was less than an hour away by train, but the classroom was an alien environment to Thayer. Not counting physical fitness classes at the YMCA, he had not been in a classroom since dropping out of high school at fifteen. How could he possibly get into Yale?

In the 1890s a bachelor's degree was not yet mandatory for admission to Yale Law School, but many students did complete their bachelor's degrees in other fields of study before starting law school. For them, the admission process was fairly simple. Candidates for admission who had not completed a college degree beforehand had to pass exams in such general subjects as history, literature, and math. Thayer studied hard, passed the entrance exams, and was duly admitted to Yale. He matriculated in 1895 as part of the largest class in the history of Yale Law School to that date: 109 students.[17]

As classes began on September 26, 1895, Thayer kept his room at the Linden and commuted between Hartford and New Haven. Every day he took the train to school—around forty miles each way. Recalling this daily experience, he remembered his early morning breakfasts more than anything: "The first recitation necessitated an early start, so I had breakfast at 5:30. This, for the sake of brevity, consisted of coffee and eggs. One morning I boiled them hard, the next morning soft, and for the sake of variety, the third morning I had them medium, but it was always eggs, boiled eggs, every morning."[18]

By the end of June 1897, Thayer had earned his LLB, passed his bar exam, and been admitted to the Connecticut state bar.[19] Instead of going directly into practice after passing the bar, he decided to do a year of graduate work at Yale to earn his master of laws. Before starting graduate school in September, he wanted to take a vacation: a bicycle tour of New England, New Brunswick, Nova Scotia, and Quebec.

The vacation let Thayer reward himself after two years of

hard work, and it helped him clear his head after so much intensive study. The main purpose behind this cycling tour, however, was to lose weight. He may have held himself to eggs and coffee for breakfast, but he obviously overindulged when it came to supper and snacks. His weight often ballooned when he did not exercise enough. During his first two years in law school, he had put on what he called "twenty-five pounds of aldermanic fat."[20] His words adapt a traditional simile: "as fat as an alderman." Needless to say, on a five-foot frame, twenty-five pounds has nowhere to hide.

Though Thayer never returned to the *Hartford Courant* as a legal reporter, the editor invited him to write occasional travel essays. Thayer chronicled many of his subsequent adventures for the *Courant*, including one that appeared under the title "Canadian Cycling." This article describes several aspects of Thayer's eight-week vacation from law school, but it says little about the bicycle he rode. Unlike *Pedal and Path*, it contains no paeans to the machine. Formerly, Thayer had taken great pride in the high-wheeled, nickel-plated Columbia Expert that got him back and forth across the United States and around Europe. "Canadian Cycling" mentions neither the model nor the brand of the bicycle he rode. Most likely, it was a Columbia, but he simply called it "an old, forty-pound machine."[21] The article does say something about the bike getting a slow leak and thus clarifies that he was riding his pneumatic, presumably the same one he had taken on his 1892 tour through New England. For Thayer, the pneumatic safety bicycle simply did not inspire the same passion as his high wheeler.

From Hartford, he headed for the Atlantic coast, which he followed through Maine. Pedaling up and down the hilly roads of coastal Maine, he could almost feel the pounds coming off. As he neared the Canadian border, he turned inland slightly. After spending the night in Calais, he crossed into New Brunswick on the road to Saint John. The day turned out to be the most dreary of his entire tour. The surrounding countryside, once well timbered, had been cleared, and most of the people who had lived there had disappeared with the trees. Only a few houses remained, and many of those were abandoned. The unimproved roads made for miserable cycling. They were "mere cart paths, deep-rutted and grass-grown." Difficult to negotiate on the pneumatic, they would have been impossible to ride on an ordinary.[22]

The day Thayer came through, a dense fog covered the land, making it difficult to see anything clearly and preventing him from either warming up or drying off. The cold, raw wind heightened his physical discomfort and gave him a sense of gloom and desolation. Sometimes he heard the sound of breakers coming from the rocky coast, but the fog was so thick he could not see the sea. He was almost ready to trade bike for train, but the rusty tracks and rotten ties of the nearby railway told him that months, perhaps years, had passed since the last train came through this bleak stretch of New Brunswick. With no other option, Thayer continued to ride, hoping to reach Saint John that night. As he approached the outskirts of the city in the gloaming, a big dog sprang from the darkness, flashing its teeth. It caught Thayer and sank its teeth into his leg. As he continued to pedal, Thayer felt something unmistakable: blood trickling down his calf.

Perhaps Nova Scotia would be more amenable. He took the ferry from Saint John across the Bay of Fundy. Thayer's account of the trip provides few details about his precise route through Nova Scotia, but he spent at least one night at the dockside hotel in Parrsboro. Known as the Land of Big Tides, this region of Nova Scotia showed him the meaning of the epithet one morning.

"If you intend to go over on the boat," the hotel proprietor said to him early that morning, "it is time you were up for breakfast."

Thayer could hardly believe what the man said. He looked out his window toward the steamer *Evangeline* but did not see a drop of water within fifty feet of the propeller. He took his time getting dressed and eating breakfast. The next time he looked out, however, the tide had come in, and *Evangeline* was ready to sail. Thayer boarded just in time to enjoy a delightful sail across Minas Basin and around Cape Blomidon, a towering precipice of red sandstone that guards the basin like a moody sentinel.

What Thayer had read about Nova Scotia conditioned how he understood the province. And what he had read about Nova Scotia was the same thing that countless other nineteenth-century Americans had read, Henry Wadsworth Longfellow's *Evangeline*: the best-loved poem by the best-loved poet in America, according to one nineteenth-century literary historian. John Seelye, a more recent literary historian, provides a different perspective, calling *Evangeline* "an oleaginous balm with a sweet smell, reminiscent of the sickroom or, worse, the schoolroom."[23]

Longfellow's scenic descriptions had raised Thayer's expectations a little too high. No way could the real-life setting approach the one Longfellow imagined. As Thayer observed, "The beauty of the famous Annapolis valley is chiefly to be found in the quiet of our own libraries, there only to be seen through the eyes of Longfellow, eyes that, in fact, never saw the land of Evangeline."[24] Thayer's little dig at Longfellow reflects the smugness of a seasoned traveler: how can you truly appreciate someplace unless you visit it?

For Nova Scotians who catered to the tourist trade, *Evangeline* offered nearly countless commercial possibilities. The steamship out of Parrsboro, which took its name from Longfellow's eponymous heroine, provides one of many examples. The slightest details of the poem offered opportunities for exploitation. The Dominion Atlantic Railway puffed itself as the "Land of Evangeline Route," quoting lines from the poem and evoking Longfellow's beautiful imagery in its promotional brochures. Merchants along the railway followed suit. Near the tracks, a billboard erected by a "Blue-Nosed" merchant alluded to, of all things, Evangeline's heifer.

Back in New Brunswick, Thayer sailed up the St. John River for part of the way, but then switched to a train to cross the province into Quebec. Chugging along at a rate of seventeen miles an hour, the New Brunswick train offered a quaint traveling experience. From Thayer's view, the engineer's consideration outweighed his common sense. Ascending one hill, the train needed all the steam it could muster. When an old sow came running from the woods onto the track, the engineer, instead of letting the cowcatcher—or, in this case, sow-catcher—do its work, blew his whistle to scare the oinker off the tracks. Blowing the whistle wasted valuable steam, dropping the pressure so much that the train nearly came to a standstill.

Upon entering Quebec, Thayer enjoyed a gorgeous ride along Lake Temiscouata, which British traveler Douglas Sladen called "thirty miles long of dark water surrounded by pine forests, and hiding in its vast depths the lordliest lake-trout of America."[25] When it comes to Thayer's tour of the lake, "Canadian Cycling" is ambiguous. His essay says he rode along the lake, but it is unclear what he rode: his bicycle or the train. After crossing the St. Lawrence, he sailed up the Saguenay River: a highlight of the trip. More chasm than river, the Saguenay is a deep, dark body of water surrounded by towering cliffs. The "River of Death" one observer called it; "Nature's Sarcophagus" said another. A contemporary guidebook cautioned, "Its overpowering sublimity and measureless desolation become oppressive to some visitors." Not Thayer. He thoroughly enjoyed its "magnificent mountain scenery."[26]

If he spent any time in Quebec City, he did not say so

in "Canadian Cycling." Other contemporary cyclists greatly enjoyed the city. C. A. Stephens, who visited with other members of his Knock-About Club during their cycling tour of Maine and Canada, said that Quebec City was "the next best thing to a tour in Europe."[27]

South of the city, Thayer pedaled through some poor-looking farm land. Its inhabitants seemed equally inhospitable, gauging by one farmer's insensitive comments. Thayer had to walk his bicycle up one hill, not because the hill was too steep but because the road was too muddy. The farmer yelled to him in French. When it became obvious that Thayer could not understand what he was saying, the farmer switched to English.

"Oh hell," the farmer said, "can't you ride such a hill as that?" Needless to say, this Quebec farmer did not leave Thayer with a good impression of the land and its people.

Not normally one to complain, Thayer comes across as a whinger in "Canadian Cycling." He details what he disliked about Canada but says hardly anything about what he liked. Regarding the highlights of the trip—the sail around Cape Blomidon, the ride along Lake Temiscouata, the sail up the Saguenay—he wrote little. Apparently, his vacation improved after he crossed from Quebec into Vermont, even more after he crossed from Vermont into New Hampshire, which was becoming one of his favorite destinations.

In the White Mountains, Thayer took a room at the Jefferson Hotel in the village of Jefferson, New Hampshire. The village offered a commanding view of the Presidential Range, and the newly renovated Jefferson Hotel was "a most worthy bearer of the illustrious statesman's name."[28] From Thayer's perspective, the hotel formed an ideal base for one- or two-day hikes into the surrounding wilderness. He enjoyed the White Mountains so much that he spent the last two weeks of his vacation here. On a two-day hike his first week in Jefferson, he stayed overnight at "The Perch," one of several camps constructed and equipped by the Appalachian Mountain Club of Boston.

Thayer ended "Canadian Cycling" with a description of these camps. Possibly the single best contemporary description of the Adirondack camps, Thayer's description bears repeating:

> When the season opens fresh beds and pillows of pine boughs are made; men hired for the purpose carry up blankets, crockery, tin dishes, knives, forks, spoons, extra suits of clothes, underwear, shoes, camp stools, folding tables, hammocks, candles, playing cards, tobacco, pipes, matches, canned goods of every variety, and at stated periods during the summer fresh bread, pies, cakes, tea, coffee, condensed milk, sugar, pepper, salt and lots of things I will not stop to mention. Everything needed for the comfort of a climber, caught in a storm or too tired to descend to his hotel, can be found at these camps. All the climber must do for himself is to find the camp, but a little caution makes that easy. As for myself, the nights I spent, lying wide-awake on the sweet smelling pine boughs, nicely tucked up in blankets, watching the wind whirl the sparks from the dying embers up into the rafters and roof of our snug little birch bark home, makes me want to forever bless the Appalachian Club of Boston.[29]

One afternoon during his second week at the Jefferson, another hotel guest asked Thayer, "What say you to going up to 'The Perch' tonight?" Having had a good time at "The Perch" the week before, Thayer said yes, of course. Aware how well-equipped the camps were, they did not bother taking any additional food or gear with them. Leaving their hotel, they walked along the highway for an hour and a half to the foot of Hunt's Trail and climbed up Mount Adams at a steady pace. Before long, they encountered a party of hikers coming down the trail.

"How about 'The Perch' to-night?" Thayer asked the other hikers.

"Oh, it's full," one replied. "There will be nine there. But 'The Cascade' is unoccupied."

"The Cascade" was located at a lower elevation from "The Perch," so Thayer and his new friend found themselves there by six that evening. They built a roaring fire and prepared dinner from food stored at the camp. The next morning they climbed Mount Jefferson and spent two hours at its peak before making their way to Crawford's Camp. During their hike that day, they came across an injured partridge, which they humanely put out of its misery. At Crawford's Camp that evening, partridge broiled in butter was the main course, butter being another staple item supplied by the Appalachian Mountain Club. Not all the camps had cook stoves, but this one did. To supplement the partridge, they fried up some ham and eggs, warmed up some apple pie, made toast, and brewed some coffee.

All the Appalachian Mountain Club asks of its visitors, Thayer explains, "is that the dishes shall be washed and the wood pile left well stocked. All the rest is free, and whosoever will may come and enjoy themselves at the club's expense." To be sure, Thayer did the dishes this evening.[30]

Bringing his eight-week Canadian vacation to a close as he cycled home from the White Mountains to Hartford, Thayer was ready to begin his graduate work at Yale Law School. During the trip, he had ridden his pneumatic more than a thousand miles. With all those miles under his belt, he could now draw that belt a couple notches tighter. Thayer successfully accomplished his main goal: he had lost those spare twenty-five pounds. No longer as fat as an alderman, George Thayer was rightfully proud of his new physique: "Nothing but muscle and bone remained and hard muscle at that, regular scrap-iron."

—•◦•10•◦•—

The Wheel and the Gun

During the years he spent with the *Hartford Courant*, George Thayer also served in the Connecticut National Guard. He first enlisted in 1889 as a member of Company K, eventually rising to sergeant. Though his autobiographical writings are fairly extensive, Thayer provides almost no details about his service in the guard. This gap is unfortunate because his guard duty coincided with significant developments involving the military use of the bicycle. Under the leadership of Colonel Charles L. Burdett, the Connecticut National Guard tested the bicycle's military viability for the first time in the history of the U.S. Army. Once again George Thayer was present to bear witness to a new chapter in the history of cycling.[1]

Born in Nantucket in 1848, Charles L. Burdett left Massachusetts for Connecticut in 1882. He settled in Hartford, where he worked as both civil engineer and patent lawyer: a dual career reflecting his talent and ambition. While living in Hartford, Burdett began cycling and also joined the National Guard. He was appointed colonel of the First Regiment in 1884. Serving as signal officer and brigade engineer, Colonel Burdett organized the signal corps of the Connecticut National

Guard. He also became active with the Connecticut Bicycle Club, the club Thayer belonged to before the Hartford Wheel Club was established. Most likely the two knew one another through their participation in club activities, but there is no indication they were friends. In the summer of 1885, Burdett joined the League of American Wheelmen.[2]

Burdett quickly became active with the LAW, not just at the state level, but also at the national level. He served as national racing chair one year, often officiating at league-sanctioned events. In addition, he took an active role in the Good Roads Movement, an effort the league initiated to improve the sorry state of American roadways. To be sure, George Thayer was not the only cyclist to get stuck in the mud on tour. In 1892 Burdett was elected national president of the LAW, a prestigious position with considerable influence. Announcing Burdett's election to the presidency, the *Illustrated American* provided an indication of the political power of the LAW, which it called "the most popular organization in the United States."[3] There can be no disputing either his dedication to cycling or his willingness to serve the cycling community, but Burdett's presidency was not without controversy. As a leader, he could be snarly and strong-headed. He was happy to lead, but anyone who questioned his leadership was doomed to feel the force of his wrath. Burdett came down hard on whoever challenged his authority, as Thayer would learn firsthand.

Though Burdett rode an ordinary when he first took up cycling, he switched to a pneumatic after he realized the wide-ranging potential of the safer, more maneuverable, and more versatile machine. Burdett's recognition of the safety bicycle's superiority got him thinking about how it could be put to military use. As a signal officer, he naturally considered the possibilities of using the bicycle to convey military dispatches.

His decision made, Burdett ordered Lieutenant Howard A. Giddings to develop a special bicycle service as part of the signal corps. He would prove to be the ideal choice to take charge of testing the bicycle as a military vehicle. Giddings did have some cycling experience, but he was not a passionate cyclist like Burdett or Thayer. He was passionate about the signal corps. Throughout his military career, Giddings would continue to experiment with the latest advances in communication technology. He was not averse to more established forms of communication: Giddings used the periodical press to make the case for the bicycle's military viability.

Carrying out Colonel Burdett's orders, Giddings shrewdly approached Colonel Pope for assistance. As a former military man, Pope was eager to do what he could to advance military technology. As the proprietor of the nation's largest bicycle company and a consummate entrepreneur and pitchman, Pope saw that supplying bicycles to the Connecticut National Guard would give him yet another way to promote Columbia bicycles. In 1891 he supplied the Connecticut National Guard with a model known as the Hartford Safety, which was a step below the top-of-the-line Columbia Safety. Though pneumatic tires were becoming the standard, Pope supplied the military version of the Hartford Safety with puncture-proof cushion tires. Neither as comfortable nor as maneuverable as pneumatic tires, the cushion tire did provide the cycling soldier with one distinct advantage: it would save him from having to fix a puncture under fire.[4]

In June 1891 Lieutenant William H. C. Bowen visited Camp Niantic to inspect the Connecticut National Guard and witness how the special bicycle service of the signal corps worked. In his report to the inspector general of the U.S. Army, Bowen expressed appreciation for the efforts of the army cyclists. Still uncertain about the bicycle's use in combat, he recognized its utility for both communication and reconnaissance. Based on what he saw at Camp Niantic, he strongly recommended that the War Department experiment with the bicycle further.

Overjoyed with Bowen's recommendation, Burdett subsequently ordered Giddings to undertake further trials at Camp Watson during the state military rendezvous in August that year. Giddings selected nine enlisted men and equipped them with Hartford Safeties, Colt repeating carbines, and pistols, intending to match them against the cavalry in a head-to-head contest. Strongly opposed to cycling soldiers, the cavalrymen were anxious to prove their own battlefield superiority in competition. They disliked the idea that some new-fangled, human-powered machine could take the place of a man and his mount. Giddings raced the cyclists against the cavalry on country roads, and the cyclists outdistanced the men on horseback. He also pitted the bicycle against the signal flag, discovering that a bicycle could deliver a message much faster than the same message could be signaled.

Only when Giddings placed the bicycle in simulated combat did it run into trouble. Attempting a retreat across the turf, the cyclists had difficulty escaping soldiers on horseback. The cavalrymen caught all the cycling soldiers but one, who escaped with a terrific burst of speed. Giddings concluded that the bicycle was indispensable for the signal department and could be useful in other military situations but hesitated to make any definite conclusions about its combat readiness. He continued his research, publishing the results as a practical manual.[5]

Given Thayer's renown as a long-distance cyclotourist, he would seem a natural for the bicycle service of the signal corps, but no evidence suggests that he was considered for a place among the Giddings nine. Lieutenant Giddings described all of his men as young and educated. Thayer, a high-school dropout in his late thirties, could scarcely be described as either young or educated. Besides, nowhere does he mention riding a bicycle for the National Guard. As a Connecticut guardsman, Thayer witnessed these groundbreaking military experiments but apparently did not participate in them.[6]

Thayer left the National Guard once he started reading law. The development of the military bicycle continued in his absence. In 1893 Pope replaced the Hartford Safety the soldiers had been riding with the top-of-the-line safety, the Columbia Light Roadster. The superior machines may have come at the instigation of Lieutenant Giddings, who was disappointed with the lower-quality machines Pope had originally supplied. The Hartford Safety had suffered some serious mechanical breakdowns during its two years of service in the Connecticut National Guard. Giddings remarked, "The highest grade wheels made are none too good for this hard service."[7]

The military version of the Columbia Light Roadster was far superior to the Hartford Safety. Pope also supplied this new military model with puncture-proof cushion tires, but otherwise it differed significantly from the previous model. With nowhere to mount a rifle on the Hartford Safety, the cyclists had to carry their carbines over their shoulders. On the Columbia Light Roadster Safety, the rifle mounted directly to the top tube of the semi-diamond frame. A set of signal flags could be mounted on the opposite side of the top tube. In addition, a box capable of holding three hundred rounds of .45-caliber ammunition hung from the top tube, fitting within the center of the frame. By strapping a bedroll to the handlebars, the cycling soldier could attach practically everything he needed to his machine.

Always keeping an eye toward the commercial potential of his products, Colonel Pope marketed the military model to the general public. Much as Jeeps would be marketed to American motorists after they had been developed for military use in World War II, the military bicycle entered the commercial market after the Connecticut National Guard had begun experimenting with them. Civilians who wanted military bicycles of their own could buy the exact same model the Connecticut signal corps rode. Using the experience of

Fig. 22. *Golden Gate, Sunset in the Yellowstone Park* depicts a cycling soldier and his wheel. His outfit closely resembles what the cyclists in the Connecticut National Guard rode (Knapp Co., 1897). Library of Congress, Prints and Photographs Division, reproduction number LC-DIG-pga-01798.

the Connecticut National Guard to puff the machine, the 1893 Columbia catalogue explains: "The Light Roadster Safeties have been the first regularly used in the United States army, and during the past year their practical utility for both courier service and for the rapid movement of organized bodies of men has been satisfactorily proved."[8] Pope marketed a modified version of the same machine as a firefighter's bicycle, which came with a fireman's axe mounted on the top tube and a fire extinguisher hanging where the ammunition box hung on the military model.

Pleased with the bicycle's performance in the signal corps, Giddings hoped to expand the military use of the bicycle. In an 1893 article on the subject for *Harper's Weekly*, he suggested further uses. He was well aware that the biggest obstacle facing the military bicycle was the cavalry, which felt threatened by the introduction of new technology and actively discouraged the military use of the bicycle. Before developing his argument, Giddings reassured readers, letting them know that he did not think that the bicycle would or could or even should replace the horse. Instead, he argued that the bicycle could serve as a valuable adjunct to the cavalry. For example, cyclists could serve as scouts, a role for which they were ideally suited: "The long journeys cyclists can make accustom them to studying the features of the country through which they pass, thus habitually training them as scouts."[9]

Cyclists could also serve in combat. Their silence gave them a considerable advantage over the cavalry, especially at night. Horses were noisy. The enemy could hear them approach and prepare for their attack. The bicycle, on the other hand, was virtually silent. It could approach the enemy from a considerable distance and take them by surprise. Giddings observed, "The moral effect of this power of stealthy approach, noiselessly and in unknown force, from distances beyond the march of infantry, must produce a feeling of nervousness and dread,

and necessitate strengthening the outposts. It would be trying work for an enemy to suddenly find bodies of infantry of
unknown reserve power appearing vaguely out of space and
behaving with cruel concreteness in the matter of bullets."[10]
Hitherto unnoticed by military historians, Giddings's description of the bicycle's strategic silence clarifies an important fact:
the military bicycle represents the first stealth technology.

The development of military technology took on a new
urgency as the nineteenth century neared its end. On February 15, 1898, the United States battleship *Maine* was blown
up in the harbor of Havana. On April 23, President McKinley
issued a call for 125,000 volunteers to serve for two years. One
month shy of his forty-fifth birthday and only a few weeks shy
of completing his master's degree, George Thayer enlisted in
the Connecticut Volunteer Infantry—under one condition.
Though he had served as a sergeant in the National Guard, now
he wanted to serve solely as a private. He continued to attend
classes at Yale until May 2, when his regiment was activated.

Thayer wrote a heartfelt letter to his sister, Florine, out-
lining his rationale for reenlisting. As he saw it, he had two
options. He could finish his master's degree and then begin
practicing law, or he could reenlist and serve his country. He
was confident that he could always finish school and become
an attorney, but the opportunity to become a soldier and test
himself in battle, something he had been longing to do all his
life, would almost surely never happen again. It was a chance
of a lifetime, the one opportunity, he told Florine, "to show
to myself and to you what stuff there was in me."[11] Though
Thayer had used bicycle touring as a substitute for going to
war in the past, it had not satisfied his longing to test himself
in the crucible of combat. He just had to enlist now. He could
not bear the thought of missing this chance.

Soon after his unit was called up, Thayer received some
good news from New Haven. The faculty of Yale Law School

had voted to recommend him for the degree of Master of Laws in consideration of the fact that he had enlisted and in view of the high standing he held in his class at the time of his enlistment.[12] George Thayer could now establish his own law practice. But first he had a war to fight.

The morning of Wednesday, May 4, 1898, Thayer left his home for the Elm Street Armory, where he would assemble with the Connecticut National Guard and the First Regiment of the Connecticut Volunteer Infantry. Recalling how he felt that morning, he ably captured his emotional state: "The time had now come—I was going to war. I went up to my room in The Linden, took a last look at all my books and things, wondered if I should ever see them again, locked the door and left the building."[13] Thayer's beautifully understated prose depicts the melancholy of a man going to war.

There was no guarantee that he actually would go to war, at least not yet. For one thing, he still had to pass the army physical. Many of those twenty-five pounds of aldermanic fat that he had worked off while bicycle touring in Canada had returned during graduate school. His weight would not affect the results of the army physical. His height could. Five feet, four inches was the minimum height for soldiers in the U.S. Army, and he was easily three inches below that. But Thayer had his cobbler fashion some extra-tall lifts for his army boots, which gave him the height and confidence to pass the physical. Becoming a soldier and fighting in the Spanish-American War meant too much for him to miss out because of a technicality.

Guardsmen and volunteers from across Connecticut assembled at the armory that Wednesday. When everything was ready, they shouldered their knapsacks and started marching up Elm Street. The city streets were so chock-full of cheering people that the column of soldiers could scarcely squeeze past. The citizens of Hartford wore red, white, and blue ribbons and waved American flags. The buildings behind them were decorated with even more American flags and other patriotic gonfalon.[14]

Several groups of soldiers preceded the First Regiment, including the bicycle brigade of the signal corps, which Giddings and Burdett had managed to keep going since 1891, though the bicycle would not be used in combat during the Spanish-American War. Imagine what history would be like if only Teddy Roosevelt had charged up San Juan Hill on a fixed-gear Columbia. For the parade through the streets of Hartford, the uniformed cyclists made an impressive sight, but they were not the ones the citizens had come to see. The people really wanted to see "the boys," that is, the men of the First Regiment, those brave soldiers like Private Thayer who had volunteered to go to war. The First Regiment was led by Colonel Burdett. Thayer was a member of Company K.

The boys marched to Union Station and boarded the train for Camp Niantic, where they would rendezvous. The short railway trip reinforced the economic significance of the bicycle to Connecticut. By no means was the Pope Manufacturing Company the only cycle maker in that state. Going through Middletown, the train chugged past the Keating Wheel Company, a manufacturer of innovative, lightweight bicycles. The Keating plant helped send off the boys by blowing its factory whistle.

During their time at Niantic, the men prepared for wherever the U.S. Army would station them. On May 10 came the time for the physical. Though Thayer was confident he could reach five feet, four inches with his boots on and lifts installed, he now learned that everyone would have to take their physicals naked. The men were weighed first and measured directly afterward. Thayer stepped from the scale on tiptoe, stayed on his toes as he walked to the measuring machine, and attempted to raise himself even higher as he stood there. Almost balancing on his toenails, he stood still until the doctor's assistant called out, "Five feet, four!"

He made it! The following Tuesday he and the other men were formally mustered into the service of the United States of America. Calling the members of the First Regiment "the boys," the citizens of Hartford were not far wrong: the average age of Company K was twenty-three.[15] Thayer was the oldest private. Having turned forty-five less than a week earlier, he was double the age of many other privates.

Since Thayer had established his literary reputation with *Pedal and Path* and perpetuated it with his contributions to the magazines and newspapers, Captain Henry H. Saunders, the leader of Company K, asked him to keep a diary of their wartime experience. Thayer agreed. After the war, he turned his diary into *History of Company K, First Connecticut Volunteer Infantry, During the Spanish-American War*, an inside narrative relating the wartime exploits of the member of Thayer's company in considerable detail. It remains a valuable resource for researching Connecticut biography.

The boys of Company K came from many different walks of life. Their occupations included some traditional ones and some new ones: blacksmith, electrician, insurance clerk, machinist, photographer, printer, salesman, stenographer, and teacher. Thayer listed Frank J. Cadwell's occupation as a "wheelman." He included brief biographies of every member of the company, heading each with an appropriate epigraph. For Private Cadwell, Thayer used lines from Longfellow's "Keramos." Though the poem refers to a potter's wheel, lines from it were often applied to cyclists:

> Turn, turn my wheel! Turn round and round
> Without a pause, without a sound.[16]

Thayer called Cadwell a "record-breaking wheelman," but he may have overstated the case. Before joining the First Regiment, Cadwell had placed in some amateur races, including a first place in a one-mile handicap race sponsored by the Veru Bicycle and Rubber Company, a New Haven retailer, but he had yet to break any cycling records.[17] Cadwell's military service would prevent him from competing in the 1898 racing season, but he would return to competition the following year with newfound success.

Colonel Burdett hoped to keep the companies of the First Regiment together, but the army ordered them to different locations along the coast of New England. Companies F and K would go to Portland to defend the Maine coast from attack by Spanish warships.

The next morning the boys of Companies F and K struck their tents, packed their gear, and proceeded to the railway station, where they cheered Colonel Burdett and the other officers who were being stationed elsewhere. Companies F and K reached Portland at eight that night and made it to Fort Preble in a pouring rain the next morning. They set up camp and then waited—and waited. Though Thayer had compared bicycle touring and military service in the past, there was a world of difference between the two, as he now realized. The cyclotourist need wait for no man. The soldier spends most of his time waiting.

Fort Preble, as Thayer could quickly tell, was ill-equipped to protect Maine, lacking sufficient armament to defend the coast. If the Spanish fleet attacked, there would be little the Connecticut volunteers could do to stop an invasion. But after a few weeks, Thayer could also tell that the likelihood of a Spanish attack was almost nil. Soldier life at Fort Preble during the Spanish-American War mainly became a matter of battling boredom.

The army food, like the weather, was dismal. Many men grumbled, but Thayer endured. He credited his stoicism to his bicycle touring, which provided him with the wherewithal

Fig. 23. This photograph depicts the swimming squad that Thayer led to Casco Bay when they were stationed in Maine at Fort Preble during the Spanish-American War. Thayer is seated in front. From George B. Thayer, *History of Company K, First Connecticut Volunteer Infantry, During the Spanish-American War* (Hartford: R. S. Peck, 1899).

to sustain hardship and privation. "I thank my stars for the rough experience the different trips on my wheel compelled me to endure, for I don't mind this at all," he wrote. "But I feel sorry for the young fellows who cannot eat salt pork three times a day as I can." Thayer's cyclotouring also helped in another way. Used to keeping all his gear in an army knapsack, he never had any trouble finding what he wanted, not even when it was pitch dark.[18]

He adjusted to life at Fort Preble by heading out to the seashore to go swimming. Every day, sometimes twice a day, Thayer led groups of men to Casco Bay. They began calling him "the commandant of the swimming squads." He explained, "The water is still so cold it makes our legs ache to stay in longer than to just duck under but the tonic of the salt freshens us up wonderfully."[19] As the summer progressed, the water got warmer, and their swims grew longer. Thayer and several others continued to enjoy swimming, even after Captain Saunders prohibited them from swimming without trunks. In one letter to her brother, Florine asked George if he felt the effects of rheumatism. He replied, "The daily swims are putting me in fine shape. I can touch my fingers to the ground with stiff knees and keep them there, all right. I must be about twelve pounds lighter than I was."[20]

Though intended to comfort him, the letters George Thayer received from his sister during the Spanish-American War were unsettling. He could tell that Florine's already precarious health was deteriorating. When she reported to him that a trip to the seashore had done nothing to improve her health, George replied with sadness and sympathy: "I am sorry to see you back home and feeling so miserably."[21] After her husband, William McCray, died unexpectedly, Florine's health declined further. William's great sense of humor had sustained his wife during her long illness; his death was her death blow. Florine Thayer McCray would die just seven weeks after her husband.[22]

The last week of June 1898 a rumor went around Fort Preble that Companies K and F would take part in the Puerto Rico campaign. The men yelled with delight when they heard the rumor, but it turned out to be just that, a rumor, nothing more. They would stay in Maine until mid-July, when they broke camp and left for Camp Alger, located in Virginia just outside of Washington DC. Here all the companies of the First Connecticut Volunteer Infantry would reunite. To Thayer's eyes, Camp Alger did not look promising. This year's camp was last year's cornfield. They erected their tents and christened streets after the different companies. With all the companies of the First Regiment back together, the boys of Company K were once again under the command of Col-

Fig. 24. Rather than sleep in an overcrowded tent during a hot
Washington DC summer, Thayer chose to fashion accommodations
of his own from pine boughs and a scrap of canvas. From George B.
Thayer, *History of Company K, First Connecticut Volunteer Infantry,
During the Spanish-American War* (Hartford: R. S. Peck, 1899).

onel Burdett, who, to their chagrin, saw drill as the best way
to reinforce discipline.

Thayer was tough enough to withstand Colonel Burdett's
rigorous daily drills, but he made one crucial adjustment to
make the nights more tolerable. A shortage of tents meant that
six men had to share each one. The idea of six men crammed
into a tent designed for four in the hundred-degree heat of a
DC summer was more than Thayer could stand. He decided
to sleep outdoors on the ground. He made a mound of dirt for
himself, covered it with freshly cut pine boughs, and stretched
a waterproof tarp over the top to protect himself from the rain.

On Monday, August 8, Thayer recorded a strange sight,
which he incorporated in the *History of Company K*: "Down

through the Virginia camp, across a small bridge, into a deep mud hole and up into our camp rode Colonel Burdett on his wheel, bumping over the uneven ground of our corn field and into K street with a rush."[23] The strong-willed Burdett had kept the signal corps of the Connecticut National Guard going, but his efforts to make the bicycle a vital part of the U.S. Army had not had much impact. Though bicycles were not used in combat during the Spanish-American War, Burdett was determined to make some kind of wartime use of the bicycle. He decided to use his as a personal military transport.

Despite the importance of the bicycle to Thayer's life, his portrayal of Colonel Burdett riding his wheel through the muddy streets of this cornfield-turned-camp borders on ridicule. Since Thayer first rode a boneshaker in the 1870s, through his touring days atop his ordinary to his switch to a pneumatic, the bicycle had always been a symbol of freedom for him. It offered the freedom to go wherever he wanted, whenever he wanted. It had taken him across the United States, through Great Britain, over the Alps, around France, and throughout eastern Canada. At Camp Alger, the bicycle assumed an opposite meaning. Their commander had a bicycle; the enlisted men did not. The bicycle represented the differences between them. Paradoxically, Colonel Burdett's bicycle symbolized the lack of freedom for the rank and file. They were stuck in camp, unable to go to war and equally unable to go home. The bicycle separated Burdett from his men, becoming a symbol of his impracticality, his overbearing authority, and his inability to relate to the men or their plight.

The war was over by the third week of August, but the Connecticut volunteers were stuck at Camp Alger, still subject to Colonel Burdett's iron rule, still forced to drill every day. The men did not regret volunteering to serve their country, but now that their opportunity to see combat was gone, they were anxious to go home and resume their lives. Though the fighting had ended, the army still needed men to serve in Cuba; according to the latest rumor, the First Connecticut Volunteer Infantry would be sent to Cuba to do garrison duty. The men groaned at that possibility. Garrison duty? Why, there was neither glory nor excitement in that. Colonel Burdett, on the other hand, was all for garrison duty: here again he was out of touch with the men. He seemed unaware that they had lives and families and careers back in Connecticut.

When they protested against being kept at Camp Alger unnecessarily, Colonel Burdett reacted swiftly, drafting a resolution, which he submitted to the men for a vote: "Resolved, That the members of this command are desirous of retracting their oath of military service to the United States for two years and want to be mustered out and go home during the present armistice and before peace is declared."[24] The colonel's ultimatum rankled the otherwise easy-going Private Thayer. Speaking about Thayer, a fellow soldier remarked, "I never heard him complain but once and that was when Colonel Burdett made us vote to retract our oath of military service."[25]

Thayer's outrage is understandable. Burdett's resolution forced him and the other men to deny their sworn commitment to fight for their country. Just because they wanted to be mustered out now that the war was over did not mean that they were any less committed to their nation. Thayer and some other enlisted men approached Captain Saunders to see if they could vote on being mustered out without retracting their oath, but Saunders said they could not. Overwhelmingly, they voted to be mustered out, even if their votes were construed as retractions of their oath.[26] In September, they left Washington to return to Camp Niantic. The last day of October, the Boys of Company K were finally mustered out.

The military bicycle fared little better than the members of Thayer's company. Burdett's commitment to the military bicycle, combined with Giddings's enterprise and ingenuity, had kept the bicycle-riding signal corps going. With Burdett's support, Giddings would sustain the military use of the bicycle to the turn of the century, but their hopes of making the cycling soldier a permanent part of the U.S. Army faded quickly after the Spanish-American War. The reactionary cavalry never accepted cyclists as their equal. Even Colonel Pope lost interest in the military bicycle and, in 1900, withdrew his support altogether. Giddings conceded defeat in 1901, ordering the signal corps of the Connecticut National Guard to come to the June encampment on horseback. Like the boys of Company K, the bicycle never did make it to the front lines.

11

The End of an Era

Once he was mustered out of the service, George Thayer could begin his legal career. Before 1898 ended, he opened a law office in the First National Bank Building on State Street in downtown Hartford.[1] It was a crowded profession. The city directory for the following year lists a total of 134 attorneys. By comparison, the list of authors in the same directory contains only two, one famous, the other forgotten: Samuel L. Clemens and a dime novelist named Edward S. Van Zile.[2] Of course, Thayer himself could lay claim to authorship, but he had long since realized what the city directory clarified: seldom did authorship provide the means to make a living. The law, needless to say, could be a lucrative career—even in a city with 133 competitors.

During his first year as an attorney, Thayer struggled to keep his head above water. Having learned patience long ago, he bided his time as he built his clientele.[3] His fortunes improved after the first year, but he found private practice somewhat dissatisfying. His cases seemed so petty. As an attorney, Thayer was involved with people who took little responsibility for themselves, people with no gumption of their own who looked to the law to solve their problems, those who would rather sue than do.

Before another year passed, Thayer's legal career changed drastically. On May 13, 1901, the Hartford prosecutor's office needed a substitute prosecutor. Having established a good reputation for his professional judgment and personal maturity, Thayer accepted the temporary appointment. As prosecutor for the day, he could go after the bad guys. And, it turned out, he was quite good at it. Word of his skill as a prosecutor quickly got around. The following month the county commissioners appointed him full time to prosecute cases concerning violations of the community's stringent liquor laws. Ginger-Ale George now had a cause to call his own.

In the coming years, he took on anyone who violated the liquor laws: bartenders, beer wagon drivers, brewers, clubmen, department store owners, druggists, grocers, hotel managers, liquor wholesalers, pool hall proprietors, restaurateurs, saloon keepers, teamsters, everyone. He came down especially hard on those who sold liquor to teens. His ongoing community service promoted athletics among Hartford youth, and he hated the thought of adults contributing to the delinquency of minors.

As Thayer's legal career flourished, he settled down like he had never settled down before. He enjoyed living in the Linden: the manager, the elevator boy, the pastry chef had all become close personal friends.[4] He was still living there when he accepted his position as prosecutor, but he soon built a large house at 45 Pleasant Street in West Hartford. The property was huge. With a frontage of 361 feet on Pleasant Street, it extended back about 1,500 feet and, therefore, contained over twelve acres of land. It also contained a small pond fed by Trout Brook. He hired George Dennison to design and build the home, which, upon completion, earned a reputation as one of the finest houses in Connecticut. Thayer moved in before the end of 1902.[5]

Such a magnificent home seems like quite an extravagance for this former budget cyclotourist, but he could afford it. His salary was not great, but during his years as prosecutor he maintained his private practice. And he also had another source of income. He funded his new home largely from what he had inherited from his sister, who had inherited her husband's estate, valued at over a hundred thousand dollars. Dying without issue, she had bequeathed her estate to her two brothers to divide equally between themselves.[6] George Thayer liquidated Florine's estate but held onto what may have been the most important part of her property—her books. Over the course of her busy, if brief life, Florine Thayer McCray had assembled a library of some 1,500 volumes, which her younger brother took possession of upon her death. Though their parents had instilled them with a lifelong love of literature, George had never amassed a great home library like Florine's. Since law school, he had assembled a pretty fair law library, but her collection gave him a wealth of pleasure reading. George was determined to keep Florine's library intact to honor her memory. There was no way he could store it in his room at the Linden. Florine's library was one factor motivating her younger brother to build a home of his own.

Thayer's professional responsibilities kept him so busy that he had little time for travel during his lawyer years. In 1899 he went to Grinnell, Iowa, to see his brother, Adelbert. Given the timing of the trip—a few months after their sister's death—this journey may have had a practical purpose: to settle her estate.[7] Whereas George used his inheritance to build a stately home in West Hartford, Adelbert used his for a summer cottage on the shores of White Bear Lake in Minnesota. Years later, George would visit Adelbert at his vacation home, where he greatly enjoyed swimming and fishing.[8]

George Thayer served as prosecutor for over nine years, three times longer than others usually spent in the office, but he finally submitted his letter of resignation in September 1910.[9] He would continue his private practice for a few more years, but stepping down as prosecutor would give him the time to do what he really wanted: teach gym classes to local youth.

He continued teaching at the Hartford YMCA, but he also began teaching gym classes in West Hartford at the town hall. He taught other classes in his new home, as well. The apparatus Thayer used to teach gym at the town hall included dumbbells, floor mats, Indian clubs, parallel bars, and a pommel horse. He taught two classes most nights, a junior class for teenage boys and a young men's class. In 1911 the junior class met from seven to eight in the evening, and the young men's class met the next hour. After their training hour ended at nine, the young men played basketball.[10]

As prosecutor, Thayer had challenged those who sold liquor to minors, but once he left the office, he approached the same social problem in a different way. Instead of going after the adults who encouraged unhealthy and immoral behavior among Hartford's youth, Thayer worked directly with the youth to encourage healthy, morally upright behavior.

Eventually retiring from private practice, Thayer left himself plenty of time to visit those parts of the world he had yet to see. Over the next decade and a half, he took numerous trips to far-flung destinations, starting in 1912 with a five-month journey to Panama, Hawaii, and Alaska. This trip formed a pattern for future journeys. The first extended vacation he had taken since his 1897 Canadian cycling tour, it was also the first he took without his bicycle.

Thayer wrote several essays about his experiences in Panama and Hawaii. In none of them does he say why he left his bicycle home. His age could have had something to do with his decision, but it seems unlikely. Though he would turn fifty-nine during this trip, he did not consider himself old. His workouts at the YMCA had helped him stay fit. He was ready for adventures that would challenge men twenty-five years younger. The bicycle, however, no longer held the charm for him that it had a quarter-century earlier. Once he abandoned his ordinary for a pneumatic, much of his passion for cycling disappeared.

Thayer's Canadian cycling tour had roughly coincided with the peak of the bicycle boom that had begun once the chain-driven, pneumatic-wheeled safety bicycle emerged in the early 1890s. By century's end, the boom was over. There were still plenty of bicycles on the road in the early twentieth century, but most served utilitarian purposes. Bicycle racing remained a popular sport, but casual riders simply quit riding. The bicycle became something boys rode to deliver newspapers and groceries, but it largely stopped being an adult recreational vehicle. For the most part, the bicycles manufactured in the United States during the early twentieth century were sturdy machines for city riding, not lightweight, long-distance touring machines. The elegance and simplicity the Columbia Expert had symbolized disappeared along the way.[11]

The experience of Frank J. Cadwell, a veteran of Thayer's regiment during the Spanish-American War, illustrates the pattern cyclists took in the early twentieth century. Cadwell remained a competitive cyclist into the first decade of the new century, placing in several events from one-mile sprints to six-day races, but by 1910, he had put away his bicycle in favor of a faster mode of two-wheeled travel: the motorcycle. Cadwell briefly raced motorcycles before becoming manager of a competitive motorcycle track in Springfield, Massachusetts.[12]

The automobile adversely affected the bicycle's history, of course. Not only did it provide an alternate means of vacation travel, it also became an obnoxious presence on the road, detracting from the pleasures of bicycle touring. In 1914 Thayer received a friendly letter from the German student he had cycled with for a few days during his 1888 European tour. The German cyclist fondly remembered the time they had spent together but explained that he no longer rode his bicycle: "I have left since many years the bicycling sport, because there is no pleasure today to make bicycle journeys in the powder excited by the auto cars."[13] Thayer's German friend was referring to dirt roads, obviously, but then as now, motorists were a nuisance on asphalt roads, too.

The invention of the internal combustion engine was not the only reason why cycling diminished in the United States during the early twentieth century. When Thayer returned from his transcontinental tour in 1886, he had compared the nationwide network of cyclists to a fraternity, an organization whose members felt strong bonds of brotherhood. No longer did cyclists share the fraternal feelings they used to share back in the days of the ordinary. Writing at the start of the twentieth century, one old-time cyclist, for instance, spoke wistfully of "the most excellent fraternal spirit that marked the early days of cycling."[14]

The feelings of brotherhood Thayer formerly experienced riding his wheel he now achieved through his work with the YMCA and other community organizations. If he had any regrets about taking an extended vacation before he left for Panama, they concerned his absence from the students in the gym classes he taught. Before he solidified his travel plans, he asked his students, all forty of them, if it would be alright if he took a lengthy trip. They unanimously voted the vacation for him.[15]

Beyond the reasons why travelers generally avoided the bicycle in favor of other means of travel, Thayer may have had some specific reasons why he left his bicycle at home. Perhaps he did not take it on his Panama-Hawaii-Alaska vacation because a bicycle would have been more of a burden than a help. The nature of this trip made walking more amenable than cycling. Panama was narrow enough to walk all the way across. Thayer had already cycled from the Atlantic to the Pacific; by crossing Panama on foot, he would be able to claim that he walked from the Atlantic to the Pacific. Besides, the canal was still under construction, and the land surrounding it contained few roads suitable for cycling. Had Thayer brought his pneumatic, he would have had to push it most of the way across.

Hawaii, too, was small enough that he could walk or sail wherever he wished. It had some excellent roads, as Thayer would learn when he got there, but he may not have known about Hawaiian roads ahead of time. For whatever reason, he decided not to bring his bicycle on this trip, nor did he bring it on the other vacations he would take in the future. Thayer's local reputation as a traveler would grow among those who read the numerous travel essays he contributed to the *Hartford Courant*, but from this point forward he would make his way afoot, not awheel.

His time in Hawaii let him enjoy many different sports. Oahu offered some enjoyable opportunities for mountain climbing. One day Thayer went up Palolo Valley to see the lake formed by the crater of an extinct volcano and the series of waterfalls the lake created. He climbed a trail alongside one waterfall, enjoying a pleasure similar to one he had enjoyed in Yosemite over a quarter-century earlier. By the time he saw the Punch Bowl and returned to where he had started, he had hiked twenty miles.

Another day he hiked through Kalihi Valley with A. M. McClure, an employee of the Honolulu YMCA. McClure put Thayer through his paces, taking him up a ridge so steep and so treacherous that they had to scramble over it on hands and knees. In his account of Hawaii, Thayer captured his precarious situation: "There were places where I found myself perched on a ridge scarcely fifteen inches wide, with a 1,000 foot precipice to one side."[16]

Interisland travel was quite convenient, so he visited other Hawaiian islands, including the Big Island. As his steamship approached Hilo, he enjoyed the scenery's stark contrasts: the steep cliffs of black lava rising from the white foam of the breakers and the dark canyons washed with waterfalls.[17] Already, the infrastructure to accommodate automobiles had developed significantly. The interisland steamers now transported motor cars, letting Hawaiian residents take their automobiles with them while island hopping. On the steamer Thayer took from Oahu to the Big Island, for example, Frank E. Thompson, a Honolulu attorney, sent his car and driver to Hilo for the use of his ten-year-old son: one of many ways Thompson spoiled the boy.

Acquainted with Thompson, Thayer caught a ride in the convertible with his friend's son and his chauffeur from Hilo to the Kilauea volcano. Thayer's account of this trip thus constitutes his earliest published description of automobile travel. Upon stepping foot on the Big Island, he "was soon being whizzed away, in the auto, from Hilo, through a dense fern forest and over a fairly level country. The morning was misty and occasionally the car skidded slightly but this gave the driver an opportunity to show his skill while the young lad, not satisfied, stood up in the back seat and yelled 'Faster, faster,' at the same time rapidly firing off a small revolver he had with him."[18]

The largest active volcano in the world, Kilauea mesmerized Thayer. He reached the edge of the cauldron at three in the afternoon, took a seat, and stayed there for several hours. As he had during his past travels, he brought some writing materials with him to this picturesque locale, which allowed him to record his on-the-spot impressions. Other tourists who came to witness the cauldron of molten lava that afternoon returned to Volcano House in time for supper. But nothing, neither hunger nor the threat of rain, could make Thayer budge from his spot. He did not return to Volcano House until three that morning. He had arranged to stay at Volcano House for four nights: every night he came back to the crater for further observations.[19]

Leaving Hilo, he headed for Maui next. As the steamer approached the island, he noticed a fine road about fifty feet above the shoreline and enjoyed watching an automobile race along the coast.[20] Maui had several excellent roads for motoring and, presumably, for bicycling, though Thayer did not evaluate their suitability for two-wheeled travel. The good roads had little impact on his Maui travel plans. He wanted to travel on horseback, to go where wheeled traffic could not, which proved to be the perfect way to see Maui.

Thayer spent the next three days on horseback riding across the island, covering a total of ninety-eight miles. During his time on Maui, he grew quite fond of Gypsy, the sure-footed, yet fickle mare that took him across the island. He had done little horseback riding since his boyhood days when he used to ride Sleepy David to school. As an adult, he had preferred a two-wheeled mount over a four-footed one. But he had not forgotten how to ride. The spirited Gypsy proved more challenging than the lackadaisical horse he rode to school, but once he adjusted to Gypsy's eccentricities, he thoroughly enjoyed the ride.

Though Thayer had planned to spend three weeks in Hawaii, Arthur Wilder and Fred Peterson, two Hawaiian classmates from Yale who had returned to Honolulu to practice law, urged him to stay longer. Once they extended their hospitality, Thayer lingered in Honolulu two weeks further, taking advantage of all that Oahu had to offer. Wilder, who had become an associate justice of the Supreme Court of Hawaii, lived adjacent to Waikiki Beach, so Thayer enjoyed watching the local men surf off the coast of Waikiki and sometimes went swimming with them. They encouraged him to try surfing.[21]

When he finally left Hawaii, Justice Wilder accompanied him to the dock. A forty-piece Hawaiian band played music to send off Thayer and his fellow passengers. As was the custom, Wilder brought several leis, which he placed around Thayer's neck shortly before he boarded his San Francisco-bound vessel. Describing his personal appearance, Thayer created a humorous caricature, depicting himself as nothing but a column of flowers topped by a shining, sun-tanned dome.[22]

Upon returning to San Francisco, Thayer had planned to travel to Seattle and then return home across Canada. But once he reached Seattle, he learned about an organized excursion to Alaska, so he decided to see the northernmost territory of the United States. Traveling along the coast of British Columbia, the steamer took a route that, for the most part, went inside the chain of coastal islands, which made for a calm, yet spectacular passage. Happily, Thayer did not need to worry about the *nausea marina* on this trip. Snow-capped mountains, glaciers, icebergs, whales: he could appreciate all that was grand in nature from the warm, sunny deck of the Alaska-bound steamer.

Trekking across Panama, mountain climbing on Oahu, volcano watching on Hawaii, horseback riding on Maui, swimming with surfers off Waikiki, whale watching along the rugged coast of British Columbia: George Thayer may have left his bicycle home, but he had not lost his sense of adventure or his sense of fun.

He planned further travels, but his plans changed in 1914, when something happened that Thayer had never imagined would happen again, at least not in his lifetime: the United States again found itself on the brink of war. It looked like the nation would go to war with Mexico. American forces stormed Veracruz and took control of its port. Three days after the occupation of Veracruz began, President Wilson mobilized the regular army and called up 150,000 National Guard troops.

Too young to have served in the Civil War, and denied combat duty during the Spanish-American War, Thayer had largely accepted that the opportunity for him to serve in combat and fight for his country had passed. The possibility of war with Mexico invigorated him. Perhaps he could still serve his country on the battlefield. Throughout his life, he had never let his age stop him from doing whatever he wanted to do, and now, though sixty, he was in good-enough shape to handle whatever the army might throw at him. He still worked out daily at the YMCA. In great shape physically and mentally, he knew he could pass any army physical, but his application process never got that far: the U.S. Army refused his request to enlist. Age, it seems, had finally caught up with George B. Thayer. Uncle Sam had no use for a sixty-year-old infantryman.[23]

He would have one more chance to go to war. On April 6, 1917, the United States declared war on Germany. Though he had been turned down when he had volunteered for service in Mexico three years earlier, he was determined to volunteer again and serve in Europe. He knew it would be difficult, but he did everything he could to volunteer. He offered to serve in any capacity, from carrying a gun to driving a mule. Eight separate times he got as far as an examining surgeon. The first seven turned him down, not because he was out of shape but because he was too old. The last of the eight examining surgeons did not reject him outright but instead required Thayer to obtain a medical certificate from the physician who attended him during his last illness. His last illness? Why, Thayer had not been sick enough to see a doctor since he had the measles when he was ten!

Thayer grew increasingly angry with every rejection. Imagine all these doctors saying he was too old for combat. Why, he would show them. These rejections motivated him to take extraordinary measures, to rise to an even higher level of fitness than he had formerly achieved. He began walking thirty-five or forty miles a day just to spite all those naysayers who said he was not fit to serve his country. In his own words, here's how he reacted to these rejections:

> I would pick myself up and for purpose of working off all my rebellious feeling, go off into the country, beyond the hearing of our local YMCA, and safely outside police jurisdiction where profanity was not indictable, I would walk for miles and miles, keeping up not the old time "hay-foot, straw-foot" but the more modern cadence and chanticle, decidedly more in keeping with my hot blood, "Damn 'em, damn 'em!" Frequently thirty-five or forty miles in a day were thus paced off with peculiar pleasure in myself and with no intended injury to any one.[24]

Once the U.S. Army proved to be a dead end, Thayer applied to both the YMCA and the Red Cross to serve in Europe. While waiting to hear from them, he did everything he could to support the war effort on the home front. Not even Armistice Day, November 11, 1918, stopped him from trying. He knew that the transition from war to peace would take time, that many American soldiers would remain in Europe for months, and that much relief work would be required. In short, he still wanted to go to Europe to serve his country.

Thayer had long been a fixture at the Hartford YMCA. Nearly everyone who worked out there knew him. But the week after Armistice Day, he simply disappeared. Where did he go? No one seemed to know. By the end of November, the mystery was solved. A close friend received a postcard from him explaining his whereabouts. When the war ended, Thayer still had an application in with the YMCA. In mid-November, he received a telegram instructing him to report to Columbia University. With thousands of other potential candidates, Thayer went through an intensive, one-week training camp that kept him busy from 6:00 in the morning to 9:30 each night.[25]

At the week's end, the YMCA sent many of the recruits home, directing the rest to Springfield, Massachusetts. Thayer was among those selected for further training at Springfield. He had made the first cut! One of his trainers at Columbia sent the following endorsement to Springfield with him: "Don't let this man's age count against him; he's a marvel."[26] The regimen at Springfield consisted of four hours of physical training a day and eight hours of lectures. At the end of the Springfield training, the YMCA made its next cut, sending home half the recruits, but not Thayer. He was among those the YMCA selected for postwar service in Europe.

A friend shared Thayer's postcards and letters with a reporter from the *Hartford Courant*, who found the story inspiring. On January 14, 1919, a feature article appeared under the title, "George Thayer 'Fools 'Em All' and Gets Across: The Smallest and the Oldest Man in the 'Y' Service Passed through Intensive Training at Age of 65." The reporter concluded, "Thus ends, or rather begins, Mr. Thayer's efforts to get into the big war game. He went up against and mastered the greatest problems in order to win out. His age was a serious handicap, but he proved beyond doubt that he was in physical condition sufficient to outclass men his junior by two score years even in the most strenuous exercises and games."[27]

The reporter generously quoted from Thayer's postcards and letters, which emphasize the arduous nature of the physical training at Columbia University and in Springfield, but he let one telling fact slip: he had actually *gained* eight pounds during the training. The YMCA training may have been rigorous, but it was not as rigorous as Thayer's own personal regimen. He ate more and exercised less during the YMCA training than he had beforehand. His Spartan diet, daily gymnastics, and anger-inspired marathon walks had left him lean and mean, as a photograph accompanying the article clearly shows. In the photograph, Thayer appears in the gym wearing a singlet. He holds a dumbbell in each hand. The muscles in both arms are clearly defined. In the parlance of modern body builders, he is ripped.

In France, the YMCA sent Thayer to Ferrières, where he was assigned to canteen duty for an American Ambulance Corps associated with the French army. His job was to man a window and sell cigarettes to the American soldiers. Lucky Strikes, Camels, Fatimas, Omars: Thayer manned that window for eight or ten numbing hours every day. Imagine it. All his effort, all his dedication, all his sacrifice had led to this: selling soldiers packs of cigarettes. He manned that cigarette window at Ferrières for three full months before being sent to Reaume.[28] The YMCA had organized an educational program at Reaume to teach college-level courses to American soldiers who remained in France. This assignment was more promising, but almost as soon as Thayer reached Reaume, the U.S. Army took over the program the YMCA had established, and Thayer found himself out of a position. He was briefly assigned to a battalion of black soldiers, but they had little for him to do.[29]

The YMCA sent Thayer back to its base hospital in Paris and put him in the athletic department. This assignment would seem more appropriate for a cyclotourist and gym teacher. Instead of working with the men, however, Thayer was put in charge of inventory. The YMCA had sent much athletic equipment to American troops stationed throughout France, and they were now returning it. Thayer was responsible for inventorying the returned equipment. The glamour of Paris: George Thayer found himself stuck in the YMCA hospital counting baseballs by the caseload.[30]

Having to sell cigarettes and count baseballs was disappointing, but perhaps anything Thayer could have done in Europe after the war would have been anticlimactic, given the extraordinary battle he fought simply to be accepted for

European service. Thayer had won his own private war when the YMCA accepted him to serve in Europe. Doing so, he had scored a victory for all senior citizens, who should not be discriminated against simply because of their age, who should be recognized for their mental and physical abilities and be given all the respect and privileges of everyone else with the same abilities regardless of age.

After ten months in Europe, Thayer returned to Hartford and to a routine that was becoming typical for his retirement: working out at the YMCA, teaching gym classes, and speaking about his travels to local civic groups. By no means was he through with traveling. He took many short walking trips in New England and planned extended walking tours elsewhere in the United States and overseas.

As the second decade of the twentieth century gave way to the third, Thayer still had not taken the journey he desired most: a round-the-world tour. Finally, on May 13, 1922, he left Hartford determined to circle the globe. He went north to Montreal and took the train to Vancouver, where he boarded a steamer for Japan. His journey subsequently took him to China, India, and South Africa. From there he sailed up the east coast of Africa to Egypt, crossed the Mediterranean to Europe, traveled the length of Italy, revisited France, and then crossed the Atlantic. The trip took nearly a year. He did not return home to Hartford until the spring of 1923, shortly before his seventieth birthday.[31]

Throughout his round-the-world journey, Thayer had contributed articles to the *Hartford Courant* documenting his trip. When he came home, he decided to write another book of travels. Instead of writing solely about his recent journey, he would make his book a compendium of a lifetime of travel. As he considered how to structure the book, he had a tough decision to make. He could organize it chronologically, presenting his personal story as an autobiography of a traveler, or he could organize it alphabetically, presenting encyclopedic chapters about different countries, illustrated with personal anecdotes. He chose the second, less egotistical option.

By presenting his travels as a series of unconnected episodes, Thayer left many questions unanswered. He included some of his bicycle-touring stories but never explained why he quit cycling and became a pedestrian. He published the book himself, awkwardly titling it *Trips to Hell and Other Countries*. The "hell" of the title refers to the Kilauea volcano that had so intrigued him in Hawaii, and, oddly, he used a picture of molten lava as his frontispiece.

Trips to Hell lacks the freshness of *Pedal and Path* and the charm of some of the traveler's tales he had published in the *Hartford Courant*. Readers interested in his bicycle-touring activities—the most important aspect of Thayer's life as a traveler—find *Trips to Hell* frustrating. The book's first cyclo-touring story, which relates Thayer's ride through Belgium in 1888, does not occur until a hundred pages in. The chapters on England, France, Germany, and Italy contain additional stories from his European cycling tour, and the chapter on the United States relates a few episodes Thayer had told at length in *Pedal and Path*. Describing his Columbia Expert in *Trips to Hell*, the machine he had glorified in *Pedal and Path*, Thayer now calls it simply "a bicycle, one of the old high ones."[32] Far from being his crowning literary achievement, *Trips to Hell* is a disappointment. *Pedal and Path*, Thayer's first book, is also his best.

In June 1928, the month after he turned seventy-five, George Thayer decided to walk from his home in Connecticut to his favorite destination, New Hampshire. He found the mountains there as beautiful as ever, but the walk home from New Hampshire would prove to be his last. While hiking along the highway through Manchester, he suffered a massive heart attack. His heart was so big one might have thought it would never give out, but finally it did. Fittingly, George B. Thayer died on the road.[33]

On Saturday, June 30, a memorial service was held in the auditorium of the William H. Hall High School, the only place in West Hartford large enough to accommodate everyone who wished to pay their respects. Members of the physical education class he conducted at his Pleasant Street home served as pall bearers. Others from the *Hartford Courant*, the YMCA, the Connecticut National Guard, and the First Regiment of the Connecticut Volunteer Infantry also attended. The large crowd at the memorial service indicated how many lives Thayer had touched. He was buried at Grove Hill Cemetery in Rockville, Connecticut.[34]

According to the terms of Thayer's will, the income from a trust fund would go to Mount Holyoke College and Yale.[35] He designated the bequest to Mount Holyoke for its physical education department, apparently as a way to honor his sister's memory by encouraging physical fitness among college women. The bequest to Yale went toward the law school. The George B. Thayer Fund, which forms part of Yale Law School's funds for general purpose and research, remains active today.

Thayer also made a bequest to Dartmouth College, specifically to the Dartmouth Outing Club.[36] Aware that many students from West Hartford would attend Dartmouth, Thayer hoped they would become active with the Outing Club. He knew from his law school days how easily students could lose sight of physical fitness as they concentrated on their studies. His bequest to the Dartmouth Outing Club would enable many college students to maintain their physical fitness and their love of the outdoors.

The Dartmouth bequest also provided another way for Thayer to honor his beloved White Mountains. The site of his first major cycling tour, the White Mountains became a place Thayer returned to at the end of other journeys as well as a place he often visited on mini-vacations. He had climbed many mountains in his life from the Rockies to Yosemite to Hawaii and the Alps: the White Mountains essentially put the world in Thayer's backyard. This range of mountains offered natural grandeur close to home, a place where George Thayer could indulge his love of cycling, walking, and being outdoors, the one place that reminded him of all the other places he had visited during a lifetime of adventure.

NOTES

1. The Century

1. W. E. Decrow, *Yale and "The City of Elms,"* 3rd ed. (Boston: W. E. Decrow, 1885), 84.

2. Decrow, *Yale and "The City of Elms,"* 84.

3. George B. Thayer, *Trips to Hell and Other Countries* (Hartford: Case, Lockwood, and Brainard, 1924), 325.

4. George B. Thayer, *Ancestors of Adelbert Thayer, Florine Thayer McCray and Geo. Burton Thayer, Children of John W. Thayer and Adaline Burton* (Hartford: Plimpton Mfg., 1894), 120.

5. Nelson Sizer, *Forty Years in Phrenology; Embracing Recollections of History, Anecdote, and Experience* (New York: Fowler and Wells, 1888), 180; Kevin J. Hayes, *Edgar Allan Poe* (London: Reaktion, 2009), 95.

6. Thayer, *Trips to Hell,* 110–11.

7. Thayer, *Trips to Hell,* 110–11.

8. Thayer, *Trips to Hell,* 168.

9. "Distinguished American Women: Florine Thayer McCray," *Ladies Home Journal* 6 (December 1888): 2.

10. Thayer, *Ancestors,* 33–34.

11. Thayer, *Ancestors,* 147.

12. Thayer, *Ancestors,* 120.

13. Thayer, *Ancestors,* 120.

14. "Boyhood Diary of George B. Thayer," *Hartford Courant,* April 17, 1915, 4; George B. Thayer, *Pedal and Path: Across the Continent Awheel and Afoot* (Hartford: Evening Post Association, 1887), 242–43.

15. George B. Thayer, *In Hell—Shut In—At the Outbreak of the Great War, 1914* (West Hartford: George B. Thayer, 1915), 34.

16. Thayer, *Ancestors*, 149.

17. "Far from His Feet," *Historical Record* 2 (January 1888): 29; "A Survivor from Stoneman's Raid," *Minock Blade*, July 8, 1886, reprinted in George Edwin Marks, ed., *A Treatise on Marks' Patent Artificial Limbs with Rubber Hands and Feet* (New York: A. A. Marks, 1888), 165–68; Thayer, *Trips to Hell*, 13; George B. Thayer, *History of Company K, First Connecticut Volunteer Infantry, During the Spanish-American War* (Hartford: R. S. Peck, 1899), 200.

18. George B. Thayer, "War-Time Economy," *Hartford Courant*, November 13, 1917, 10.

19. "Boyhood Diary," 4.

20. "Boyhood Diary," 4.

21. "Boyhood Diary," 4.

22. "Boyhood Diary," 4.

23. "Distinguished American Women," 2.

24. Thayer, *Ancestors*, 157–58.

25. Trebor Ohl [pseud.], "Mrs. Florine Thayer McCray," *Queries* 5 (May 1889): 142–44.

26. Thayer, *Ancestors*, 161; Thayer, *Trips to Hell*, 67, 96, 298, 450, 477; "George B. Thayer Rejoices Because He Now 'Is in It,'" *Hartford Courant*, February 7, 1919, 3; Thayer, *Pedal and Path*, 216; Thayer, *In Hell*, 22.

27. Thayer, *Ancestors*, 161.

28. Thayer, *In Hell*, 23.

29. "George B. Thayer Appointed," *Hartford Courant*, June 25, 1901, 5; "George Thayer 'Fools 'em All' and Gets Across," *Hartford Courant*, January 14, 1919, 6.

30. "Tolland County Mass Meeting," *Hartford Courant*, October 22, 1868, 2.

31. "Distinguished American Women," 2; Ohl, "Mrs. Florine Thayer McCray," 142.

32. Dio Lewis, "Story of the Lexington School," *To-Day* 1 (April 5, 1873): 440–41.

33. Thayer, *Pedal and Path*, 216–17.

34. Thayer, *Trips to Hell*, 528.

35. Thayer, *Trips to Hell*, 528.

36. Thayer, *Trips to Hell*, 13.

37. Thayer, *Trips to Hell*, 13.

38. Karl Kron, *Ten Thousand Miles on a Bicycle* (New York: Karl Kron, 1887), xcvii.

39. Thayer, *Pedal and Path*, 15.

40. George B. Thayer, "Any Man Can Go to College If He Wills To," *Association Men* 41 (May 1916): 418.

41. Thayer, *Ancestors*, 121.

42. Florine Thayer McCray and Esther Louise Smith, *Wheels and Whims: An Etching* (Boston: Cupples, Upham, 1884), 74–75.

43. Thayer, *Ancestors*, 122.

44. "Matters and Things in New York," *Milwaukee Daily Sentinel*, December 14, 1868.

45. "From Our New York Correspondent," *Vermont Watchman and State Journal*, February 10, 1869.

46. "The Velocipede in Boston," *Boston Daily Advertiser*, February 4, 1869.

47. "The Velocipede: A Humorous View of the Two-Wheeled Vehicle," *Milwaukee Daily Sentinel*, January 28, 1869.

48. George B. Thayer, "The Evolution of the Bicycle," *Frank Leslie's Illustrated Newspaper*, October 5, 1889, 159.

49. Jess J. Gant and Nicholas J. Hoffman, *Wheel Fever: How Wisconsin Became a Great Bicycling State* (Madison: Wisconsin Historical Society Press, 2013), 25.

50. Thayer, *Ancestors*, 34.

51. Kevin J. Hayes, *An American Cycling Odyssey, 1887* (Lincoln: University of Nebraska Press, 2002), 23.

52. Thayer, "The Evolution of the Bicycle," 157.

53. "Big Bicycle Riding," *New Haven Evening Register*, August 25, 1884.

54. "Big Bicycle Riding," *New Haven Evening Register*, August 25, 1884.

55. "A Hundred Miles in Thirteen Hours," *Hartford Courant*, August 26, 1884, 2; "Personal," *Buffalo Courier*, September 5, 1884; "Personal," *Evening Republic* (Buffalo), September 5, 1884; *San Francisco Bulletin*, September 10, 1884.

56. Kron, *Ten Thousand Miles*, xcvii.

2. The White Mountains

1. Trebor Ohl [pseud.], "Mrs. Florine Thayer McCray," *Queries* 5 (May 1889): 144; "Wheels and Wheelmen," *Salt Lake Herald*, June 2, 1889.

2. Florine Thayer McCray, "Love on Wheels," *Peterson's Magazine* 91 (1887): 271–74.

3. Ohl, "Mrs. Florine Thayer McCray," 143.

4. George B. Thayer, *History of Company K, First Connecticut Volunteer Infantry, During the Spanish-American War* (Hartford: R. S. Peck, 1899), 151; Ohl, "Mrs. Florine Thayer McCray," 142.

5. "From Many Pens," *Fort Worth Daily Gazette*, April 19, 1886.

6. Ohl, "Mrs. Florine Thayer McCray," 142.

7. "A List of New Books Published by Cupples, Upham and Company," in Walter Besant and Henry James, *The Art of Fiction* (Boston: Cupples, Upham, 1885), 90.

8. "The Girls and Their Tricycles," *Hartford Daily Courant*, October 21, 1885.

9. McCray, "Love on Wheels," 272.

10. Florine Thayer McCray and Esther Louise Smith, *Wheels and Whims: An Etching* (Boston: Cupples, Upham, 1884), 38, 164.

11. McCray and Smith, *Wheels and Whims*, 46.

12. "Literary Notes," *New Haven Evening Register*, June 10, 1884, 2; "Wheels and Whims," *Congregationalist*, July 31, 1884, 256; "Current Literature," *Literary World* 15 (August 9, 1884): 265–66; "Literature," *New York Herald*, August 31, 1884, 15.

13. "Among the Books," *Outing and the Wheelman* 4 (July 1884): 307–8.

14. *National Union Catalog: Pre-1956 Imprints*, 754 vols. (London: Mansell, 1968–1981), no. M0029735; "Hartford (Conn.) Notes," *New York World*, May 9, 1886, 16.

15. "For and about Women," *Buffalo Evening News*, February 13, 1886.

16. "It May Be of Interest," *The Record* (Mt. Kisco), June 10, 1887.

17. Pope Manufacturing Co., advertisement, *LAW Bulletin*, July 2, 1885, 1.

18. George B. Thayer, *Pedal and Path: Across the Continent Awheel and Afoot* (Hartford: Evening Post Association, 1887), 172, 180.

19. For a good biographical sketch of Professor Williams, see William Richard Cutter, ed., *New England Families: Genealogical and Memorial*, 4 vols. (New York: Lewes Historical Publishing, 1915), 2: 980–81.

20. Thayer, *Pedal and Path*, 3.

21. George B. Thayer, "'Joe Hawley Was My Hero, and I Never Had But One,' Writes George B. Thayer," *Hartford Courant*, October 25, 1914, A14; "Notes of the Wheel," *Hartford Courant*, November 25, 1885, 1.

22. George B. Thayer, "Two Days of His Trip," *Hartford Daily Courant*, December 5, 1885, 1.

23. McCray and Smith, *Wheels and Whims*, 116.

24. "Another Trans-Continental Bicycler," *Outing*, May 1886, 236.

25. George B. Thayer, "The White Mountains," *LAW Bulletin*, January 22, 1886, 52.

26. Quoted in *New England: A Handbook for Travellers*, 7th ed. (Boston: James R. Osgood, 1883), 159.

27. C. A. Stephens, *The Adventures of Six Young Men in the Wilds of Maine and Canada; or, The Knock-About Club* (London: Dean and Son, 1884), 21.

28. Thayer, "White Mountains," 52.

29. Thayer, "Two Days," 1.

30. Quoted in Muriel Lydia Seymour, "Our Trip to the 'Old Man of the Mountain,'" *Granite Monthly* 55 (August 1923): 389.

31. Thayer, "White Mountains," 52.

32. *The White Mountains: A Handbook for Travellers*, 4th ed. (Boston: James R. Osgood, 1882), 258.

33. Thayer, "White Mountains," 52.

34. Thayer, "White Mountains," 52.

35. Thayer, "White Mountains," 52.

36. Jean Bobet, *Tomorrow, We Ride*, trans. Adam Berry (Norwich: Mousehold Press, 2009), 113.

37. Thayer, "Two Days," 1.

38. Thayer, "Two Days," 1.

39. Thayer, "Two Days," 1.

40. Thayer, "White Mountains," 52.

41. "Notes of the Wheel," 1.

42. "Notes of the Wheel," 1; Thayer, *Pedal and Path*, 162.

3. The Road to Omaha

1. "Notes of the Wheel," *Hartford Daily Courant*, November 25, 1885, 1.

2. George B. Thayer, *Pedal and Path: Across the Continent Awheel and Afoot* (Hartford: Evening Post Association, 1887), 5–6.

3. Thayer, *Pedal and Path*, 127.

4. Karl Kron, *Ten Thousand Miles on a Bicycle* (New York: Karl Kron, 1887), xcvii.

5. "4224 Miles on a Bike," *Evening Star* (Washington DC), October 22, 1886; "The Twenty Mile Road Race," *Hartford Daily Courant*, June 19, 1886, 2; "Across the Continent: Mr. George B. Thayer Returns from His Long Bicycle Trip," *Hartford Daily Courant*, October 23, 1886, 1.

6. Thayer, *Pedal and Path*, 127.

7. Thayer, *Pedal and Path*, 7.

8. Harold Elvin, *The Ride to Chandigarh* (New York: Macmillan, 1957), 4.

9. Kron, *Ten Thousand Miles*, 621.

10. George B. Thayer, "The Evolution of the Bicycle," *Frank Leslie's Illustrated Newspaper*, no. 1777, October 5, 1889, 160.

11. Karl Kron published *Ten Thousand Miles on a Bicycle* by subscription, and he listed his 3,196 subscribers by name in the book. Listing the names of subscribers in a book was not unusual; what makes Kron's list stand out is that he provided two lists, one alphabetical, the other analytical. Titled "Directory of Wheelmen," the analytical list organizes Kron's

subscribers by place of residence and club membership. In addition, it gives the profession of many subscribers and mentions offices they held in their local club and in the LAW. Since Kron gathered such information from his subscribers in 1886, the year Thayer took his transcontinental tour, the offices listed in *Ten Thousand Miles* are the ones Kron's subscribers held when Thayer met them. Information about club members and offices held mentioned here comes from Kron's list of subscribers and will not be documented separately. Incidentally, George B. Thayer was one of Kron's early subscribers: no. 192.

12. Kevin J. Hayes, "Pedalling Preachers: Clergymen and the Acceptance of the Bicycle, 1881–1887," *Cycling History 20: Proceedings of the 20th International Cycling History Conference*, ed. Gary W. Sanderson (Cheltenham: John Pinkerton Memorial Publishing Fund, 2010), 17–22.

13. Thayer, *Pedal and Path*, 8.

14. Thayer, *Pedal and Path*, 15.

15. Thayer, *Pedal and Path*, 19.

16. "Among the Books," *Outing* 13 (February 1889): 463.

17. Kevin J. Hayes, *An American Cycling Odyssey, 1887* (Lincoln: University of Nebraska Press, 2002), 28.

18. Thayer, *Pedal and Path*, 23.

19. Thayer, *Pedal and Path*, 23.

20. "Sporting Notes," *Syracuse Daily Journal*, April 23, 1886.

21. C. W. Nairn and Henry Sturmey, eds. *The Cyclist and Wheel World Annual* (Coventry: Iliffe and Son, 1884), 198.

22. "Our Monthly Record," *Outing and the Wheelman* 4 (July 1884): 313.

23. Thayer, *Pedal and Path*, 30.

24. Thayer, *Pedal and Path*, 30.

25. Thayer, *Pedal and Path*, 33.

26. Thayer, *Pedal and Path*, 35.

27. Thayer, *Pedal and Path*, 33.

28. Thayer, *Pedal and Path*, 37.

29. Thayer, *Pedal and Path*, 37.

30. Thayer, *Pedal and Path*, 37.

31. Thomas Stevens, *Around the World on a Bicycle*, 2 vols. (New York: C. Scribner's Sons, 1887–1888), 1: 82–83.

32. Thayer, *Pedal and Path*, 37–38.

33. Thayer, *Pedal and Path*, 40.

34. Thayer, *Pedal and Path*, 41.

35. "4224 Miles on a Bike," *Evening Star* (Washington DC), October 22, 1886.

36. Thayer, *Pedal and Path*, 44.

37. "Bicycle Budget," *St. Louis Post Dispatch*, October 4, 1886, 7.

38. "Sporting Notes," *Rocky Mountain News* (Denver), May 31, 1886, 2.

39. George Edwin Marks, *A Treatise on Marks' Patent Artificial Limbs with Rubber Hands and Feet* (New York: A. A. Marks, 1888), 165–68; George B. Thayer, *Trips to Hell and Other Countries* (Hartford: Case, Lockwood, and Brainard, 1924), 543.

40. "George Thayer Fools 'Em All and Gets Across," *Hartford Courant*, January 14, 1919, 6.

41. Hayes, *American Cycling Odyssey*, 158–62.

42. "Gathered News," *Brown and Holland News* 2 (September 1883): 197; Thayer, *Pedal and Path*, 80.

4. The Way to San Francisco

1. George B. Thayer, *Pedal and Path: Across the Continent Awheel and Afoot* (Hartford: Evening Post Association, 1887), 85.

2. Thayer, *Pedal and Path*, 88–89.

3. Thayer, *Pedal and Path*, 89.

4. William H. Thomes, *California; as It Is and Was: A Journey Overland from Boston to the Golden State and Return* (Boston: DeWolfe, Fiske, 1887), 125; Emily Pfeiffer, *Flying Leaves from East and West* (London: Field and Tuer, 1885), 123.

5. Thayer, *Pedal and Path*, 92–93.

6. Thayer, *Pedal and Path*, 93.

7. Thayer, *Pedal and Path*, 93–94.

8. Thayer, *Pedal and Path*, 98.

9. Thayer, *Pedal and Path*, 99.

10. Thayer, *Pedal and Path*, 104.

11. "Wheel Notes," *Salt Lake Herald*, July 11, 1886, 8.

12. Florine Thayer McCray, *The Life-Work of the Author of Uncle Tom's Cabin* (New York: Funk and Wagnalls, 1889), 238.

13. Thayer, *Pedal and Path*, 108–9.

14. Thayer, *Pedal and Path*, 110.

15. Kevin J. Hayes, *An American Cycling Odyssey, 1887* (Lincoln: University of Nebraska Press, 2002), 123–26.

16. George B. Thayer, *Trips to Hell and Other Countries* (Hartford: Case, Lockwood, and Brainard, 1924), 534.

17. Thayer, *Pedal and Path*, 120.

18. Thayer, *Pedal and Path*, 120.

19. Thayer, *Pedal and Path*, 122–23.

20. "Across the Continent on a Bicycle," *Arizona Sentinel*, August 21, 1886; "By Wheel: A Bicycler on His Way Across the Continent," *Los Ange-*

les Daily Times, August 25, 1886; "From Sea to Sea on a Bicycle," New York Times, September 20, 1886, 10; Karl Kron, Ten Thousand Miles on a Bicycle (New York: Karl Kron, 1887), xcvii.

21. George B. Thayer, "Travelling Unarmed on a Bicycle," Youth's Companion, July 24, 1890, 400.

22. Thayer, Pedal and Path, 123.

23. Thayer, Pedal and Path, 127.

24. Thayer, Pedal and Path, 127.

25. "Wheel Notes," Salt Lake Herald, July 11, 1886, 8.

26. Thayer, Pedal and Path, 135–36.

27. "A Wheelman on a Journey," Salt Lake Herald, July 29, 1886; "Across the Continent," Sacramento Daily Record-Union, September 8, 1886.

28. Riaan Manser, Around Africa on My Bicycle (Johannesburg: Jonathan Ball, 2007), 173.

29. George B. Thayer, "Bicycling Friendships with Animals," Youth's Companion, May 29, 1890, 295–96.

30. Thayer, "Bicycling Friendships," 295.

31. Thayer, Pedal and Path, 137.

32. "Across the Continent on a Bicycle," Sacramento Daily Record-Union, October 1, 1887.

33. "4224 Miles on a Bike," Evening Star (Washington DC), October 22, 1886; Thayer, Pedal and Path, 142.

34. Thayer, Pedal and Path, 147–48.

35. Thayer, Pedal and Path, 149.

36. Thayer, Pedal and Path, 154.

37. Thayer, Pedal and Path, 157.

38. Thayer, Pedal and Path, 157.

39. "From Sea to Sea," 10.

40. Tom Kevill-Davies, The Hungry Cyclist: Pedalling the Americas in Search of the Perfect Meal (London: Collins, 2009), xiii.

41. Thayer, Pedal and Path, 157–58.

42. Thayer, Pedal and Path, 158.

43. Frank Moore, ed., Anecdotes, Poetry and Incidents of the War: North and South, 1860–1865 (New York: for the subscribers, 1866), 391.

44. Tim Mulliner, Long Ride for a Pie: From London to New Zealand on Two Wheels and an Appetite (Aukland: New Holland, 2006), 73. The episode that closes this chapter comes from Thayer, Pedal and Path, 161–62.

5. Eastbound and Down

1. George B. Thayer, Pedal and Path: Across the Continent Awheel and Afoot (Hartford: Evening Post Association, 1887), 173.

2. Thayer, *Pedal and Path*, 173.

3. Thayer, *Pedal and Path*, 181–82.

4. Thayer, *Pedal and Path*, 188.

5. Thayer, *Pedal and Path*, 194–95.

6. Thayer, *Pedal and Path*, 195.

7. Florine Thayer McCray, *Environment: A Story of Modern Society* (New York: Funk and Wagnalls, 1887), 193.

8. Thayer, *Pedal and Path*, 198.

9. Thayer, *Pedal and Path*, 201.

10. Thayer, *Pedal and Path*, 201, 227; George B. Thayer, "Travelling Unarmed on a Bicycle," *Youth's Companion* 63 (July 24, 1890): 399; George B. Thayer, *Trips to Hell and Other Countries* (Hartford: Case, Lockwood, and Brainard, 1924), 530–31.

11. Thomas Stevens, *Around the World on a Bicycle*, 2 vols. (London: Sampson Low, Marston, Searle, and Rivington, 1887–88), 1: 21–22.

12. Kevin J. Hayes, *An American Cycling Odyssey, 1887* (Lincoln: University of Nebraska Press, 2002), 139.

13. Thayer, *Pedal and Path*, 210–11.

14. Thayer, *Pedal and Path*, 212.

15. Thayer, *Pedal and Path*, 210–14; Sandra Opdycke, "Crandall, Prudence," *American National Biography*, ed. John A. Garraty and Mark C. Carnes, 24 vols. (New York: Oxford University Press, 1999).

16. Thayer, *Pedal and Path*, 228.

17. Thayer, *Pedal and Path*, 218–19.

18. Thayer, *Pedal and Path*, 224.

19. Thayer, *Pedal and Path*, 224; "The Wheelmen's Parade," *St. Louis Daily Globe-Democrat*, October 2, 1886, 8; "The Cycler's Success," *St. Louis Post-Dispatch*, October 2, 1886, 7.

20. Thayer, *Pedal and Path*, 225; "The Wheelmen's Parade," *St. Louis Daily Globe-Democrat*, October 2, 1886, 8; Karl Kron, *Ten Thousand Miles on a Bicycle* (New York: Karl Kron, 1887), 487–88.

21. "Weird Wheelmen," *St. Louis Post-Dispatch*, October 1, 1886, 8; "The Wheelmen's Parade," 8.

22. "Weird Wheelmen," 8.

23. Thayer, *Pedal and Path*, 230.

24. Thayer, *Pedal and Path*, 232.

25. "4224 Miles on a Bike," *Evening Star* (Washington DC), October 22, 1886.

26. Thayer, *Pedal and Path*, 238.

27. Thayer, *Pedal and Path*, 239.

28. Thayer, *Pedal and Path*, 241.

29. Thayer, *Pedal and Path*, 242–243.

30. "4224 Miles on a Bike," *Evening Star* (Washington DC), October 22, 1886.

31. Thayer, *Pedal and Path*, 243–44; "Across the Continent," *Hartford Courant*, October 23, 1886, 1.

6. From New England to Old

1. "Across the Continent," *Hartford Daily Courant*, October 23, 1886, 1; "A Long Ride," *St. Louis Daily Globe-Democrat*, October 23, 1886, 4; "Odd Gleanings," *St. Albans (VT) Daily Messenger*, October 28, 1886, 2; "Latest News Items," *San Francisco Daily Evening Bulletin*, November 2, 1886; "A Long Trip," *Atchison Daily Globe*, November 11, 1886; "A Long Trip— Over 4000 Miles Across Country on a Bicycle," *Canadian Wheelman* 4 (December 1886): 19.

2. George B. Thayer, *Pedal and Path: Across the Continent Awheel and Afoot* (Hartford: Evening Post Association, 1887), 4.

3. "Wheel Notes," *Salt Lake Herald*, December 5, 1886, 5.

4. "Wheel Notes," 5.

5. George B. Thayer, "Tourist Thayer at Home," *LAW Bulletin* 3 (November 17, 1886): 498.

6. George W. Nellis, "Cycling in America," *Herkimer Citizen*, May 24, 1887; Kevin J. Hayes, *An American Cycling Odyssey, 1887* (Lincoln: University of Nebraska Press, 2002), 13.

7. Karl Kron, *Ten Thousand Miles on a Bicycle* (New York: Karl Kron, 1887), xcvii.

8. Thayer, *Pedal and Path*, 4.

9. "Among the Books," *Outing* 13 (February 1889): 463.

10. "Editor's Library," *Wildwood's Magazine* 2 (March 1889): 204.

11. Kron, *Ten Thousand Miles*, xcvii; George B. Thayer, *Trips to Hell and Other Countries* (Hartford: Case, Lockwood, and Brainard, 1924), 30.

12. Stephen B. Goddard, *Colonel Albert Pope and His American Dream Machines: The Life and Times of a Bicycle Tycoon Turned Automobile Pioneer* (Jefferson NC: McFarland, 2000), 66–90.

13. Kron, *Ten Thousand Miles*, xcvii; "Across the Continent," *Sacramento Daily Record-Union*, September 8, 1886.

14. Kron, *Ten Thousand Miles*, 769; George B. Thayer, "The Evolution of the Bicycle," *Frank Leslie's Illustrated Newspaper*, no. 1777 (October 5, 1889): 158.

15. Thayer, *Trips to Hell*, 308.

16. Thayer, "Tourist Thayer," 498.

17. Thayer, *Pedal and Path*, 180.

18. "Going Abroad," *Brooklyn Daily Eagle*, June 9, 1888, 6.

19. Thayer, *Trips to Hell*, 151.

20. "To Try European Roads," *New York Times*, June 7, 1888, 8.

21. "Personal Intelligence," *Washington Post*, June 12, 1888, 4.

22. "Going Abroad," *Brooklyn Eagle*, June 9, 1888, 6; "Logs of Transatlantic Lines," *Glasgow Herald*, June 20, 1888.

23. "Going Abroad," *Brooklyn Eagle*, June 9, 1888, 6; "Logs of Transatlantic Lines," *Glasgow Herald*, June 20, 1888.

24. Maynard H. Jephson, "From Monmouth to Midlothian," *London Bicycle Club Gazette* 5 (November 1, 1882): 247.

25. *Black's Tourist's Guide to Derbyshire: Its Towns, Water-Places, Dales, and Mansions*, 16th ed. (Edinburgh: Adam and Charles Black, 1888), 57; Elizabeth Robins Pennell, "Our Journey to the Hebrides," *Harper's New Monthly Magazine* 77 (1888): 490.

26. [Owen Seaman], *Nauticus in Scotland: A Tricycle Tour of 2,462 Miles, Including Skye and the West Coast* (London: Simpkin, Marshall, 1882), 39.

27. Thayer, *Trips to Hell*, 477.

28. G. W. Burston and H. R. Stokes, *Round about the World on Bicycles* (Melbourne: George Robertson, 1890), 245.

29. James Lennox, *A Road Guide to the Southern Scottish Counties* (Dumfries: J. Anderson and Son, 1885), 66; [Eliza Archard Conner], "Edinburgh, Dryburgh, and Abbotsford," *Literary World* 13 (August 26, 1882): 282.

30. [Seaman], *Nauticus in Scotland*, 7; Lennox, *Road Guide*, 55.

31. George B. Thayer, "Bicycling Accidents in Europe," *Youth's Companion* 63 (May 15, 1890): 263.

32. Thayer, "Bicycling Accidents," 263.

33. Lennox, *Road Guide*, 52.

34. Kevin J. Hayes, "Baedeker Guides," in *Literature of Travel and Exploration: An Encyclopaedia*, ed. Jennifer Speake, 3 vols. (London: Fitzroy Dearborn, 2003), 1: 58.

35. Thayer, *Trips to Hell*, 154.

36. E. R. Shipton, "Cycling," in J. F. Muirhead, *Great Britain, England, Wales, and Scotland* (Leipzig: Karl Baedeker, 1887), xxv.

37. C. W. Nairn and Henry Sturmey, eds. *The Cyclists and Wheel World Annual* (Coventry: Iliffe and Son, 1884), 173.

38. Alfred Nixon, "John-O'-Groats to Land's End on a Tricycle," *Wheelman* 1 (November 1882): 131; Elizabeth Robins Pennell, "From Cathedral to Cathedral," *Chautauquan* 11 (June 1890): 324.

39. Pennell, "From Cathedral to Cathedral," 324; "A Durham Pilgrimage," *Musical News* 2 (January 1, 1892): 6; [Eliza Archard Conner], "Cambridge and Durham," *Literary World* 13 (September 9, 1882): 297.

40. Muirhead, *Great Britain*, 369.

41. Thayer, *Trips to Hell*, 171.

42. George B. Thayer, "Wheeling through Europe," *Atchison Daily Champion*, November 9, 1888, 8.

43. Thayer, *Trips to Hell*, 174.

44. George B. Thayer, "Evolution of the Bicycle," 160.

45. George B. Thayer, "Cheap Cycling," *Boston Daily Globe*, October 22, 1888, 5.

46. Thayer, *Trips to Hell*, 34.

47. J. F. Muirhead, *London and Its Environs*, 5th rev. ed. (Leipzig: Karl Baedeker, 1885), 141.

48. Thayer, *Trips to Hell*, 153.

7. The Grand Tour

1. Karl Baedeker, *Belgium and Holland* (Leipzig: Karl Baedeker, 1888), 108.

2. George B. Thayer, *Trips to Hell and Other Countries* (Hartford: Case, Lockwood, and Brainard, 1924), 102.

3. Thayer, *Trips to Hell*, 102–3.

4. John Foster Fraser, *Round the World on a Wheel* (1899; reprinted, London: Thomas Nelson and Sons, 1919), 23.

5. Thomas Stevens, *Around the World on a Bicycle*, 2 vols. (London: Sampson Low, Marston, Searle, and Rivington, 1887–88), 1: 123; George B. Thayer, "Wheeling through Europe: A Bicycle Tourist Tells How Enjoyable Such Traveling Is," *Auburn Bulletin*, November 6, 1888. This article, which originally appeared in the *New York World*, was also reprinted in the *Atchison Daily Champion*, November 9, 1888, 8, and *Spirit of the Times* (Batavia NY), November 17, 1888.

6. Thayer, *Trips to Hell*, 190.

7. George B. Thayer, "Cycling down a Mountain Side," *Atchison Daily Champion*, December 24, 1888.

8. Thayer, "Wheeling through Europe."

9. George B. Thayer, *In Hell—Shut In—At the Outbreak of the Great War, 1914* (West Hartford: George B. Thayer, 1915), 17.

10. Quoted in C. L. Freeston, *Cycling in the Alps with Some Notes on the Chief Passes* (London: Grant Richards, 1900), 181.

11. George B. Thayer, "Travelling Unarmed on a Bicycle," *Youth's Companion* 63 (July 24, 1890): 400.

12. George B. Thayer, "Biggest Volcano Now Burnt Out," *Hartford Courant*, August 22, 1912, 12.

13. Karl Baedeker, *Switzerland, and the Adjacent Portions of Italy, Savoy, and the Tyrol* (Leipzig: Karl Baedeker, 1877), 142.

14. Frank R. Stockton, *Personally Conducted* (New York: Charles Scribner's Sons, 1889), 130; Thayer, *In Hell*, 18.

15. Thayer, "Wheeling through Europe," 8.

16. G. W. Burston, and H. R. Stokes, *Round about the World on Bicycles* (Melbourne: George Robertson, 1890), 201.

17. "Another World's Tour on Bicycles," *Pall Mall Gazette*, June 6, 1889.

18. Thayer, *Trips to Hell*, 310.

19. Burston and Stokes, *Round about the World*, 201.

20. Thayer, "Travelling Unarmed," 399–400; Thayer, *Trips to Hell*, 310–12.

21. Eliza Archard Conner, *"E.A." Abroad: A Summer in Europe* (Cincinnati: W. E. Dibble, 1883), 293.

22. George B. Thayer, "Bicycling Friendships with Animals," *Youth's Companion* 63 (May 29, 1890): 296.

23. George B. Thayer, "Cheap Cycling," *Boston Daily Globe*, October 22, 1888, 5.

24. George B. Thayer, "Cycling in Europe," *Milwaukee Daily Journal*, November 20, 1888.

25. Stevens, *Around the World*, 1: 113.

26. Thayer, "Wheeling through Europe."

27. Thayer, "Wheeling through Europe."

28. Karl Baedeker, *Paris and Its Environs* (Leipzig: Karl Baedeker, 1884), 290, 292.

29. "Continental Roads," *London Bicycle Club Gazette* 3 (May 14, 1880): 70.

30. Thayer, "Cycling in Europe."

31. Inglis Sheldon-Williams, *A Dawdle in France* (London: A. and C. Black, 1926), 1.

32. Thayer, "Cycling in Europe."

33. Thayer, "Cycling in Europe."

34. Thayer, "Cycling in Europe."

35. Joseph Pennell, and Elizabeth Robins Pennell, *Our Sentimental Journey through France and Italy* (London: Longmans, Green, 1888), 168–70. Joseph and Elizabeth are listed as coauthors. He did the illustrations; she wrote the text.

36. Thayer, *Trips to Hell*, 188–89.

37. Pennell, *Our Sentimental Journey*, 211.

38. Pennell, *Our Sentimental Journey*, 227; Sheldon-Williams, *A Dawdle in France*, 189.

39. Thayer, "Cycling in Europe."

40. Thayer, "Cycling in Europe."

41. William L. Sachtleben and Thomas G. Allen, "Cycling Round the World," *Penny Illustrated Paper and Illustrated Times*, October 18, 1890, 253.

42. George B. Thayer, "Bicycling Accidents in Europe," *Youth's Companion* 63 (May 15, 1890): 263–64.

43. Laurent Fignon, *We Were Young and Carefree: The Autobiography of Laurent Fignon*, trans. William Fotheringham (London: Yellow Jersey Press, 2010), 39.

44. Thayer, "Bicycling Accidents," 264.

45. Thayer, "Bicycling Accidents," 264.

46. Thayer, "Bicycling Accidents," 264.

47. Thayer, *Trips to Hell*, 186–88.

48. Thayer, "Wheeling through Europe."

49. Thayer, "Cycling in Europe."

50. "Cyclist Thayer's Tour," *Boston Sunday Globe*, October 7, 1888, 5.

8. The Rise of the Dwarf

1. George B. Thayer, "Cycling Down a Mountain Side," *Atchison Daily Champion*, October 24, 1888; Thayer, "Wheeling through Europe," *Atchison Daily Champion*, November 9, 1888; Thayer, "Cycling in Europe," *Milwaukee Daily Journal*, November 20, 1888; Thayer, "Cycling in Europe," *Bismarck Daily Tribune*, January 5, 1889; "Cycling in Europe," *Mohave County Miner* (Mineral Park, Arizona Territory), March 23, 1889.

2. W. I. Harris, "Sketches of Baseball Writers," *Athletic Sports in America, England and Australia*, ed. Henry Chadwick (Philadelphia: Hubbard Brothers, 1889), 593.

3. George B. Thayer, "The Evolution of the Bicycle," *Frank Leslie's Illustrated Newspaper*, no. 1777 (October 5, 1889): 157.

4. Thayer, "Evolution," 157.

5. Thayer, "Evolution," 157.

6. Thayer, "Evolution," 159.

7. "Editor's Open Window," *Outing* 8 (1886): 483.

8. Pope Manufacturing Co., *Columbia Bicycles* (Boston: Pope Manufacturing, 1887), 20; Gormully and Jeffrey Mfg. Co., *American Cycles, 1887* (Chicago: Gormully and Jeffrey, 1887), 18.

9. Gormully and Jeffrey Mfg. Co., *American Cycles, 1887*, 18.

10. Pope Manufacturing Co., *Columbia Bicycles* (Boston: Pope Manufacturing, 1889), 25.

11. F. Prial, "'Cycling," in *Athletic Sports in America, England and Australia*, ed. Henry Chadwick (Philadelphia: Hubbard Brothers, 1889), 693.

12. Andrew Ritchie, *Quest for Speed: A History of Early Bicycle Racing, 1868–1903* (El Cerrito CA: Andrew Ritchie, 2011), 225.

13. *Bicycle Clubs Gameboard*, ca. 1896 (Library Company of Philadelphia, GC-Games [P.2011.32]).

14. Prudential Insurance Company, *Clippings on Bicycle Accidents, 1896-*(Lilly Library, Indiana University).

15. "Wheelman Cornell's Career," *New York Times*, September 6, 1889, 5.

16. "The Wheel at Hartford," *Boston Daily Advertiser*, September 3, 1889.

17. "The Wheel," *Daily Inter Ocean* (Chicago), September 5, 1889, 2.

18. Peter Nye, *Hearts of Lions: The History of American Bicycle Racing* (New York: Norton, 1988), 35; "George M. Hendee, Bicycle Ex-Racer," *New York Times*, June 18, 1943, 21.

19. "Two Records Broken: The Second Day's Bicycle Racing at Charter Oak Park," *New York Times*, September 4, 1889, 2.

20. "Two Records Broken," 2.

21. Thayer, "Evolution," 158.

22. Thayer, "Evolution," 158–59.

23. Stephen B. Goddard, *Colonel Albert Pope and His American Dream Machines: The Life and Times of a Bicycle Tycoon Turned Automobile Pioneer* (Jefferson NC: McFarland, 2000), 5.

24. Thayer, "Evolution," 159–60.

25. Thayer, "Evolution," 160.

26. Karl Kron, *Ten Thousand Miles on a Bicycle* (1887; reprinted, Croton-on-Hudson: Emil Rosenblatt, 1982), 769.

27. "St. Paul Wheelmen," *St. Paul Daily News*, October 12, 1889, 4.

28. Susan Belasco, *Stowe in Her Own Time: A Biographical Chronicle of Her Life, Drawn from Recollections, Interviews, and Memoirs by Family, Friends, and Associates* (Iowa City: University of Iowa Press, 2009), 155.

29. Eliza Putnam Heaton, "The Daughters of Eve," *Galveston Daily News*, May 12, 1889, 9.

30. "Sporting Notes," *Sacramento Record-Union*, February 28, 1891, 3; "At the Rink," *Sacramento Record Union*, March 1, 1891, 8; "Clever Bicycling," *Sacramento Record-Union*, November 30, 1891, 3.

31. Andrew Ritchie, *Flying Yankee: The International Cycling Career of Arthur Augustus Zimmerman* (Cheltenham: John Pinkerton Memorial Publishing Fund, 2009), 42–43.

32. George B. Thayer, "Bicycling Accidents in Europe," *Youth's Companion* 63 (May 15, 1890): 263–64.

33. Thayer, "Bicycling Accidents," 263–64; Thayer, "Bicycling Friendships with Animals," *Youth's Companion* 63 (May 29, 1890): 295–96; Thayer, "Travelling Unarmed on a Bicycle," *Youth's Companion* 63 (July 24, 1890): 399–400.

9. The Swish of the Fat Pneumatics

1. George B. Thayer, "Have the Facts Learned," *Hartford Courant,* January 4, 1892, 4.

2. "Connecticut," *Springfield Republican,* October 1, 1889, 7.

3. "Wheel Club Gymnasium," *Hartford Daily Courant,* March 15, 1893, 2.

4. Pope Manufacturing Co., *Columbia Bicycles* (Boston: Pope Manufacturing, 1887), 25.

5. "Classified List of the Books Placed in the Library from July 15 to August 15, 1901," *Monthly Bulletin of Books Added to the Public Library of the City of Boston* 6 (August 1901): 312; Commonwealth of Massachusetts, *Report of the Library of the State Library for the Year Ending September 30, 1895 and Sixteenth Annual Supplement to the General Catalogue* (Boston: Wright and Potter, 1896), 188; Library of Congress, *American and English Genealogies in the Library of Congress,* 2nd ed. (Washington: GPO, 1919), 1103.

6. George B. Thayer, *Ancestors of Adelbert Thayer, Florine Thayer McCray and Geo. Burton Thayer, Children of John W. Thayer and Adaline Burton* (Hartford: Plimpton Mfg., 1894), 146.

7. Andrew Ritchie, *Quest for Speed: A History of Early Bicycling Racing, 1868–1903* (El Cerrito CA: by the author, 2011), 228–31.

8. David V. Herlihy, *Bicycle: The History* (New Haven: Yale University Press, 2004), 246.

9. H. G. Wells, *The Wheels of Chance, The Time Machine* (London: J. M. Dent, 1946), 181.

10. Rouse, Hazard, and Co., *Extraordinary Reductions in 1893 and 1894 Patterns: Big Money for Dealers . . . Special Bargain List* (Peoria: Rouse, Hazard, [1894]), unpaginated.

11. "Bike and Bloomers," Chicago *Daily Inter Ocean,* June 30, 1895. A regular column in the *Daily Inter Ocean,* "Bike and Bloomers" consists of bicycle jokes culled from newspapers across the nation. It forms a valuable but so far largely untapped resource for cycling historians.

12. George B. Thayer, "After His Ancestors: In the Hill Country with a Pneumatic," *Hartford Daily Courant,* July 13, 1892, 3.

13. G. W. Burston and H. R. Stokes, *Round about the World on Bicycles: The Pleasure Tour of G. W. Burston and H. R. Stokes* (Melbourne: George Robertson, 1890). Thomas Gaskell Allen Jr. and William Lewis Sachtleben, *Across Asia on a Bicycle: The Journey of Two American Students from Constantinople to Peking* (New York: Century, 1894), relates part of their round-the-world journey. David V. Herlihy briefly retells their story as part of *The Lost Cyclist: The Epic Tale of an American Adventurer and His Mysterious Disappearance* (Boston: Houghton Mifflin Harcourt, 2010).

14. Thayer, "After His Ancestors," 3.

15. Thayer, "After His Ancestors," 3.

16. George B. Thayer, "Any Man Can Go to College If He Wills To," *Association Men* 41 (May 1916): 418.

17. Frederick C. Hicks, *History of the Yale Law School to 1915* (Union NJ: Lawbook Exchange, 2001), 210.

18. Thayer, "Any Man Can," 418.

19. "Lawyers," *American Lawyer* 5 (July 1897): 326.

20. George B. Thayer, "Canadian Cycling," *Hartford Courant*, September 9, 1897, 12.

21. Thayer, "Canadian Cycling," 12.

22. Thayer, "Canadian Cycling," 12.

23. Thomas B. Shaw and Truman J. Backus, *Shaw's New History of English Literature; Together with A History of English Literature in America*, rev. ed. (New York: Sheldon and Company, 1884), 439–41; John Seelye, "Attic Shape: Dusting Off Evangeline," *Virginia Quarterly Review* 60 (1984): 22.

24. Thayer, "Canadian Cycling," 12.

25. Douglas Sladen, *On the Cars and Off: Being the Journal of a Pilgrimage Along the Queen's Highway to the East, from Halifax in Nova Scotia to Victoria in Vancouver's Island* (London: Ward, Lock and Bowden, 1895), 33.

26. Charles G. D. Roberts, *The Canadian Guide-Book* (New York: D. Appleton, 1899), 109; Thayer, "Canadian Cycling," 12.

27. C. A. Stephens, *The Adventures of Six Young Men in the Wilds of Maine and Canada; or, The Knock-About Club* (London: Dean and Son, 1884), 220.

28. J. M. Cooper, "Jefferson," *Granite Monthly* 25 (August 1898): 78.

29. Thayer, "Canadian Cycling," 12.

30. Thayer, "Canadian Cycling," 12.

10. The Wheel and the Gun

1. Robert A. Smith, *Merry Wheels and Spokes of Steel: A Social History of the Bicycle* (1972; reprinted, San Bernardino: Borgo Press, 1995), 227.

2. "Applications for Membership, LAW," *LAW Bulletin* 1 (July 16, 1885): 57, lists "Charles L. Burdett, Connecticut Bicycle Club, Hartford, dated July 13, 1885."

3. Personals, *Illustrated American*, March 5, 1892, 119.

4. Karl Edwards, "Giddings' Mounted Infantry: Connecticut's First Signal Corps and the Bicycle," *Wheelman*, no. 41 (1992): 9.

5. Howard A. Giddings, *Manual for Cyclists: For the Use of the Regular Army, Organized Militia, and Volunteer Troops of the United States* (Kansas City MO: Hudson-Kimberly, 1898).

6. Thayer, "Canadian Cycling," 12.

7. Howard Alden Giddings, "Cyclist Infantry: The New Branch of the Military Service," *Harper's Weekly*, February 11, 1893, 135.

8. Pope Manufacturing Co., *Columbia Bicycles* (Boston: Pope Manufacturing, 1893), 27.

9. Giddings, "Cyclist Infantry," 135.

10. Giddings, "Cyclist Infantry," 135.

11. George B. Thayer, *History of Company K, First Connecticut Volunteer Infantry, During the Spanish-American War* (Hartford: R. S. Peck, 1899), 152.

12. Thayer, *History of Company K*, 155.

13. Thayer, *History of Company K*, 141.

14. "Cheers and Tears: First Regiment Off for the War," *Hartford Courant*, May 5, 1898, 1.

15. Thayer, *History of Company K*, 59.

16. Thayer, *History of Company K*, 25; Kevin J. Hayes, *An American Cycling Odyssey, 1887* (Lincoln: University of Nebraska Press, 2002), 55–56.

17. Thayer, *History of Company K*, 25; "Bicycle Races at Wallingford," *Hartford Courant*, July 26, 1897, 9; "Labor Day Races," *Hartford Courant*, September 3, 1897, 6; "Moonlight Club Races," *Hartford Courant*, September 6, 1897, 11; "Three Records Broken: Great Bicycle Races at Waterbury," *Hartford Courant*, September 10, 1897, 1; "New Amateur Mile Record," *Hartford Courant*, September 20, 1897, 9.

18. Thayer, *History of Company K*, 170–71, 208.

19. Thayer, *History of Company K*, 199.

20. Thayer, *History of Company K*, 207.

21. Thayer, *History of Company K*, 274, 280.

22. "Death of Colonel M'Cray," *Hartford Courant*, January 23, 1899, 8; "Mrs. Florine T. M'Cray," *Hartford Courant*, March 13, 1899, 3.

23. Thayer, *History of Company K*, 263.

24. Thayer, *History of Company K*, 284.

25. Quoted in Thayer, *History of Company K*, 74.

26. Thayer, *History of Company K*, 289.

11. The End of an Era

1. "Lawyers," *American Lawyer* 6 (1898): 466.

2. *Geer's Hartford City Directory* (Hartford: Hartford Printing Company, 1899), 595–96.

3. George B. Thayer, "Any Man Can Go to College If He Wills To," *Association Men* 41 (1916): 418.

4. George B. Thayer, *History of Company K, First Connecticut Volunteer Infantry, During the Spanish-American War* (Hartford: R. S. Peck, 1899), 143.

5. "West Hartford," *Hartford Courant*, September 5, 1917, 5; "Geo. B. Thayer Gives Home to West Hartford," *Hartford Courant*, July 25, 1917, 2; City Personals, *Hartford Courant*, December 27, 1902, 14.

6. "Colonel M'Cray's Estate," *Hartford Courant*, February 6, 1899, 4; "Will of Mrs. Florine M'Cray," *Hartford Courant*, March 21, 1899, 5; "Pastor Gets Auto and $445 in Cash in West Hartford," *Hartford Courant*, May 19, 1916, 10.

7. City Personals, *Hartford Courant*, June 8, 1899, 7.

8. "The Kind of Pickerel in White Bear Lake," *Hartford Courant*, July 22, 1909, 18.

9. "G. B. Thayer Resigns," *Hartford Courant*, September 5, 1910, 6.

10. "West Hartford: Athletic Training at Town Hall," *Hartford Courant*, January 17, 1911, 15.

11. David V. Herlihy, *Bicycle: The History* (New Haven: Yale University Press, 2004), 294.

12. "Kramer's Great Finish," *New York Sun*, June 27, 1904, 6; "Close Finish at Vailsburg," *New York Sun*, July 17, 1904, 9; "Kramer Wins at Vailsburg," *New York Sun*, August 1, 1904, 6; "Race Meet at New Orleans Planned," *Motorcycle Illustrated*, March 15, 1910, 15.

13. Quoted in George B. Thayer, *Trips to Hell and Other Countries* (Hartford: Case, Lockwood, and Brainard, 1924), 190.

14. "LAW Official Report," *Good Roads Magazine* 32 (October 1901): 20.

15. George B. Thayer, "Journeying Afoot across Isthmus," *Hartford Courant*, June 7, 1912, 16.

16. Thayer, "Midnight View of the Caldron of a Volcano," *Hartford Courant*, August 17, 1912, 10.

17. George B. Thayer, "Biggest Volcano Now Burnt Out," *Hartford Courant*, August 22, 1912, 12.

18. Thayer, "Midnight View," 10.

19. Thayer, "Midnight View," 10; Thayer, *Trips to Hell*, 76.

20. Thayer, "Biggest Volcano," 12.

21. Thayer, "Biggest Volcano," 12.

22. Thayer, "Biggest Volcano," 12.

23. George B. Thayer, *In Hell—Shut In—At the Outbreak of the Great War, 1914* (West Hartford: George B. Thayer, 1915), 34.

24. George B. Thayer, "George B. Thayer Rejoices Because He Now 'Is in It,'" *Hartford Courant*, February 7, 1919, 3.

25. "George Thayer 'Fools 'Em All' and Gets Across," *Hartford Courant*, January 14, 1919, 6.

26. Quoted in "George Thayer 'Fools 'Em All,'" 6.

27. "George Thayer 'Fools 'Em All,'" 6.

28. "George Thayer Fires in France," *Hartford Courant*, April 29, 1919, 7; "George Thayer Back, Still Young at 67," *Hartford Courant*, November 2, 1919, 17.

29. "George Thayer Back," 17.

30. "George Thayer Back," 17.

31. "Thayer to Speak on World Tour," *Hartford Courant*, April 21, 1923, 6.

32. Thayer, *Trips to Hell*, 530.

33. "G. B. Thayer Found Dead on Highway," *Hartford Courant*, June 29, 1928, 6.

34. "Hold Funeral Service for George B. Thayer," *Hartford Courant*, July 1, 1928, A1.

35. "3 Colleges Benefit by Thayer Will," *Hartford Courant*, August 31, 1928, 7.

36. "3 Colleges Benefit," 7; David O. Hooke, *Reaching that Peak: 75 Years of the Dartmouth Outing Club* (Canaan NH: Phoenix Publishing for the Dartmouth Outing Club, 1987), 28.

INDEX

Belgium, 117, 131–33, 143, 223
Bellows Falls (VT), 32
Berkeley Athletic Club, 160
Bernardston (MA), 31
Bicycle of Cathay (Stockton), 135
bicycles. *See* boneshakers; ordinaries; riding rinks; safety bicycles; tandems; tricycles; velocipedes; *and names of individual marques*
"Bicycling Accidents in Europe" (Thayer), 169
Birlo, P. J., 161–62
Blaine, James G., 18
Bleak House (Dickens), 9, 121
Bobet, Jean, 36
Bodega Bay (CA), 95
Bohemiene (*pseud.* Florine Thayer McCray), 21
Bois de Boulogne, 140–42
Bolton (CT), 179
boneshakers, 14–16
Boston (MA), 8, 14, 41, 106, 155, 188
Boston Globe, 150
Boston Saturday Evening Gazette, 21
Bowen, William H. C., 192–93
Brattleboro (VT), 32
Bridal Veil Falls (Yosemite), 83
British Columbia, 217
British Museum, 129
Brixen (UT), 79
Brooklyn, 77–78
Brooklyn Daily Eagle, 118
Brooklyn Times, 21
Brown, Mrs. (hotelkeeper), 127–28
Brown, Samuel, 59, 65
Brown University, 27, 96–97
Bubble (Maui), 135
Buffalo (NY), 18, 54–55, 58, 79
Buffalo Bicycle Club, 54
Buffalo Evening News, 27
Bull Run, First Battle of, 6
Bully (France), 147
Burdett, Charles L., 190–92, 199, 201, 204–7

Burke, Thomas Henry, 130
Burlingame, Maxy W., 2
Burnside (CT), 179
Burnside's Bridge, 110
Burston, G. W., 121–22, 136–37, 177; *Round about the World on Bicycles*, 177–79
Burton, Adaline, 2
Burton, George W., 110
Byron, George Gordon, sixth baron, 140

Cadwell, Frank J., 200–201, 212
Calais (France), 183
Calaveras Big Trees, 82–83
California, 21, 41, 53, 66, 77, 80, 89, 92–93, 95, 97, 103, 111, 118
Calistoga (CA), 93
Canada, 183, 186–88, 198, 205, 211–12, 217
"Canadian Cycling" (Thayer), 183, 186–88
Canandaigua Bicycle Club, 53
Canary, D. J., 165, 167
Cannes (France), 148–49
Cap of Liberty (Yosemite), 85
Cape Blomidon (Nova Scotia), 185, 187
Cardington (OH), 59
Casco Bay (ME), 202
Catherine of Aragon, 128
Catskill Mountain House, 50
Cavendish, Lord Frederick, 130
Cave of the Winds, 70–71
Centennial Exhibition, 115
Central Italy and Rome (Baedeker), 150
Chamard, F. J., 66
Chamberlain, Everett, 15
Champs Elysées, 140
Charity Organization Society (Hartford), 171–72
Charleston (SC), 7, 28
Charter Oak Park (Hartford), 160–62
Chautauqua Institution, 16, 181
Chepachet (RI), 2

Dickens, Charles, 9–10, 121; *Bleak House,* 9, 121; *David Copperfield,* 9; *Nicholas Nickleby,* 9, 11; *Oliver Twist,* 9; *Our Mutual Friend,* 9; *Pickwick Papers,* 9; *Tale of Two Cities,* 9

Dominion Atlantic Railway, 185

Donohue, Peter J., 151

Dryburgh Abbey (Scotland), 122

Dublin, 130

Du Maurier, George, 177; *Trilby,* 177

Dunlop, John Boyd, 174

Durham (England), 126–27

Durham Cathedral, 126

Durham City Cycling Club, 127

dwarf bicycles. *See* safety bicycles

East Hartford (CT), 3, 179

East Springfield (NY), 82

Echo Lake (White Mountains), 36

Edam (steamship), 118–19

Edinburgh, 120–21

Egypt, 118, 150, 222

El Capitan (Yosemite), 83, 85

Elk Falls (KS), 102, 104

Ellington (CT), 11

Elm Street Armory (Hartford), 198

El Paso (TX), 77

Elvin, Harold, 45–47; *Ride to Chandigarh,* 45–47

Ely (England), 126

Emporia (KS), 104

England, 4, 28, 115, 122–30, 136, 158, 223

English Channel, 131

Environment (McCray), 117

Erie Canal, 52, 54

Essone (France), 143–44

Euclid (OH), 55

Europe, 27–28, 117–18, 130–31, 133, 147, 150–51, 169, 213, 218–22

Evangeline (Longfellow), 185–86

Evangeline (steamboat), 185

"Evolution of the Bicycle" (Thayer), 153, 163, 181

Fabyan (NH), 37–38

Ferrières (France), 221

Fighting Temeraire (Turner), 130

Firehole (Yellowstone), 99–101

First Connecticut Volunteer Infantry, 190, 197–207, 224

First National Bank Building (Hartford), 208

First National Mine, 74–75

Five Forks, 6

Florence, 150

Flume (White Mountains), 35–36, 70

Folsom, Omar W., 119

Fonda (NY), 52

Fontainebleau, 143

Fort Preble, 201–3

Fort Schuyler Wheelmen, 52

Fountain Geyser (Yellowstone), 99–100

Fourteenth Illinois Cavalry, 7

France, 28, 117, 140–47, 150, 158, 205, 221–23

Franconia Notch (White Mountains), 33

Frank Leslie's Illustrated Newspaper, 151–52, 160, 166, 168

Fraser, John Foster, 132–33

Freehold (NJ), 161

Free Will Baptist Church, 2

French Riviera, 150

Funk and Wagnalls, 117

Garden of the Gods (CO), 73

Garfield, James A., 55

Garrison, William Lloyd, 104

Gascogne (steamship), 118

Georgetown (KY), 108

Georgia, 7

Germany, 117, 130, 131–33, 136, 158, 218, 213, 223

Giddings, Howard A., 191–97, 199, 206–7

Gilbert and Sullivan, 99: *Mikado,* 99–100, 106

Glasgow, 118–20, 128, 147

Goat Island, 54

Good Roads Movement, 191

Gormully and Jeffrey, 155–56; American Safety, 156; Grand Army of the Republic, 28, 79, 89, 91–92, 96

Grand Cavern (CO), 68

Gray, C. Theron, 82

Great Britain, 27, 117–18, 121, 125, 131, 169, 205

Great Britain, England, Wales, and Scotland (Muirhead), 125

"Great Stone Face" (Hawthorne), 33

Greece, 118, 150

Greenfield (MA), 31

Green River (WY), 76–78

Greenwich (CT), 48

Grimsel Pass, 134–35, 137

Grinnell (IA), 63, 210

Grinnell College, 63

Haleakala Volcano, 135

Half Dome (Yosemite), 85

Halfway Hotel (WY), 98

Halfway House (CO), 71

Hall Preparatory School, 11

Harper's Magazine, 177

Harper's Weekly, 5–6, 62, 110, 196

Harris, W. I., 151

Hartford (CT), 10, 17, 21–22, 27, 105, 110, 113–16, 118, 151–52, 154–55, 160, 162, 164, 173, 181, 183–89, 190, 198–200, 208–9, 211, 222; Charter Oak Park, 160–62; City Hall, 115; Connecticut State House, 115; Elm Street Armory, 198; First National Bank Building, 208; Hartford Public Library, 115; Linden Hotel, 181, 198, 209–10; Opera House, 115; Union Station, 115; Young Men's Christian Association (YMCA), 172, 211–13, 218–19, 224; Young Men's Institute, 115

Hartford Bicycle Tournament, 152, 156, 160–65, 167–68

Hartford Courant, 5–6, 8, 18, 22, 29, 110, 171, 173, 177, 181, 183, 190, 214, 220, 222–24

Hartford Evening Post, 42, 113–15, 117

Hartford Globe, 21

Hartford Wheel Club, 116, 152, 155, 163, 172, 191

Hasley, J. A., 66–82

Havana, 197

Haverhill (MA), 41

Hawaii, 135, 211, 213–17, 223, 225

Hawthorne, Nathaniel, 10, 33, 37–38; "Ambitious Guest," 38; "Great Stone Face," 33

Hawthorne, Rose, 10

Hawthorne, Una, 10

Heaton, Eliza Putnam, 167

Hendee, George, 162–63

Higgins, George F., 66

high wheelers. *See* ordinaries

Hilo (HI), 215–16

History of Company K (Thayer), 200, 204

Hockanum River, 2, 4

Holyoke (MA), 31

Honolulu, 214, 216

House of Commons, 129–30

Houston (TX), 77

Howells, William Dean, 96; *Modern Instance*, 96

Hudson River, 50

Hugo, Victor, 132

Hurlbutt, William, 48

Ice Grotto (Rhône Glacier), 135–36

Illinois, 61–62, 107

Illustrated American, 191

India, 45, 222

Indiana, 59, 86, 107, 142

Indianapolis, 58

Indian Territory, 102

Intra (Italy), 137–39

Iowa, 44, 53, 63

Irving, Washington, 48

Is Darwin Right? (Denton), 104

Italy, 117, 131, 137, 138, 150, 223

Ives, F. F., 160, 162

James, Sam R., 52

January, John W., 6–7, 12, 61–63

Wheels of Chance (Wells), 174
White Bear Lake (MN), 210
White Mountains, 20, 29, 33, 70, 187,
 189, 224–25
Whitman, Walt, 49
Wilder, Arthur, 216–17
Wilderness, 6
Wildwood's Magazine, 114
Willey, Samuel, Jr., 37
Willey House, 37–40
Williams, Alonzo, 27–28, 53, 96–97, 117
Williams, Mr., 102–3
Williams Canyon (CO), 70
Williamsport (MD), 109
Wilson, Woodrow, 217
Windermere (CT), 4, 6, 9–11, 173
Windermere Woolen Company, 4–5,
 7, 13

Winsor, Tom, 180
Woodman, Charles M., 64
Wynkoop, T. S., 119
Wyoming, 75–78, 81

Yale Law School, 182, 189, 197, 216, 224
Yale University, 45
Yellowstone National Park, 98–99, 101
York (England), 126
Yosemite, 79, 82–86, 89, 91, 214, 225
Young Men's Christian Association
 (YMCA), 53, 182, 211–14, 218–22, 224
Youth's Companion, 168–70
Yuma (AZ), 77

Zborowski, Anna, comtesse de Mont-
 saulnin, 145
Zile, Edward S. Van, 208
Zimmerman, Arthur A., 161–63, 168